What Matters in English Teaching
Collected Blogs and Other Writing

Barbara Bleiman, English & Media Centre

Written by Barbara Bleiman

Edited by Andrew McCallum and Lucy Webster

Editorial assistance: Maria Pettersson and Claire Pollard

Cover design: Rebecca Scambler

Thanks to Dan Clayton for his contributions to Chapter 11 'Teaching English Language'

© English and Media Centre, 18 Compton Terrace, London, N1 2UN

First published, 2020

Printed by: Stephens and George Ltd

ISBN: 9781906101664

Acknowledgements

'Quend Plage-les-Pins' by Helen Tookey (*City of Departures*, 2019) is reprinted here by kind permission of Carcanet Press Limited, Manchester, UK

Every effort has been made to trace and acknowledge copyright, but if accidental infringement has been made, we would welcome information to redress the situation.

About Barbara Bleiman

Barbara studied English at Somerville College Oxford (1973-6). She completed a PGCE at the Institute of Education, London University, where she was awarded the Storey Miller Prize for the highest grade in her year in any subject (a combination of her final examination mark and teaching practice). She taught full-time in London schools for 10 years, ending up at Islington Sixth Form Centre where she was initially Head of English, and then a member of SLT working cross-phase with the local FE college before the two institutions merged as City & Islington College. In the late 1980s she did a one-year secondment as an Advisory Teacher at the English Centre and then continued to work both there and at Islington Sixth Form Centre in part-time roles while bringing up her children. More recently, she became Co-Director of EMC, first alongside Michael Simons and latterly with the current Director Andrew McCallum. She stepped down at the end of 2015 but continues to work part-time for EMC, as well as pursuing her own fiction writing.

Both at EMC and previously for commercial publishers, she has written or co-written a number of award-winning resources, across a range of areas of English, including A Level, poetry, Shakespeare and language, as well as writing numerous articles, chapters for books and blogs. Since 2001, Barbara and Lucy Webster have edited *emagazine*, EMC's quarterly print subscription magazine for A Level students.

She has managed several research projects for external agencies including: a DfE funded Best Practice Research Scholarship Project (BPRS) on A Level; a Learning Skills Network (LSN) project on English and work-related learning; a Teacher Development Agency (TDA) project on underachieving writers, and an intergenerational speaking and listening project funded by Paul Hamlyn. Most recently she has led EMC's project on group work, *It's Good to Talk*.

Over her 40 years in education she has been a consultant to a number of external agencies, including QCDA, the Nuffield Science GCSE project and several Awarding Bodies. She was a member of the QCA English 21 planning group and worked with Teachers TV. Along with Andrew McCallum, she represents the English and Media Centre on the Common English Forum. She was on the Poetry Book Society Board from 2007-1010 and is an RSA fellow.

In 2019 Barbara was awarded the NATE Award for Outstanding Contribution to the Teaching of English.

Barbara Bleiman's collection of writings on 'what matters in English' is a refreshing reminder of the conversation that is English. She sets her considerations in the historical and contemporary contexts of English education, engaging with wider discourses of English as a school subject. Absolutely essential reading for anyone involved – or interested – in the teaching of English.

Dr Rachel Roberts, University of Reading

This book is exactly what I needed! It has clarified my thinking (especially about how and what we read with young people), made me both ask questions about my practice and think carefully about what I want to develop and do more of in the future. I love how well it situates current debates in the history of English teaching, whilst also being so up to date. The balance between very personal, anecdotal experience and wider research makes it a collection which is helpful, thoughtful, insightful and engaging.

Myfanwy Edwards, Head of English, Richmond upon Thames School

This is a book which should be read by all teachers of English. It is published at a crucial moment for the subject, when reflection is more important than ever. And Barbara Bleiman is uniquely well-positioned to analyse the forces acting on how the subject is conceived of and taught, whether from academia, from government and official institutions, or from grass-roots movements and social media.

Framed by two seminal speeches on the state of the subject, from 1991 and 2019, this collection of articles, blogs and specially-written pieces is at once a lesson in history and a manifesto for the future – an objective survey of what is, with passionate advocacy for what might be.

All of the pieces here are rooted in a deep knowledge of theory and of the literature around English teaching. However, they also draw on rich, personal experience and recent, important work with teachers in schools. Descriptions of practice provide persuasive evidence of – and a remarkably practical guide to – what matters in English.

However, what perhaps most powerfully pervades the book are the words of pupils themselves. Glimpsed in extracts from written work, and in transcripts of recorded talk, these are the authentic voices which Barbara puts at the heart of her practice and of her vision for English.

James Durran, Local Authority Advisor North Yorkshire

This book should be essential reading for all student teachers of English. English teachers know in their hearts what English is, and 'what matters', but staying true to that conviction can be challenging when working in increasingly prescriptive, 'one-size-fits-all-subjects' contexts. Barbara presents powerful arguments to counter much of today's narrative around 'what works' by returning to the fundamental question of 'what matters,' while simultaneously offering tried and tested, practical approaches to implement in classrooms right away. I know I will dip into it again and again. To have Barbara's extensive wisdom and experience compiled into one highly readable volume is invaluable, and English classrooms up and down the country, not least my own, will be far richer for it. A lighthouse in the storm for teachers at all stages of their career. Thank you, Barbara!

Amy Druce, Lead English Teacher, School 21

Contents

Acknowledgements

If I were to offer all the thanks I might want to, to all the people who have contributed either directly or indirectly to this book, the acknowledgements would stretch over many pages. Everything I believe, understand and know about English teaching has come from collaborative work and discussion with others – teachers, academics, educators, school students and above all my colleagues at EMC over many years – in the past Michael Simons, Sabrina Broadbent and Jenny Grahame and also my current brilliant colleagues, Andrew McCallum, Lucy Webster, Kate Oliver, Emma Barker, Lucy Hinchliffe, Dan Clayton and Claire Pollard.

I do want to mention a few other people though, whose own work has been particularly valuable to me and who feature in chapters in the book. A huge thank you to Robert Eaglestone, both for his own superb writing on English and for his long-standing collaborations with me personally and with the work of the English and Media Centre. Thank you too to all the amazing teachers involved in EMC's group work project *It's Good to Talk* and, in particular, Richard Long, a teacher whose work I very much admire.

I would also like to thank those in NATE, LATE, the English Association, University English, CLPE, UKLA, University College London Institute of Education, James Durran and others with whom I have many shared ideas and values. Finally, thank you to all the teachers and students I have had the pleasure and privilege of working with in over 43 years in education.

Foreword

The first blog that Barbara Bleiman wrote for the English and Media Centre was *Is 'what works?' the only question educational research should be trying to answer?* For me, it's one of the key pieces in this brilliant collection. Early on, it challenged a growing orthodoxy, now fully embedded across swathes of the educational landscape, that was leading to a narrowing of possibilities for young people. Nowhere was this more the case than in secondary English. In the name of 'what works?', prominent, often reactionary voices in tune with government thinking, were placing limits on what students could do: *don't read that; don't write like that; don't speak like that; don't even speak at all!*

Modestly, with intelligence, rigour and determination, Barbara advocated an enlightened alternative. This alternative is based on her phenomenal understanding of how language and literature work and, more importantly, how this relates to teaching and learning. Its starting point is the expectation that young people can read challenging texts; they can write for a range of audiences and purposes; they can think and speak for themselves and express their ideas cogently. They need guidance and intervention from a teacher along the way, and they need to be immersed in language and literature that will help develop what they already know, but they bring an array of riches to the classroom which we ignore at our peril. One of the joys of this book is that it so insightfully critiques deficit models of English teaching that diminish the humanity of our young people, while simultaneously offering valuable alternatives.

It's a mystery to me that approaches of the kind promoted by Barbara (not just in this book, but in her published classroom resources that have been used by millions of students during her four decades in education, and in the courses she has run for thousands of teachers) are not in the ascendancy. That's not to say that they aren't currently being practised in classrooms up and down the country. They are. English teachers are a resourceful bunch and will always find ways to teach that which they know to be valuable and important, whatever the external pressures working against them. But it is to recognise that we operate in strange times: times when much of what goes on in secondary English classrooms is unrecognisable from the vibrancy and variety of the discipline at university level. And where rich traditions of language and literature pedagogy – stuff that really works – are overlooked in favour of general educational theories that are at best irrelevant to English, at worst damaging to its long-term future and the future of our young people.

The title of this book clearly offers a gentle riposte to the 'what works' agenda critiqued in that first blog. There need not, of course, be a discrepancy between 'what works' and 'what matters'. But the latter has to be our starting point. We need to recognise (and continuously debate) what matters and then make sure we implement this in ways that work. Anyone looking for a blueprint for how to do this is holding the solution in their hands.

Andrew McCallum, Director English and Media Centre, March 2020

Introduction

What is the real English – the genuine article – that we should be making available to our students? What should it contain, how should it be taught, what does it look like in terms of student work and outcomes, when it's served up at its very best – the gourmet meal that all students should eat, rather than the cheap, fast-food version that some may end up consuming, with little refinement or nutritional value? This book seeks to explore these fundamental questions and hopes to offer some answers for today's English teacher.

The English and Media Centre[1] has had a surprisingly consistent view on the issues raised by these questions, over the five decades of its existence as a development centre, publisher and provider of CPD for English teachers. Our specific practices and thinking have developed and evolved over that period, as we have continued to strive to be relevant and helpful to English teachers over times of significant change, but our key values and underlying principles have retained their essential core.

At the heart of EMC's philosophy right from the outset in the early 70s was a mantra of practice – theory – practice, always starting with the classroom and ending with it, but bringing to bear any valuable theoretical thinking, both from the past and the present. Expressed a little differently now, perhaps with the word 'research' incorporated within 'theory', that mantra is still informing all of our work, and is at the heart of this book too. I hope people reading this book will take away with them important ideas and values about how to *do* English teaching – not just abstract academic ideas but practical ways of thinking that can inform what we actually do with students in English. It's a book for practitioners, not a book for theorists or educational researchers. The informal style, and light-touch approach to research, is intended to make it both a good read and a book that is useable and illuminating for teachers actually doing the job of being an English teacher right now. Most of the texts I refer to have been talked about, weighed up and applied in our dialogues as a team at EMC, and in our work with teachers and in classrooms. The research and theories presented here are ones that we believe to be valid, significant and useful. But the treatment of them in the book will not be exhaustive or comprehensive – I will not be attempting to cover every view on every issue, just those we have found most helpful.

More than anything else, this book opens up a set of conversations. It revisits themes and ideas in different ways. It engages with current debates but situates them in a broader context, drawing lessons from the past as well as posing possible directions for the future. It tries to make links and connections and bring English teachers into a wide range of ongoing discussions about what the subject is and what it should be.

---

1. The English and Media Centre is also known by the abbreviation EMC. From now on, the book will use the shorter version.

A Timeline – Key Events in English Teaching

1921	*The Teaching of English in England* (Newbolt Report).
1947	London Association for the Teaching of English (LATE) established.
1963	National Association for the Teaching of English (NATE) established.
1965	Introduction of CSEs as an alternative to O Level. There were 3 'modes' with varying patterns of assessment. Mode 3 was 100% coursework, marked by the school.
1966	International Dartmouth Conference held in USA, with UK and US educationalists focusing on English in education.
1967	*Growth Through English* (John Dixon).
1970	*Language and Learning* (James Britton).
1971	*Language in Use* (Peter Doughty, John Pearce and Geoffrey Thornton) .
	Teaching London Kids magazine first issue.
1975	ILEA English Centre established (becoming EMC, an independent charity, in 1990).
	A Language for Life (The Bullock Report) with, among other things, the first notions of language across the curriculum.
1976	Callaghan's 'The Great Debate' speech, initiating the idea of a national curriculum.
1977	Introduction of AEB 753 AL English Literature syllabus, leading to AEB 660, with 50% coursework.
1983-87	ILEA initiatives on race, class and gender.
1985-98	The National Writing Project.
1987-93	The National Oracy Project.
1988	*Report of the Committee of Inquiry into the Teaching of English Language* (The Kingman Report).
	Education Reform Act.
	Introduction of GCSEs, replacing CSE and O Level as a single exam for all. English GCSE was 100% coursework.
1988-89	First statutory National Curriculum introduced. Programmes of Study published 1988 and 1989 for first teaching September 1989.
1989	*English for Ages 5-16* (The Cox Report).
1989-92	Language in the National Curriculum (LINC project).

1992	First publication of schools' league tables.
1993	KS3 SATs first introduced.
1995	New updated National Curriculum (after Dearing Report).
1998	National Literacy Strategy (NLS) launched for primary.
1999	New National Curriculum for first teaching September 2000 (David Blunkett, Secretary of State for Education).
2000	Curriculum reform of A Level, with the start of AS as both a standalone qualification and a staging post towards A Level.
2001	National Literacy Strategy extended to Secondary with the KS3 Framework for Teaching English: Years 7, 8 and 9.
2008	New National Curriculum (Ed Balls, Secretary of State for Education).
2009	Ofsted report: *English at the Crossroads*.
2010	GCSE specifications for three English subjects: English, English Language and English Literature. Students took either English or both of the other two. GCSE coursework was replaced by Controlled Assessment (60% for English and English Language – 40% written, 20% speaking and listening).
	First application of the Ebacc in League Tables.
2012	Ofsted report: *Improving Literacy: Moving English Forward*.
2013	New National Curriculum for first teaching September 2014 (Michael Gove, Secretary of State for Education).
	Introduction of Creative Writing A Level.
2015	New A Level specifications introduced with a maximum 20% coursework. AS became a standalone qualification: a return to linearity.
	New GCSE specifications with no coursework or Controlled Assessment, no American texts.
2016	Introduction of Progress 8 as part of the accountability measures.
2018	Final examination of Creative Writing A Level, first introduced in 2013 and withdrawn in 2015 reforms.

1. Way Back Then
Ruskin Conference on English Teaching, 1991

In 1991, when I was in my mid-thirties, I was asked to speak at a conference about the state of English in universities and schools. I had been a Head of English in an inner-city sixth form college, a senior teacher in charge of the college's vocational and pre-vocational courses and had completed a year as an advisory teacher at the English Centre (now EMC). The conference was called 'The Future of English'. I had fifteen to twenty minutes allocated to me. Addressing an audience comprised mainly of university academics in English and associated subjects, I used the time to flag up the most pressing issues for the subject, from the perspective of a practitioner who also engaged strongly with research and wider thinking about English and education.

It's interesting to look back at that speech now, and reflect on what has stayed the same and what has changed. At the end of this book is my Harold Rosen Lecture, a speech I made nearly thirty years later, in July 2019, to the NATE conference in Chester. It was only after writing and delivering the 2019 speech that I returned to the one written some thirty years earlier. What struck me was how many common strands there were. In both, I talk about the following: the distortions on the subject brought about by the constant churn of political interventions, however well meant; the impact of an over-emphasis on assessment; fundamental, underlying principles about who education is for; the valuing of students themselves and what they bring to the process of learning. In the Ruskin speech, I talked about both language and literature and the pressing concerns of the time. But I also chose to raise issues about vocational and pre-vocational English, questioning the role of teachers not just in offering to students an entry into an academic subject but also in preparing them to meet the demands of future life, as workers, citizens, informed adults and people with leisure time and broader cultural lives. At the time, this particular role for English was being hotly contested. Many English teachers felt it was pandering to the needs of employers and would detract and distract from the literature and creative writing that had always been at the heart of the subject. Now this debate seems, rather surprisingly, absent. It has stopped being so much of a battleground. Is that because we all simply agree that literacy is of prime importance and agree on what we mean by that? Or has literacy now shrunk to academic literacy – what gives students access to the curriculum? Have English teachers forgotten our role in looking beyond the academic discipline to wider obligations to all students, regardless of whether they wish to carry on with the subject in future years, and beyond the functional, to a kind of literacy that enriches your whole life? The blogs and writings in this book try to answer these questions and more. But first, here's that early Ruskin speech. Perhaps, after reading it, you might want to turn straight to the Harold Rosen lecture on page 187 and compare – or, instead, wait and read it at the very end, to reflect on the subject in the first decades of the millennium and how and why it has changed.

The Ruskin Speech

What has happened to English in the 1970s and 80s? I'll try to address the question from my own personal experience as a practising teacher over that period of time. I taught in London comprehensives in the mid 70s and in the early 80s as Head of English, then Senior Teacher at Islington Sixth Form Centre. I was an ILEA English Advisory Teacher for a year and I am currently teaching part-time, working freelance and as a parent.

What I describe will inevitably be a partial perspective; teaching for fifteen years in London, I have been especially influenced by the London radical teaching network – LATE, Teaching London Kids, the ILEA English Centre[1] – and the work of the London Institute of Education. Many of the examples I quote are drawn from the work of these organisations.

I'll aim to look at just three issues that seem to me to have been important during the 70s and 80s.

- First, what we have felt to be important about Language.

- Second, what our changing approaches have been towards the teaching of Literature.

- Third, and looking into the future here, how we have responded to the demand that English should teach skills for working life.

In 1976 I went to the Institute of Education in London. A few months previously I had been an English undergraduate at Oxford and towards the end of my course had attended a conference at Ruskin College with Raymond Williams and Terry Eagleton where, with some unease, I began to confront the idea that my three years in the Bodleian could have been spent in rather different ways. However, I threw off the challenge, partly no doubt because of the insecurity it produced, but partly because I found it difficult to engage with theory in the abstract. I wanted something that would make sense of the practical issues that were before me.

The Institute was bubbling with debate and ideas and the theoretical arguments and practice seemed to feed into each other, with a real relationship between theories of learning and what goes on in the classroom – the case for mixed-ability teaching, challenging conventional wisdoms about how children read, applying theories of language and learning to develop strategies and materials to teach with.

The key issue for me was on Language and Culture, arising out of the Rosen/Bernstein debate.[2] Exciting work was being done in the classroom by people like John Richmond, allowing pupils their own voice, encouraging and valuing language variety and informing teachers themselves about the dialects and languages in their classrooms.[3]

---

1. Now the English and Media Centre.

2. The linguist Basil Bernstein argued that working-class children had a 'restricted code' of language, whilst middle-class children operated within an 'elaborated code'. Harold Rosen strongly critiqued this theory in an article called 'Language and Class', published in 1972.

3. *Becoming Our Own Experts* (1982). Teachers were becoming their own experts and undertaking their own research in the classroom. Language diversity was seen as a resource rather than a problem.

Community publishing projects were publishing working-class writing and texts like *In the Melting Pot*, written by a Hackney school student, became a symbol of what we, radical English teachers, were trying to do. Publishing pupils' work was a way of giving them a sense of their own worth and part of the shift away from the canon and towards offering a broader range of texts, drawing on pupils' own experience.

Knowledge about language was seen as very important, with books like the English Centre's *The Languages Book* aiming to teach pupils about language and power and the nature of different kinds of discourse.

There were also broader initiatives on the language demands of the whole school curriculum. The work of Barnes and Britton led to teachers examining the language of subject areas and the extent to which that language was a barrier to pupils' learning.[4] In the 70s, the focus was very much on changing the language of the subject areas to allow for the more personal and familiar. However, in recent years, the issue has been re-visited and some radical teachers are taking a different stance, thinking afresh about whether one has an obligation to teach working-class pupils about the language of different kinds of discourse. The Rosen/Bernstein debate remains alive, fuelled by recent work in genre theory and by re-evaluations of how we teach language in getting to grips with the National Curriculum.[5]

Throughout the 70s and 80s there has been a right-wing bandwagon (often led by the popular press) to change the agenda, to narrow English teachers' interests in language to the teaching of grammar, to force on us misguided ideas about the teaching of literacy and to exhaust us into submission by a thousand and one ways of quantifying and assessing language development rather than teaching it. From graded assessments, through records of achievement and into the National Curriculum inordinate amounts of time and energy have been spent resisting attempts to contain English and reduce it to its lowest common denominator. All credit is due to the radical English teaching lobby; in key places the arguments have been won and the National Curriculum, for all one's doubts about the assessment element, does embody much of what we would consider to be good practice in English. On the Language issue for instance, the National Curriculum Programmes of Study, with their emphasis on appropriate uses of language for different purposes and audiences, encourage good practice. The Knowledge About Language requirements generally avoid a narrow emphasis on the teaching of a particular notion of grammar but take us into many of the spheres of interest raised in the 70s, about language and culture, language and power, purposes and audiences and different kinds of discourse.

---

4. Barnes and Britton's work is referred to in other chapters. Key texts on language across the curriculum include *From Communication to Curriculum* (Barnes,1974) and *Language, the Learner and the School* (Barnes, Britton and Rosen, 1971)

5. In Australia, educational linguist Jim Martin and others built on Halliday's theories of functional linguistics to identify the social purposes of language use – explaining, describing, arguing, reviewing, recounting, narrating – and the ways in which these can be seen as 'genres' with set, predictable structures and conventions. These, they argued, could be made explicit and specifically taught.

The 80s have seen us obsessed with the assessment of language development, largely because this has been forced upon us. But the influence on teachers of the developments of the 70s has been powerful enough to allow that assessment to be successfully steered towards a model of language development with which we remain broadly in sympathy.

Turning to my second issue, the teaching of Literature, what have our concerns been over the 70s and 80s?

In my experience, in the late 70s, race became the central issue, with the emergence of the National Front in schools, the founding in 1978 of ALTARF (All London Teachers Against Racism and Fascism) and the perceived need not merely to offer a curriculum that was multicultural but that was anti-racist as well. English teachers argued particularly strongly for the banning of racist texts from schools, drew up criteria for the selection of texts, looked for positively anti-racist texts. Publishing houses were gradually being forced to offer different kinds of texts and opinion-forming bodies like the ILEA English Centre encouraged the study of particular texts, like *Roll of Thunder Hear My Cry*, by producing anti-racist teaching material to go with them.

Again in the late 70s, a gender group was set up at the English Centre, with teachers on secondments from schools and advisory teachers.

As with race, the main initial concern in terms of literature teaching was with what kinds of texts are taught in schools – eliminating sexist texts, looking at how many texts were by women writers, providing materials to encourage teachers to use feminist texts or texts that provide a female perspective. From this starting-point the group produced important work on other aspects of gender and English.

In terms of gender and race, the debate on literature has moved on. We have made significant advances in the terms we set ourselves in the 70s. Overtly misogynist and racist books are less in evidence. LEA initiatives, such as ILEA's on Race, Gender and Class have, at the very least, legitimised a kind of basic commitment to anti-racist and anti-sexist teaching. One example of how far we have moved can be found in looking at what is taught in A Level Literature courses, where most syllabuses now offer more texts by modern women writers and opportunities to study world literature, written in English.

On the increasingly popular AEB 660 syllabus, it is common to find teachers choosing writers like Alice Walker, Maya Angelou, Derek Walcott, Fay Weldon and so on.

While as a teacher in the 70s I was delighted with these changes, as a 90s teacher I can see some of the limitations. Now our emphasis has shifted, from what kinds of texts we read to approaches to texts, whatever they may be, and to the making of meaning. Here we have drawn on developments in the universities and in literary theory and have been strongly influenced by Media Studies and its growth within English. The search for the perfect socialist/feminist text has been somewhat undermined by the work done by people like Gemma Moss in her book *Un/popular Fictions* and the approaches taken to media texts, which encourage us to ask not questions about the value of texts but questions about the nature of texts: their means of production, their historical and cultural contexts, the different ways in which we make meaning from them and the influence of our gender, race and class upon that whole process. The authoritative reading of a text has gone out of the window and I would argue that this is not just among committed, theoretically-orientated teachers, but is also influencing wider current practice.

Is it that English teachers up and down the country are reading the latest books on literary theory and applying them in the classroom? I think not. Changing approaches to texts have come partly from the world of literary theory but also from direct experience within the classroom and, most important of all, through the exchange of ideas amongst practising teachers.

First, I think there has been the influence of Media Studies. Approaches to Media texts have influenced English teachers' ways of dealing with other texts, particularly at GCSE. Second, in that Leavisite bastion of A Level, teachers have become increasingly dissatisfied with what they can offer, partly by contrast with the empowering approaches of GCSE and partly because of witnessing daily the failure of their students to make sense of the traditional textual approaches. Growing numbers of A Level teachers have been opting for alternative syllabuses, maybe at first because they simply want the freedom to choose their own texts but in the process of meeting as consortia and exchanging ideas, there has been a gradual filtering through of new approaches to those texts, regardless of whether those teachers have read the theory behind them or not.[6] Third, the general shift in the classroom from an interest in the content and the teacher to the learner makes the shift of emphasis from author and text to the reader particularly welcome.

I do think it is worth noting the way in which new approaches to texts have spread. It has been through practical collaboration over making classroom material, through networks of committed teachers such as in NATE and LATE, teachers on secondments as Advisory Teachers or doing part-time MAs, meetings of alternative A Level Consortia and in-service training courses. For instance, the work of Advisory Teachers at the ILEA English Centre on two publications, *Changing Stories* and *Making Stories*, was a very important attempt to provide classroom resources that would ask different questions of texts and provide a useful model for teachers to develop their own material on the texts they are teaching.

When I was an Advisory Teacher at the English Centre recently, we worked with a group of practising teachers, in collaboration with Jane Miller at the Institute of Education and Kenneth Ramchand at the University of the West Indies to produce teaching material on Jean Rhys's novel *Wide Sargasso Sea* that would provide A Level teachers with new approaches to a text. This kind of collaboration between school teachers and university teachers seems to me be very important for future developments in English teaching, yet it is all too rare.

---

6. AEB 753, introduced in 1977, included open book exams and 30% coursework. It later became AEB 660 and in the 1980s coursework rose to 50%. These were fully accredited A Level courses, chosen by large numbers of schools.

Of course, now in the 90s, many new teachers are coming into the system, whose own experience has been of a non-Leavisite A Level and degree course and this will no doubt have an important influence on the teaching of literature in the future.

In looking at the teaching of language and the teaching of literature, I have looked back over the late 70s and 80s. My third area of concern takes me more towards the future.

In the 70s, as a young teacher I was wedded to the idea of an almost exclusively literature-based English curriculum. Language work arose largely from personal experience or from books. Any attempt to see English as providing skills for work was anathema and I can even remember howling down a representative from the Schools Council Industry Project at a LATE conference, who was later to become a close working colleague and friend. One can see the extent of radical English teachers' opposition to a skills approach in an article by Roy Goddard in *English and Education* in 1985, in which he bemoans the introduction of TVEI[7] and CPVE (two pre-vocational education initiatives introduced in KS4 and KS5, the first as a general pre-vocational initiative for all students and the second as a vocational route for students who might otherwise have been doing GCSE resits). He says that TVEI was the Government's attempt 'to wrest the educational orientation of schools away from the needs, interests and capacities of children towards the demands of industry' and he suggests that 'Its function is, quite simply, to reintroduce selection in secondary schools.' For Goddard, 'it is part of the project of the new vocationalism to hinder and discourage any form of teaching which tries to provide students with the means of critically investigating the conditions of their existence and of exploring questions of value and meaning.'

The view he expresses echoes that of many radical teachers at the time, and some today. However, the introduction of TVEI had some effects which would have perhaps rather startled such critics as Roy Goddard. It became clear that rather than consigning less able students to a lower status vocational route, TVEI was having the most powerful impact on the so-called able, supposedly more academic students. They were taking up the opportunities offered by TVEI and finding them a refreshing change from some of the more sterile approaches of academic learning. Many of the approaches within TVEI, trying to make the curriculum more student-centred, more practical and related to contexts in the community and beyond the classroom, were having the reverse effect to that anticipated and were not only making pupils more committed to their work but also allowing them to, in Goddard's words 'investigate the conditions of their existence and explore questions of value and meaning'. The students quoted in Peter Medway's TVEI Evaluation Project at Leeds University, who analysed the use of new technology in their school, or worked and wrote for adults with learning difficulties or who evaluated their work experience for different audiences, were all engaged in the kind of non-literary English that I think all students, of whatever ability, should be engaged in.

---

7. TVEI, the Technical and Vocational Education Initiative, was the first major national government intervention in the school curriculum, set up to support the development of pre-vocational education (1983-97).

Now in the 1990s, there is a growing belief that English should offer the best of the academic and vocational traditions to all students at 16-19 and that there are some lessons to be learnt from vocational education in the 11-16 curriculum. At 16-19, the debate is hotting up, with widespread calls for a unified system of academic and vocational education, where all students would follow modules with academic and vocational slants. What we need is a new definition of English at 16-19, one which draws on the best of both traditions.[8] If we can free ourselves from the stranglehold of A Level it may well be that the new concepts of English that emerge will open the way for a broader notion of English in general, not only in incorporating the idea of teaching language for life but also by broadening our ideas about what texts should be studied, to include the texts that surround us in our ordinary lives.

So, rather than feeling threatened by the growth of vocationalism, I feel the opposite, that if English teachers take vocational education seriously and influence it in the way that they have influenced the development of the National Curriculum, it could be part of a transformation of English teaching that we would really welcome. The relationship between the academic and the vocational is the next big curricular battle that we need to be part of – it encompasses issues about how we teach language and what we want to teach as literature and it is an area in which we could do with some help from our colleagues in the universities, both in exploring the underlying issues and in developing practical ideas about what kind of curriculum we should be arguing for.

References for Chapter 1

Barnes, D. 1974. *From Communication to Curriculum*. Harmondsworth: Penguin.

Barnes D., Britton, J. and Rosen, H. 1971. *Language, The Learner and The School*. Harmondsworth: Penguin.

Finegold, D., Keep, E., Miliband, D. Raffe, D., Spours, K. and Young, M. 1990. *A British Baccalaureate: Overcoming Divisions Between Education and Training*. London: IPPR.

Goddard, R. 1985. 'Beyond the literary heritage: meeting the needs in English at 16-19'. In *English in Education* 19 (2).

Moss, G. 1989. *Un/popular Fictions*. London: Virago Press.

Richmond, J. et al 1982. *Becoming Our Own Experts*. London: The Talk Workshop Group. ILEA English Centre: London.

Rosen H. 1972. 'Language and class'. In ed. Richmond, John. 2017. *Harold Rosen: Writings on Life, Language and Learning, 1958-2008*. London: UCL Institute of Education Press.

---

8. The idea of replacing A Levels and vocational qualifications with a single, unified qualification was fuelled by IPPR's report, The British Baccalaureate, written by David Miliband and Michael Young, among others.

2. What English Is and What It Could and Should Be

This section starts by questioning what English as a subject is, and how it's been characterised in the past. It goes on to explore what it should be like now, looking at the direction that it has been going in more recently, arguing that it is in danger of losing its way. This is followed by a recent piece highlighting the dangers of a focus on small procedures as opposed to bigger concepts and a much earlier article, from 1997, looking at the teaching of literary texts, asking what we mean by offering challenging texts in English classrooms. This last piece is interesting for the way it gives a window onto an earlier period of English teaching but it also offers some ideas that are applicable to today's dilemmas – about the canon versus diverse texts, about classroom pedagogy and what we consider to be rich experiences of the subject.

2.1 Where we've come from and why it matters

When the English Centre was set up in 1975 to support all English teachers in Inner London schools, it was founded on a set of principles and practices that were remarkably uncontentious among English teachers themselves. While some individuals or groups of teachers may have dissented, there was nevertheless an extraordinary commonality of thinking about the big questions facing teachers of the subject, especially among those teachers who were most active and engaged in their work – the Teachmeet, TeamEnglish, ResearchED teachers of their day. This homogeneity of views may seem rather surprising from today's perspective, where almost everything is contested, teachers (English teachers not least), are in different camps and pin their flags to very different masts.

These are just some of the kinds of things that an English teacher in the 1970s and early 1980s[1] would have been likely to take pretty much for granted:

- That students' own creative writing was a rich source of self-expression and nourished their broader personal and educational development.

- That students' interests and enthusiasms should be capitalised on, in the selection of topics and texts; they would enjoy the work, work harder and learn more if they felt 'engaged' with what they were doing.

- That canonical texts were important but that offering students diverse texts from their own worlds and cultures was a vital bridge between home identity and school learning; in valuing the one, you made it possible to extend out into the other.

---

1. *English for Ages 5 to 16*, known as the Cox Report (1989) identified five ways of characterising the subject: Personal Growth; Cross-curricular; Adult Needs; Cultural Heritage; Cultural Analysis. Which of these has been foregrounded has fluctuated over the years but until recently all have informed English teachers' thinking. It's interesting to see how these ideas were embedded in practice in English teaching of the 1970s and 80s. See 'Real English versus Exam English' on page 26 for more on this.

- That students had a voice in the classroom that needed to be heard, in classroom dialogue, in group work, in performance, in the development of oracy as a tool as well as an essential means of developing thinking in the subject.

- That the spoken language of students needed to be respected, since the way we speak expresses who we are, and though students needed to learn how to adopt new voices for new occasions, students' own language, as influenced by their class, gender, age or cultural identity, needed to be accepted, celebrated and valued.

- That English was the subject, more than any other, where students would find their identity.

- That knowledge about language was about much more than just correct spelling, punctuation and grammar, and that developing understandings about language in use should be at the heart of what we do.

- That understanding the media and exploring media texts were fundamental aspects of the English curriculum.

- That English was the subject where students would learn to love books and that one of the key purposes of English was to allow them to become confident and enthusiastic readers in their adult lives.

- That in English students would make strong relationships with each other and with their teacher, because the subject itself was all about identity and human experience.

- That English was a subject that students loved. If asked, many, if not most, would say English was their favourite subject.

Could one say the same of today's English teaching environment? Almost certainly not. The demands and constraints of the current educational world, with its high stakes testing and accountability culture, have meant that many of these aspects of teaching English are under pressure and no longer taken for granted. In their hearts, teachers may well believe in many of these things but will be subject to powerful forces that mitigate against them. Equally, some of these previous 'givens' have become grounds of serious disagreement and debate. Ideas about a literary canon, student engagement, pupil voice and 'correctness' in spoken language, for instance, are all hotly contested areas.

Where did these givens come from, and what has happened to disrupt the dominance of these views? You could read a book like Simon Gibbons' *English and Its Teachers: A History of Policy, Pedagogy and Practice* to find out all about this long and fascinating story. This book, on the other hand, isn't a history; it's a practical and committed look at the subject and how it's being taught now, with a glance backwards to see how current approaches have changed. So instead of telling the whole story, in the first part of this chapter I'm going to give a lightning tour of some key thinkers, influences and ways of thinking about being an English teacher from that period. Later in the book, in discussing particular aspects of English teaching, I'll come back to some of them in more detail.

In the 1970s and 80s, as is the case now, some of the key thinkers and influencers were not academic researchers but rather teachers with their ideas firmly rooted in the classrooms in which they taught. That may come as something of a surprise. Yesterday's 'experts' were, in their own way, very much like today's teachers wanting to inform themselves and develop their practices online, in blogs, on Twitter, in self-supporting groups of teachers. Harold Rosen, for instance, who went on to become professor at the Institute of Education, developed his ideas about English teaching in the 1950s as a Head of Department at what was then Walworth School, an inner city comprehensive. Michael Simons, who set up the ILEA English Centre, had been a classroom teacher in Wandsworth. He went on to have a hugely significant role in the development of the subject, through his work at EMC, including setting up the *English Magazine* (later the *English and Media Magazine*), starting to create resources for English classrooms that could be shared widely, and acting as a guiding light and advocate for media education, both in English and as a separate subject.

Just as with the current highly active, enthusiastic teachers using social media platforms, who offer each other ideas online or who meet voluntarily on their weekends to share expertise, teachers like John Richmond, the many teachers who attended LATE conferences or started up the magazine *Teaching London Kids* or went to NATE conferences, or met up at the English Centre (later EMC) for after school interest groups, were all fervently working to develop their practices. Some were investigating their own classrooms to do research of their own, or contributing to projects run by the English Centre. This classroom research had some of the same flavour as current teacher-led research but perhaps with more emphasis on trying to understand what's happening in the complexity of classrooms, rather than trying to apply and test out single strategies and solutions – an investigative rather than a 'proof of efficacy' orientation. This kind of research was rooted in underpinning ideas drawn from the work of sociologists, psychologists, linguists, child behaviour experts and educationalists, in much the same way as today. Harold Rosen's contributions were multiple. The most important centred around his passionate advocacy and understanding of storytelling, in all its varieties both written and oral, his valuing of students' own experiences and language in the classroom, his recognition of the social nature of learning, his understanding that language should be at the heart of learning not just in English but across the curriculum (the language across the curriculum initiatives of the 70s morphed into a rather differently focused 'literacy across the curriculum' that resurfaced as part of the National Literacy Strategy of the late 1990s.[2])

The work of Harold Rosen, Douglas Barnes, John Dixon and others drew on thinkers, linguists and psychologists like Vygotsky but they also put a premium

---

2. The National Literacy Strategy was introduced by the Labour Secretary of State for Education, David Blunkett, published in 1997, introduced into primary schools in 1998 and extended to Secondary in 2001, as the Key Stage 3 National Strategy Framework for Teaching English: Years 7, 8 and 9.

on classroom research, alongside philosophical or theoretical thinking on a more abstract plane. Dixon's major work, *Growth Through English*, emerging from the Dartmouth Conference of 1966, placed a fresh emphasis on pedagogy alongside content and involved a re-thinking of what was meant by knowledge. Classroom transcripts and film clips were regarded as highly valuable, and were the subject of close scrutiny, in CPD and in departmental discussions. Barnes, Britton and Rosen's *Language, the Learner and the School*, showed learning in action not just in English but in other subjects and was seminal in revealing what dialogue between students can do to develop knowledge in English and across the curriculum.

Looking at student work, whether in group discussion or student writing, was a vital element in understanding what was involved in English the subject, how students learned and what constituted 'good work'. To that extent, the English teacher of the late 1970s and 80s was a privileged one. They were likely to attend weekly, or fortnightly, departmental meetings after school, dedicated wholly to talking about the curriculum content and methods of teaching in the department. They would be regularly engaged in looking at examples of student writing (through coursework moderation in particular) and in constant dialogue with colleagues about their practices. It was a time when teachers could open up about uncertainties and insecurities, could ask for help and make judgements about their students' progress that were largely devoid of fearfulness of terrible repercussions. Whether they were judged to be good teachers by their peers, their students or their students' parents mattered a lot, but not in the same way as now. It was a question of professionalism and pride, not fear of retribution from on high. Constant observation and assessment, linked to performance and pay, alongside league tables and performance measures, had not yet laid a cold, dread hand on the teacher's shoulder. Teachers did not need to justify their students' achievements, spend disproportionate time on exam preparation to get them to achieve in external assessments or worry unduly about how their results would impact on them and their school.

The idea that students' own identities are worth taking seriously in English classrooms has a long history. It emerged out of two different traditions, a linguistic and a cultural and literary one, which overlapped. In the 1970s there were fierce arguments between Basil Bernstein, who argued that working-class children had a 'restricted code' in their use of language, and Harold Rosen and academic linguists like William Labov, who resisted this 'deficit' view.

Rosen, Labov and others argued that all varieties of English are 'correct' and of equal value linguistically (if not socially and politically). They recognised that the ways in which people speak are bound up with their sense of who they are and their confidence in themselves, in much deeper ways than simply being 'schooled' in order to shift from one way of speaking to another.

These same debates are now being played out in discussions of vocabulary and language 'gaps', in decisions about how to treat students' use of non-standard varieties of English in both talk and writing, in the classroom and even the playground, and in a more modern revisiting of the deficit debate in discussions of a cultural capital 'vacuum' among working-class children. The work of many contemporary linguists negates the idea of a deficit, but rather suggests the flexibility and range that is available to young people that they are capable of exploiting to the full. Rob Drummond's (2018) research into the language of students in a pupil referral unit explores the ways in which their rich uses of language in their own groups is subject to shifts and changes in different contexts. Sali A. Tagliamonte in her introduction to *Teen Talk: The Language of Adolescents* (2016), a book based on a vast database of young people's talk, goes as far as to say that, rather than being a cause for concern, 'teenage language is critical to the advancement of language evolution and society itself.'

Rosen's work from a more cultural and literary perspective, emphasised the importance of starting with students' own experiences and cultures, respecting and valuing everything they brought with them into the classroom. We can see the influence of this approach in the radical shifts in thinking about which texts are worthy of study in English classrooms. When I was at school in the 1960s, I read George Bernard Shaw, George Eliot, Elizabeth Bowen and pre-twentieth century poetry at KS3. For O Level, the contemporary poets I studied were all white men – Clifford Dyment, Ted Hughes, James Kirkup (only one of whom has turned out to be a major figure, by today's reckoning.) By the time I started teaching in the 1970s, I was able not only to teach canonical texts but also bring in local young writers, *Best West Indian Short Stories*, writing by Alan Sillitoe, Beverley Naidoo, Farukh Dhondy and others. Joan Goody, who chaired NATE's Multicultural Education committee played a huge role in valuing students own heritage and identities, championing knowledge about books written in English from other cultures. In those days, given patterns of migration to the UK and London in particular, texts from the Caribbean featured strongly. Community literacy initiatives sprang up, with bookshops like Centerprise in Hackney publishing the work of writers who would normally not have even thought of themselves as writers, let alone have access to a publishing house to publish their work. This movement to celebrate and publish ordinary people's writing and value both their lives and their creativity, spilled over into schools, with many schools publishing anthologies of their own students' work and making the students' own writing part of the reading curriculum of the school. EMC published several collections of stunning student writing – authentic, powerful, well-written accounts of the lives of young people and what mattered to them. They included real-life accounts and fictional stories, poetry as well as prose. For teachers of those times, it's hard to forget the powerful impact on classes of reading Chelsea Herbert's *In the Melting Pot* (1970s), or sharing Saroeun Ing's extraordinary account of suffering in Cambodia under the rule of the Khmer Rouge and her family's flight to Thailand and then on to England. These student stories became the stimulus and inspiration for other students in classrooms up and down the country to both read for pleasure and write their own stories. EMC's *In the Melting Pot, Our Lives* (1980) and *More Lives* (1987) were bought in sets by schools and were among the most popular texts in the history of the Centre.

This sense of greeting the students and taking them on a journey that started 'where they were at' has been part of a pretty solid consensus between teachers, students, government and Awarding Bodies, till relatively recently. In all the earlier versions of the National Curriculum, however much one might argue over number of texts or the labelling as 'other' or 'different', the idea of texts from diverse cultures was firmly embedded. Even the current iteration of the National Curriculum for KS3 and 4, slimmed down as it is, cites 'seminal world literature' as a curriculum requirement. And yet many English teachers are now embracing an idea of 'cultural capital' that includes predominantly or even exclusively canonical English texts from past eras and excludes diverse texts that might represent the cultural worlds of students in their classrooms. Text choice is just one example of the ways in which English validates or invalidates, includes or excludes, students' own identities, experiences and starting-points.

A further key figure from the 1970s whose work continues to resonate is Douglas Barnes. He was hugely influential in demonstrating, through classroom research, the ways in which children learn through exploratory talk, using extensive transcript material to analyse how and why such talk helps students to take school knowledge, incorporate it into their existing frames of thinking and make it their own. His work was based on 'constructivist' views of the nature of learning, where the participant is an active 'constructor' of knowledge. The social nature of learning, developed in the work of Vygotsky (for instance in his seminal work *Thought and Language*, 1934) was key to Barnes' thinking and finds its successors in much of the work of EMC from the 1970s to today, in the work of academics like Neil Mercer and his colleagues and in the newer initiatives of schools like School 21 with its associated Voice 21 project.[3]

Key thinkers and influencers about language teaching came from the field of linguistics. Michael Halliday's work on functional grammar gave us a new way of thinking about how grammar works and how it could be taught – not through fixed word classes and labelling exercises but through thinking about the grammatical functions of words and syntactic combinations.[4] Ron Carter's seminal work in the LINC project (1989-1992), arising from the Kingman Report on the teaching of language, demonstrated how well-founded linguistic knowledge could be translated into classroom study, introducing students to ideas about the differences between spoken and written language, the origins, features and status of standard English as compared with other varieties, the ways in which language varies according to purpose, context and audience, as well as class, gender, race, age and geographical location. The LINC resources included classroom activities and transcripts of dialogues between children, exemplifying the ways in which they could further their knowledge through talk. The legacy of the LINC project can still be found in most English classrooms, even now that explicit teaching about

---

3. School 21 in Stratford, East London was opened in 2012 as a free school, with a vision to do education differently and re-think how to prepare students for life in the 21st century. Voice 21 arose out of it as a wider initiative to support oracy education in other schools.

4. Halliday's groundbreaking work of the 1960s and 70s gained wider recognition in 1985 with the publication of *An Introduction to Functional Grammar*.

language, for its own sake, has largely disappeared from the KS3 and KS4 formal requirements.

Media Studies was a relatively new discipline in the 1970s, carving out a niche for itself in the universities and in schools too but media *education*, alongside subject Media, was also seen as important for all students and found its 'natural' home within English, where discussion of literary texts could easily, and fruitfully, be extended to texts of all different kinds, from newspapers and magazines to photographs, films and TV programmes[5]. Textual analysis and cultural studies engaged in many similar practices and processes and could inform and enrich each other. Equally, creating media texts was closely related to creating traditional English texts. Writing stories *and* newspaper articles, screenplays *and* plays, stories *and* comics or photostories, writing comment and opinion *and* making photodocumentaries could draw on the common features and also flag up and make use of the distinctive and significant elements of the different media. Media was an enrichment not an optional add-on. And as it developed, it was also seen as something that all students should be entitled to, not just for the creative opportunities it offered but also as a necessity to teach media 'literacy' in a world in which critical understanding of the media was ever more vital. At EMC, it was also always a source of jokey ribbing between the media 'experts' and the rest of us that the media activities always seemed like such good fun, for students and teachers alike – from storyboards, simulations and advertising campaigns to short films and photographic montages. We all wanted to be doing the media work – and so did students.

Mostly, it was educational material about the subject itself that English teachers read in the 1970s to early 2000s but there were a few broader influences. For instance, in the 1960s, the educational psychologist Jerome Bruner put forward the notion of the spiral curriculum, suggesting that students don't learn in entirely linear ways but need to revisit concepts in different ways in order to consolidate learning and come back to ideas in new, more sophisticated ways. One contemporary descendent of that may be the whole idea of 'interleaving', returning to an idea rather than assuming that once taught everything is learnt and remembered. That link to Bruner and his work, interestingly, is rarely made.

Another important thinker in the early years was Paolo Freire. It's certainly not the case that all English teachers at the time were radical thinkers, reaching for their copy of *Pedagogy of the Oppressed* at every opportunity, but as a group, they were probably more interested in ideas about the empowerment of their pupils than most, and would have been likely to have known about movements to democratise schools and give students a voice.

---

5. Media education is not fully represented in this book. This is not because I don't think it is a very important part of the English curriculum. I do. However, it has never been an area of particular expertise for me, either in my work as a teacher in schools or in my work as a consultant at EMC. I have always deferred to the greater knowledge of others, most especially my colleague of many years, Jenny Grahame, whose understanding, wisdom and immense practical inventiveness in the field of Media Studies and media in English are unparalleled. More recently, Claire Pollard has taken over this role and continues to inform and enrich my thinking about everything to do with media education.

The 1970s and 80s are often seen as the 'progressive years'. It's interesting to think what it meant to be a progressive English teacher in that period. Sometimes I can see little relationship between the progressive teacher I aspired to be, and the term that is bandied about now – often pejoratively to describe all kinds of beliefs and tendencies that are just as alien to me now as they might have been then, when I'd have happily accepted that label. Ideas like learning styles, no teacher talk, brain gym, growth mindset, WALT, WILF, SOLO, flipped learning, 'whizzy' lessons or anything else that claimed to be worth doing just because it was fun, would have been as much of an anathema to me and my colleagues then as they are now. They did not emerge in the so-called 'progressive' era but much later, in the period during and after the introduction of the primary National Literacy Strategy (1998) and the KS3 Framework for Teaching English: Years 7, 8 and 9 (2001). Many of them, ironically, emerged much more recently, promoted by not very progressive tweeters and bloggers who became interested in generic ideas about pedagogy promoted by international educational writers and 'gurus'.

Interestingly, while talking about progressivism in the 1970s, it's worth pointing out that the majority of schools – with some rare public exceptions that regularly made the press – were not really all that 'progressive'. A narrative that suggests that all schools were doing project work, cross-curricular activities, discovery-based learning with the teacher contributing very little, or happily allowing students to run riot, is far from the truth. Most schools were striving to achieve orderly, disciplined classes in which children learned. My first school, a comprehensive in Tottenham, had school uniform, desks in rows, students lined up outside the door to come in and expected to stand up when adults entered and a Senior Management Team who strongly favoured silent classrooms and looked askance at group work. It was not to my taste, and I moved quickly to what I saw as being a more conducive environment (where teachers talked a lot but students did too). It is probably fair to say that the general mood *was* a bit different, in particular because there was more scope for English teachers to create a strong 'ethos' of their own and take professional responsibility for the way the subject was taught. The views of a good Head of English on how the subject should be taught were generally listened to.

Why does it matter to think about this past and these ideas? It seems to me that it offers a broader perspective, and perspective is a vital thing in a fast-changing world. Every teacher comes into the profession at a particular moment. It is easy to imagine that your particular moment is what teaching English *is*. But with the swings and roundabouts of change in education, not least of all the massive rethinking involved in the National Literacy Strategies of the early 2000s, English has undergone seismic shifts. Those teachers who entered the profession as trainees in the early 2000s, for instance, some in their particular brand of training going into a single school and then continuing their careers in that same school, may well have encountered English teaching of a radically new variety that had thrown away much that came before; it had abandoned some of the givens I have listed above and added new ones, in response to a much more target-driven, anxious culture of accountability. Many of these academically able trainees were placed in schools in special measures, at the toughest end of that accountability culture; rightly they baulked at some of the givens they were expected to accept and bizarre practices they were required to undertake. But they didn't necessarily have the historical understanding of the subject to be able to make full sense of the shifts, nor were they necessarily in departments with stable long-term staffing, where well-established, confident Heads of Department could help steer a sane course through the curriculum upheavals and assessment pressures, in the light of their understanding of what was best (and worst) about the English of previous periods. These new teachers simply found themselves doing things that didn't make sense to them, for reasons they couldn't understand, and in ways that were not necessarily effective for their students. This is also true for anyone starting out as an English teacher in today's schools, entering into a set of practices and conventions that have arisen at a particular moment. Whether it's PEE[6] and its associated acronyms – or a rejection of them – or triple marking of books, or no marking at all, or putting learning objectives up at the start of lessons, or always having a plenary, or never having a plenary, teachers need to be able to see what's ephemeral and what's likely to last. Knowing that the subject can be something else, and has been something else, and undoubtedly will be a little different in the future, can give you this perspective and a chance to question – it wasn't always like this; is this how it should be now?

And if the answer is no, or we have grave doubts, then we have to ask, how *should* it be now? English is undoubtedly a complicated subject that it's hard for others, not working within it, to fully understand. However, I would argue that its messiness is part of what makes it what it is. There is a glue that binds the seemingly disparate elements together; in my view that glue is the interrelationships between things – the fact that reading makes us better writers and writing makes us better readers, for instance. It's the relationship between talk and writing. And it's the connection between literary understandings and non-literary knowledge – that we read and write functional texts better, with more acuity and insight if we are also engaged in literary reading and have the kind of linguistic sensitivity that comes from that. And it's also the relationship between knowing about language and learning how to use it well. English is, indeed, a bit of this and a bit of that, but the this and that, when combined in a sustained and well thought-through curriculum, add up to make a highly patterned, intricate quilt, rather than random scraps and threads. A warm one too.

---

6. PEE stands for Point Evidence/Example, Exploration. Other more elaborate variations abound, including PEEL (Point, Evidence, Exploration, Link) and PETAL (Point, Evidence, Technique, Analysis, Link).

2.2 Real English versus Exam English – the case for authentic experience

This article was originally published in *The Use of English* (Volume 69, No 3, Summer 2018) and subsequently on EMC's blog. It seeks to offer a rationale for teaching the subject in ways that are authentic, allied to practices in academic English, and likely to engage the interest of students sufficiently for them to choose to study it at higher levels, rather than being a distorted version focused mainly on examination results at GCSE.

In a wide-ranging report commissioned by the government in the late 1980s, Brian Cox led a working party that surveyed and commented on the state of English teaching, in order to make recommendations for the first ever National Curriculum.[1] As part of the report Cox identified five different ways of conceptualising English: Personal Growth, Cross-curricular, Adult Needs, Cultural Heritage and Cultural Analysis. He set out what teachers and the educational community understood the role of the subject to be and recognised the importance of all of these things. Different schools, departments or even individual teachers within a department, might give greater weight to one or other of these aspects of the subject and that seemed to be tolerated, in those more 'permissive' times. Personal Growth perhaps looks like a rather dated phrase now. This may be not just because there's been a swing away from that kind of language in relation to education but also because the focus has shifted somewhat from 'what students get out of the subject' at an emotional level – what it does to them as an individual in terms of their broader development and sense of self – and more towards what knowledge they have obtained – what it has taught them in purely academic terms. It doesn't necessarily mean to say it's still not considered by some to be important, but perhaps it's become subsumed to some extent in newer terms like 'creativity' or 'critical literacy' and maybe it's seen more as a prerequisite for learning knowledge, rather than a 'good' in its own right. What isn't on that list at all, however, is 'Assessment' or 'Passing GCSEs and A Levels'. And yet, in the current climate of high stakes testing and accountability, surely this would have to appear, probably quite high up in the minds of the students themselves, as well as their teachers. We all have anecdotal stories to tell about Year 7 classrooms in which a GCSE question is up on the board as the starting-point for learning about poetry, or where students are thinking about what they will have learned before they have learned anything at all. Local authority advisor, James Durran, quoted an example on Twitter recently that can stand in for all of these kinds of experiences. On going into the classroom of a really good teacher and asking a Year 7 'What is English?' the student said, 'Analysing texts' and when asked 'Why?' the reply came 'To prepare for tests.'

---

1. The Cox Report (1989) *English for ages 5 to 16* is a key document in the history of English teaching. It took evidence from a huge number of individuals and organisations involved in the teaching of the subject, across all phases and including writers, linguists and other academics. The commentary on many aspects of the subject still resonates in today's world.

Amanda Spielman has noted this shrinking of educational horizons to assessment and only assessment. In a key speech in June 2017 at the Festival of Education at Wellington College, she said:

> One of the areas that I think we lose sight of is the real substance of education. Not the exam grades or the progress scores, important though they are, but instead the real meat of what is taught in our schools and colleges: the curriculum.

The teachers we meet at EMC seem to feel as if they're between a rock and a hard place. They want their subject to be the enriching, rewarding and intellectually challenging subject that they themselves found it to be. They want it to fulfil many of Cox's purposes. But their schools' regimes for tracking pupils and the pressure towards results seem to run counter to that and departmental time is taken up with targets and data rather than allowing them to develop a consensus on what they want the subject to be for their students. On the courses we run, for GCSE and A Level (and now increasingly at KS3), there is always that tension between what teachers would like to be able to do and what they feel they have to do.

At EMC we have been drawing on our knowledge of the past, our close scrutiny of the full spectrum of examination specifications and our opportunities for broader thinking, to argue that the two are not as mutually exclusive as sometimes appears. Indeed, we'd argue that good results across all attainment levels are only possible if students are really engaging with the subject in ways that are valid and legitimate in terms of the wider practices that we know to constitute it, in the academic world and in literary and linguistic life beyond the classroom. If English in schools becomes 'exam English' or 'school English', with no real connection to the 'real English' or 'full English' that can be found in other contexts, then students will engage in ways of thinking and writing that will neither fulfil any of Cox's roles for the subject, nor get them the best possible grades in exams.

Let's take one practical example of this from A Level English – the assessment of students' use of contextual knowledge to explore literary texts in ways that illuminate the text. There's nothing wrong with teaching students to think about texts in their contexts. It's a central plank of much contemporary criticism, alongside the more 'intrinsic' critical approaches that are associated with close reading. However, the focus on contexts as an assessment tool, and an explicit assessment objective, both at A Level and GCSE, has brought with it a distortion of its true role in 'real English'. As critics like Peter Barry would argue, a large amount of 'distant' historical or biographical context turns English into History, and it is really the 'adjacent' contexts, where something is very closely relevant to a particular text, that can shine fresh light on the text itself.[2] Often those adjacent contexts are cultural, or generic or literary – part of the intertextual web in which any single text sits. But sadly, now that context is assessed, with a weighting given to it and a set number of marks, it is in danger of losing its way. Many students understandably come to believe that 30% of marks on context means 30% of an

---

2. Barry's *Literature in Contexts* (2007) distinguishes between 'adjacent' and 'distant' contexts. He takes up this same issue in EMC's book for A Level students, *The Literature Reader*.

essay spent writing about the context, often a rather distant one, often historical rather than literary, all too often including the kind of historical generalisations that would make a genuine historian turn pale and shudder. We've all read those paragraphs in essays in which all women were downtrodden in Shakespeare's day, every American text can be seen as exemplifying the American Dream and anything that happens to a woman in any Victorian novel is the result of patriarchy.

Interestingly, Examiners' Reports for A Level all recognise the problem, and have done so for a very long time, ever since contextual knowledge first appeared as an assessment objective as part of the curriculum reforms in 2000 (frequently referred to as Curriculum 2000). There has been a consistent message over the years, almost a plea from the examiners, to put context in its proper place, to value quality over quantity and to recognise that simply telling the examiner a great deal about the world beyond a text will gain students very few marks. Since 2000, we have been collecting quotations from Examiners' Reports to this effect and using them on courses with teachers. Nothing has changed – the message remains the same – except that perhaps now, with a new, higher weighting at A Level, the message has become even more urgent.[3]

Talking to colleagues who focus more on GCSE, and in conversation with some of the Awarding Bodies, the same seems to be true there.

So despite the Awarding Bodies' explicit statements in Examiners' Reports, and the training done by organisations like our own, there still seems to be immense pressure on teachers to be doing the very things that are neither helpful to their students in getting good grades, nor good practice within the subject itself.

One answer to this, for us, has been to try to encourage the teachers we meet to step back from the assessment objectives and to encourage their students, at the start of the course, to do the same. Just as a Year 7 doesn't need to see a GCSE question, so a GCSE or A Level student doesn't need to know that 30% of a component goes on context, right from day one. Rather, they need to start applying contextual knowledge in well-judged ways and learn what it means to do that. On a recent training day on 'Contexts and Criticism', my colleague Lucy Webster and I started the day with a broad consideration of what the subject English is, drawing on the work of academics like Robert Eaglestone and Peter Barry. Eaglestone (2017) describes the two fundamental literary critical approaches that characterise the subject, those that are intrinsic and those that are extrinsic.

> Some critics claim that intrinsic types of criticism lead to 'objective' readings, the idea that texts can be independent of their historical, social and personal context, and that 'literary-ness' makes a text a valuable work of art, which is worth studying in its own right [...] In contrast, extrinsic methods of interpretation take it for granted that the literary text is part of the world and rooted in its context. An extrinsic critic considers that the job of criticism is to

---

3. Examples from 2017 A Level series: Edexcel: 'Contextual factors need treating with as much discrimination and subtlety as the play itself.' OCR: 'Some students, unfortunately, thought they had to force in all sorts of information, ideas or assertions about historical and biographical contexts, much of which was sweeping and not well understood.' AQA B: 'It is also important to guard against the use of over-simplified, contextual generalisations which often amount to nothing more than unconvincing assertions.'

move from the text outwards to some other, not specifically literary, object or idea. Such critics use literary texts to explore other ideas about things in the world, and, in turn, use other ideas to explain the literary text.

We argued that, if students are to understand what is legitimate and insightful use of contextual knowledge, they need to know what place contextual knowledge has in the subject at large. They need to read examples of what it can do to your reading of a text and see how critics can make brilliant use of it, not to show off, not as mere decoration, nor as proof of knowledge, but as a way of reading a text differently and better, constructing an argument that draws on ideas beyond the text. Before ever mentioning assessment, or AOs, before suggesting that you need to 'get a bit of context in to score marks' or say, 'contextually', in order to draw the examiner's attention to the fact that you're talking about contexts, it's worth offering extrinsic information on a text under discussion and asking students to think hard about the validity and usefulness of applying that information. They ought to be able to reject the idea of using it because it's not fruitful, as well as deciding that it really does help support a particular interpretation or give a fresh angle on the text. Later, as they begin to get closer to the exams, it will be worth looking at examples of student writing where it's done really well, in relation to a particular component, essay or mark scheme, at a point where they themselves will have some ideas about what kind of contextual comment really pays its way. But shaping all the teaching around marks and mark schemes is unlikely to produce good writing in any terms – in the broader world of 'real English' or in the narrower world of the exams themselves.

One very important reason for ensuring that students have an authentic experience of the subject, as the means by which they also achieve highly, is to do with the future of the subject as a whole. After some worrying reports that English A Levels were not recruiting well, EMC conducted a survey in September 2017. There are obvious structural reasons for the dip in numbers that all subjects suffered with the shrinking of AS entries, but it seemed, anecdotally, that English might be doing worse than most. Our survey of over 100 schools and colleges, of different types and sizes, suggested that these fears were justified. English Literature, in our surveyed centres, was down by about 16%, English Language by 17% and Language and Literature by 26%. We asked for teachers' views on the possible reasons for this. The reasons given were complex, and included the view that STEM is being highly promoted in schools, as well as at university level, at the expense of English and the Humanities. But there was a fairly significant number of people who expressed the belief that though the new GCSEs were in some ways rigorous and could be seen to be good preparation for A Level, they were also narrow in focus and students had not enjoyed them. The students viewed English as difficult, high pressure and unengaging. The teachers felt that the content of the new GCSEs had, in some cases, been a 'turn-off'. Now some of this might be the effect of the first two years of teaching and the first set of exams, always a difficult time for teachers and students. Some too might be to do with the pressure on English teachers being passed on to students. But whatever it is, it is clear that for the life cycle of English as a subject (from school to university to degree to PGCE and back into school), we need to address the fact that students may be being switched off the subject.[4] If the backwash from these new GCSEs begins to be felt at KS3 too, as seems to be increasingly the case, if KS3 becomes no more than an extended period of preparation for exams several years down the line, then we are in serious trouble. Stories of students disliking the subject or being unclear about its value will be heard more and more frequently and will put the subject itself at risk. Our students need to understand what 'real English' is, if they are going to want to take it further. They need to have the excitement of entering into the kinds of disciplinary conversations that make the subject what it is. Eaglestone (2017) describes this well for A Level students and new undergraduates:

> Just as a mathematician (obviously) doesn't learn all the (infinite) answers to all the (infinite) mathematical problems but ways of thinking about and solving them, and just as a geographer learns to think about space and locations in certain specific ways, so English teaches students to think 'as' critics. This may once have been, but is no longer, a sort of monolithic, fixed identity; rather, it is a mobile, developing sense of a range of questions and ideas about the literary, widely defined, and [...] characterised by dissensus.

At EMC, we've been arguing that this should be the case at every level – at KS3, as well as at GCSE and A Level. So, for instance, when students of all ages learn about poetry, they should be engaging with the big and exciting ideas about what poetry is and what it can do, how it differs from prose and the impact it has on readers – not just using it as a means of teaching literary terms like alliteration and metaphor, as labels to pin to examples. Though students are only examined on their knowledge about language at GCSE in limited ways, KS3 should be an opportunity to investigate and explore issues and ideas about language in use, in ways that linguists would recognise as consistent with their practices at a higher level, because it will increase their alertness to how language works and give them access to thrilling ideas about language that will spark their imaginations and thinking. They should read widely, read diverse texts and – as the American educationalist Arthur N. Applebee has said so eloquently – understand much more about the canon by seeing it freshly, through the lens of other, diverse cultures and traditions. If we want students to wow both us and their examiners with the cogency and validity of their arguments, the vigour of their thinking and the integrity of their approach, we need to teach them in that spirit. And we'd argue that that isn't just idealistic fluff, or the thing that we'd all love to have time for but can't do. It's the pragmatic answer to high achievement, as well as the way of making students love the subject, so safeguarding its future.

---

4. The results of the EMC survey have been borne out in the most recent statistics for A Level entries. Figures published by the Joint Council for Qualifications (2019) show a 31% decline across all three English subject specialisms between 2012 and 2019, with a 13.5% decline between 2018 and 2019. The decline in A Level English Language and Literature is most alarming, with a 56% reduction since 2011. The picture is almost as bad for A Level English Language, where the figure is 42%. For A Level English Literature the number is 25%. Sources: Joint Council for Qualifications (2012 and 2016-19) and GCE Inter-Board Statistics for breakdown of figures for different subjects in 2012. EMC's 2019 follow-up survey suggests a continuing, worrying decline.

2.3 Global moves and local operations – big picture thinking in English

This blog, written in July 2018, was a response to a growing trend in secondary English to teach small features of texts – terms and devices at word or phrase-level. Formulaic approaches became the norm. What seemed to have gone missing in action were thoughts, ideas and genuine responses. The validity of the point in PEE[1] was becoming all but irrelevant, certainly far less important than following the formula, and students were increasingly at risk of focusing all their attention on going through the motions of a process rather than developing significant and valid ideas and responses to texts. Many English teachers always had doubts about this approach. Increasingly there has been a questioning of the use of formulaic frameworks, though for some the abandonment of the rigid structure of response has proved challenging, not least of all because of the expectations of senior management, for whom the security of seeing a neat 'system' in place can sometimes outweigh concerns about its genuine efficacy. For many new teachers, their whole experience of English teaching has been in a system that privileges this kind of response. This continues to be a concern, not only for those involved in English in education but also for Awarding Bodies, who counsel strongly against teaching in formulaic ways. To throw light on this issue, this blog draws on a substantial piece of research in the United States in 2012. The research was about student writing and the dangers of focusing student attention on forms, structures and details at the expense of bigger ideas. My blog extends this idea beyond writing to a consideration of the subject as a whole.

In a fascinating piece of research published in May 2012, in the *Journal of Adolescent and Adult Literacy*, Thomas DeVere Wolsey, Diane Lapp and Douglas Fisher undertook an enquiry into academic writing, exploring student and teacher perceptions and a possible gap between the two. Their focus was cross-curricular, rather than the subject of English. Here's how they describe the two aspects of academic writing:

> Academic writing might be conceptualised in terms of global moves and local operations (Wolsey, 2010). Global moves include attention to the work of others. Such moves embrace working with discipline-specific content, summarising others' contributions to the discourse, anticipating objections, and situating one's point-of-view within the work others have done.
>
> Local operations, by contrast, demand the language user's knowledge of conventions such as word choice, use of discipline-specific terms, use of passive voice and choice of pronouns, or complex sentence construction.

What they discovered, in essence, was that teachers were teaching what they termed 'local operations' but were, in fact, valuing 'global moves'. High performance in a subject was much more associated with global moves and less with local operations. They observed that students who assiduously concentrated on local operations were

---

1. PEE stands for Point Evidence/Example, Exploration. Other more elaborate variations abound, including PEEL (Point, Evidence, Exploration, Link) and PETAL (Point, Evidence, Technique, Analysis, Link).

frustrated to discover that despite fulfilling all of these small procedural directives in relation to their writing, they were still being graded poorly by their teachers.[2]

Why might the teachers have been focusing their pedagogic attention on the smaller things, rather than the aspects of writing that they really valued, deep down, and that emerged strongly in their grading? One key reason seems to be that the bigger, broader aspects of what makes for good writing in the subject were more intangible, less easy to pin down, more conceptual rather than procedural and therefore harder to teach. Teachers felt that they were working to develop students' writing by focusing heavily on 'local operations' even when, ultimately, this was a lesser aspect of good writing in their subject.

Wolsey, Lapp and Fisher say:

> Excessive attention to usage and mechanics can be counterproductive to students' understanding of global moves (Beach & Friedrich, 2006). Local operations do matter, but students struggle with local operations to convey meaning in contexts that require navigating the complex conceptual understandings that teachers value.

They also explore some fascinating issues around the question of how 'apprentice' writers either authentically take on the qualities of writing in the subject, developing 'expertise in deep and meaningful ways' or simply 'replicate knowledge' by mimicking the outward features of writing in the subject.

If all of this is true, it has profound implications for the way we work with students on their writing in English. It has chimed with some of our thinking about what's happening in writing in English from KS3 through to A Level, so we've been using this research on CPD courses and in other contexts to explore the idea that we're possibly placing too much attention on small aspects of writing, at the expense of deeper understandings about what it means to 'do' English and write well about texts in the subject discipline. In looking at two essays by students in an A Level exam, for example, one of which received a much higher grade than another, we've been able to unpick what really matters in writing in the subject. The one student wrote clearly, neatly and accurately, following all the procedural advice one might give to students about use of quotation, backing up evidence, correctly referring to events and characters and so on. This same student ticked all the boxes on mentioning contextual information, acknowledging the potential for different interpretations and so on but not in the 'deep and meaningful' ways described above. The other script was a much scrappier piece of writing, full of spelling mistakes, punctuation and other technical errors. Yet this second piece was awarded a higher mark by the examiners in the exam, and in several 'outings' in CPD sessions, most teachers have also decided, ultimately, that it deserved a higher mark than the more technically accurate and well-written script. Why? Because it had good ideas about the text. Because it answered the question with

---

2. Interestingly, since this blog was first written, we are observing that more teachers are not only teaching local operations but also beginning to *value* them, the form and formula taking precedence over the quality of thinking. This is perhaps unsurprising, given that many teachers are now entering the profession who were themselves taught in this way.

insight. Because it drew on broader understandings – generic and contextual – in convincing and valid ways. In other words, because the ideas it expressed were more authentic, interesting and persuasive in relation to the text and demonstrated understanding of how we work on texts in the subject as a whole. Of course, this student needed to work on areas of weakness – his spelling, punctuation and lapses in his expression undoubtedly brought his mark down. However, his good ideas were rewarded more highly than the emptier fluency of his classmate. It's been reassuring to see that both the Awarding Body and most teachers we've worked with have been in full agreement about this, and it has implications for what we spend our time doing with students. The very committed, hard-working, good writer of the less convincing script needs to spend more time developing her ideas, subjecting them to scrutiny and finding ways of expressing them crisply, rather than focusing on the 'local operations' that she feels she needs to undertake to pass an exam. Having spent two years worrying about local operations she has found herself with very little to say. Fundamentally, she needs to write well in the subject, not focus on the small details of writing well for an examiner.

We've been using this global moves and local operations idea to explore with teachers what we actually mean by 'global moves' in our subject, in other words what it is that a critical essay, or a close reading, or a comparative piece of writing, or an analysis of a poem involves, within the discipline of English. This means thinking bigger and more broadly, talking about what the academic discipline of English is all about, looking at good examples of writing in the subject to see what the writer has done, understanding the way in which personal insights can be examined and justified, recognising the role of contextual knowledge, rather than just performing an 'operation' with a bit of context.

Recently, I've begun to think that Wolsey's idea of 'global moves' and 'local operations' has a much more extensive application to our current pedagogy and practices in the subject than I'd previously considered. It seems to me that, since the introduction of the National Literacy Strategy, and the subsequent ongoing focus on lesson objectives, targets for improvement and levels, we have become fixated on 'local operations' in all aspects of the subject. The reasons are much the same as for writing. If you're trying to 'pin down' things to teach, and what has been learnt, it's so much easier to do that on local operations. You can give yes/no answers to whether a student has shown that they can use sentence punctuation in an end of term assessment, or whether they have identified a fronted adverbial, or noticed a metaphor, or used paragraphing or spelt a word correctly. It's much harder to quantify the great idea they had about an extract from *Strange Case of Dr Jekyll and Mr Hyde* that revealed to you something you'd never thought of before. Or to know how to assess the way in which a student has drawn on their own wider reading to make insightful comments about the way a particular text fits into a broader genre.

Local operations are important – of course they are. They need to be taught. Students who don't punctuate, or paragraph, or set out quotations clearly and accurately on the page, or fail correctly to name poems or poets, or seem wobbly about the use of literary terms, need to fix that. They need to be taught these things and how to do these things. But if the focus of attention is exclusively on these, or even predominantly on them, then the more complicated global moves risk being forgotten.

Here's a little example of how the global moves/local operations idea can extend well beyond academic writing. You're starting to teach a novel at KS3. Let's say it's a Neil Gaiman novel such as *Coraline*. Local operations might be all the small things that are involved in that particular novel – the names of the characters, what they do in the novel, a chapter by chapter exploration of what happens, the identification of metaphors, a close look at some aspects of the language by homing in on individual words and phrases. You get to the end of the novel and ask the students what they remember about the novel. They can tell you the names of characters, what happened and a few particularly memorable aspects of language, in the close detail of the text. Local operations.

Let's think what we might mean by global moves on that same novel. Can your students tell you about how novels work, how readers read, how people talk and write about texts, how genres operate and authors work within them, how this particular novel fits within its genre and what is most interesting about how it's been written? Have they considered how YA fiction as a whole has grown up, changed and developed over time, so that this novel does what it does in the way that it does in this particular period? Do they understand why the choice of this text was made by you, what you're hoping for them to get out of it, what additional pleasures and understandings might come from studying as an 'expert' student of literature, rather than just reading it as an 'amateur' reader? Do your students understand the idea of intertextuality, that all texts have echoes of other texts within them? Do they know how you can have some big overarching ideas about the text that are then worth justifying and verifying by going back in, to see if those ideas are true, and then perhaps finding new ideas as you do that, that take you in fresh directions?

The implications of this might be that, in studying that Neil Gaiman novel, these kinds of activities and angles would be worth pursuing:

1. Students might consider their prior reading (or watching), to share understandings about this before starting to read the novel, and then think about how Gaiman uses, adapts or subverts the Gothic genre in his writing. This understanding of texts in their generic context is a global move.

2. Before reading the first chapter you might ask students to explore what they expect from a novel. This activates their broader knowledge and experience of what a novel is and gives them a springboard for making observations and judgements about the Gaiman novel. This is another global move.

3. A student of literature goes beyond just reading and enjoying, to take a more 'expert', close, analytical look at how texts work and how they are read. It's worth making this explicit to students. It's a global move. So here, students might begin to think about how novels usually start, what 'contract' they

set up with the reader in their first few lines, or first chapters, and how the playing on expectations works – through suspense, foreshadowing, new plot developments and so on. They might then look at the Gaiman opening in the light of this. What 'contract' does he set up with his reader? What expectations does it raise?

4. What makes Gaiman's writing (and this novel) unique, special, different from that of other writers you've read. What would you say to someone who'd not read it before, to distinguish it, say, from the writing of Mark Haddon in *The Curious Incident of the Dog in the Night-time* or another YA writer?

5. In introducing this text to other people who've not come across it before, what would you identify as being most significant about it, most special and different from other texts by other writers? Making judgements about information and ideas that are most relevant/least relevant, most interesting/ least interesting is part and parcel of thinking about the defining features of texts.

Global moves and local operations are, of course, both important, but rather than imagining that the global comes automatically via the teaching of the local, I think I'd argue the other way around, that if we understand the big picture of what the subject entails, why we're looking at texts in the way that we are, then we'll be able to fit the detail into that bigger schema or mental picture. Conceptual understanding comes first, rather than the other way around, in order for the two to work in tandem with each other.

So, let's re-evaluate what we're doing in the light of this. Let's think – as many teachers are already doing – about whether a few small learning objectives are really worthy of our attention at the start of each lesson, or whether longer term, bigger, more sustained and important objectives are what our subject is really about, despite the fact that it is less easy to prove that pupils have 'done' them and 'learnt' them in a simple, one-off moment of learning. Global moves are where success in the subject lies and we do our students a disservice if we pretend that they are not.

2.4 Challenge and text choice – walking the tightrope

In 1997, I was teaching part-time at Islington Sixth Form Centre and working two days a week at EMC. I had a group of second year A Level students and chose *Beloved* by Toni Morrison as a set text. I taught it as a coursework text for the AEB 660 A Level Literature specification.[1] Many schools had decided to teach it, but often with some trepidation because of its searingly painful, powerful subject matter and the high demands it makes on the reader through its extraordinarily rich and complex patterns of narrative structure and style. It is one of the most 'challenging' (and rewarding) books one might read as an adult so what might inexperienced readers make of it?

I wrote this article for the *English and Media Magazine*, the magazine that EMC used to publish for English teachers up until 2001. There are a number of elements of what I wrote then that still seem highly relevant to current debates: what constitutes challenge in texts; how we help students cope with such texts; what culturally diverse texts have to offer; how texts help students develop as readers and writers; what happens when students work on texts in dialogic ways, with group work as part of the process.

The students in the group I taught were both of mixed attainment and culturally diverse; this was a non-selective, inner city sixth form college. Interestingly, of the students who speak in the talk transcripts included in the piece, at least two went on to become English teachers themselves (one currently a Second in Charge of English in outer London). A third, who does not feature in these conversations, also went on to become an English teacher.

When we choose texts for study with a group of students we walk a tightrope and ask them to step out onto that tightrope with us. If the text is too difficult and demanding, the tightrope too high, we are in danger of crashing collectively, or individually, to the ground. They might never want to step out onto it again. If the tightrope is too low, everyone will have the confidence to step out, most will cross it at high speed and make it to the other side, knowing that if they fell the ground would be just beneath them. But have they experienced the same sense of excitement and exhilaration? Do they feel how brave they have been and how they have achieved something they didn't think possible before, something that required a departure from firm ground? If we raise the tightrope high, we need to provide safety nets to reassure those who are afraid of stepping out and catch those who might fall.

We walk this tightrope with any group of pupils that we teach, from Year 7 through to the most competent of A Level groups. Often the instinctive reaction is to err on the side of caution, teaching to the middle or selecting texts that we feel will be 'within' the capabilities of the majority of the pupils rather than 'beyond' them.

---

1. AEB 660 was a 50% coursework A Level syllabus that offered plenty of scope for choice of texts and approaches, alongside some defined requirements such as Shakespeare and coverage of all the major genres. In the department I led, we chose to include many texts from diverse cultures, alongside a nineteenth-century novel, pre-twentieth-century poetry and other established, canonical texts. As part of their A Level course, students invariably ended up reading many more texts than they do now.

This instinct is a natural one, deriving from the best of intentions. We want to protect pupils from failure. We want them to 'enjoy' texts. We don't want them to be 'put off' by difficulty. But what do we know about the way that pupils respond to texts that could be perceived as 'beyond' their abilities?[2]

What makes *Beloved* a challenging text?

Beloved is a hugely powerful and complex text on many different levels. Its subject, slavery, is one that demands and provokes strong feelings and disturbances in the reader. Morrison herself has said that she was 'almost frightened' of tackling the area of slavery: 'It never occurred to me to go into that area. I never thought I had the emotional resources to deal with slavery.' Her decision to focus on the experience and psychological impact of slavery on individuals makes the novel all the more intense and disturbing. She says,

> You see the other slave books focused really heavily on the horror of the institution, the physical brutality and the sort of abstract way in which a group of lovely people were being forced to do something because they were being brutalised. What I wanted to do was to put the locus, the heart of the story, within the minds of the slaves themselves and have the white people sort of drift away and be a kind of background as far as characters are concerned so that what you have is the system itself.

The reader cannot choose to be a detached bystander, observing the events of this novel.

As Antonia Byatt has said,

> she gives you no option but to inhabit her world. You can't read it as though you were looking on.

The intention behind the book is, Morrison says, to 'insert this memory that was unbearable and unspeakable into the literature' and the book itself is focused on memory and how memory works, both for individuals and for a whole society. The structure and style of the narrative mirrors the complex and fitful processes of memory. As characters gradually piece together their individual and collective histories, as a patchwork of interlocking memories, so the reader has to piece together the narrative from fragments, with different voices telling and re-telling the story and unearthing the pain that they have tried to bury. This makes for a highly unconventional narrative, full of gaps that the reader has to work to fill in.

Woven into the narrative are patterns of imagery and symbolism that reverberate with significances that are not only literary but also historical and cultural. So, the 'tree' on Sethe's back, the scar left after she is beaten by her white slave owners, has many associations: the trees on which black men were lynched, the tree of life with all its religious connotations, the idea of the family tree and the sense of continuity and family history which was wrenched from slaves, the trees in the southern landscape, with all their beauty and scope for offering spiritual comfort, despite

---

2. In an EMC blog published in September 2019, 'What Makes a KS3 Novel Challenging?' Andrew McCallum explores many of these same issues in relation to the current debates about difficulty and challenge in the choice of texts for KS3.

being part of a landscape that also represented torture, despair and dispossession. Such a rich use of symbolism forces the reader to draw on all his or her reserves of cultural and literary awareness. A first reading is just the beginning. Subsequent readings and discussion of the text pay rich dividends.

Beloved is challenging for other reasons too. Whilst it operates powerfully at the level of realist narrative (in the telling of the story of what happened to Sethe and her children, her husband's mother, Baby Suggs, and the man who becomes her lover, Paul D) the realism of the story co-exists with elements that are more mystical and mysterious. Beloved, the character who appears in their lives and forces them to unbury their past, is an extraordinarily elliptical creation, a character whose very complexity allows her to represent or be suggestive of many different kinds of experience of slavery. As Linden Peach says,

> The sense of fracture which is at the heart of the book – together with a concomitant sense of healing – is maintained, if not actually initiated, by the slippage of the signifier 'Beloved' throughout the novel. On one level Beloved subverts the notion of the outraged mother figure as an outraged ghost-daughter intent upon claiming the mother who killed her for herself alone, but she eludes precise definition. At first she appears to be the spirit ghost of the murdered baby, but no sooner has the reader acquired this hold on her than she reappears, or seems to reappear, in the form of a young woman.
>
> Eventually she appears to represent not a single child but the pain and anguish of the 60 million black people who have been enslaved, tortured and killed. As a character, then, Beloved is commensurate with the fantastical in African literature which is usually traceable back to concrete, social and historical events. But Beloved moves from one plane of reference to another, literally destabilising the novel which also moves with an equally destabilising effect from one narrative plane to another.

So what might relatively inexperienced readers make of such an 'epic' text?

Group work on the text

Three weeks after starting to read *Beloved* the class split up into small groups to prepare presentations on some of the early sections of the novel. In the transcript extract that follows, Alex and Ezra are reporting back to the whole group on their section. It is interesting to see the depth of their response even at this early stage.[3]

Alex: We found the very beginning of section five quite interesting. We didn't really know what to think of it at first and then after reading it through several times we thought, 'A fully dressed woman walked out of the water.' We thought this was quite a significant sentence at first because maybe it's a suggestion that there was a reincarnation happening or something like that because she was coming through the water and there are a lot of images about water, her being thirsty and Paul D. says, 'She said she was thirsty. Mighty thirsty look like.'

---

3. Though the emphasis of this article was not on group work, it is interesting to read the transcript of student group talk with that issue in mind. The 'seminar' approach, where students prepare a topic or section of the text in groups and collectively report back to each other was a key element of my teaching in the 1980s and 90s. Increasingly it is having to fight for its place in English classrooms. See Chapter 5 for more on this.

Ezra: It seems to be a reincarnation because of the context. Later on in the story you hear about how she was asking about earrings, and things she brought up, things she wouldn't have known nothing about but she does know about them. At the time, they don't really ask any questions but at the end of one of the chapters, I've forgotten which one, Denver asks the question, 'How does she know about this?' or something, so it kind of links. And plus, because Beloved the ghost's just disappeared and this woman's appeared out of the water just like that.

Alex: You get the impression of something emerging through, or out of the water rather than walking through the water. That's why she's still wet.

She's come right out of the water. And there's also quite a few quotes that Paul D. says. He says 'There's something funny about that girl,' and that suggests he thinks that there's something wrong, not wrong, but just something strange. And then he says 'But I seen her pick up the rocker,' I mean, that's virtually impossible.

Ezra: There's something else that comes up about the water, the way that the narrative style goes back to Denver's birth, about how water broke, and how they almost sank because there was so much water and that links back into Beloved wanting more water. So that's part of Morrison's narrative technique again.

Jean: Well, she has this thing where Sethe goes for a wee and it lasts for ages and it's almost like her waters breaking again. So, when Beloved's reborn, it's like literally inside her. It happens again, if you know what I mean.

Ava: We do think that she's a reincarnation of the baby because, as you said, the baby disappeared, the ghost disappeared and then Beloved appeared. But also there are lots of little things about her that suggest she's like a baby. Like there's lots said about her skin, how soft and baby-like her skin is, in Section 5, 'Her skin was flawless' '...baby hair before it bloomed and roped into the masses,' so there's stuff about that and, the way she's incontinent as well, so she can't control her bladder, you know, like a baby.

Ezra: In one of the chapters it says how she's totally dependent. She needs Sethe. Everyday she goes and greets her and it shows like how kind of babyish she is. She could have just brought her forward and just explained that she is a ghost and that she's come back but she said it like this is a new person, a new character. She doesn't make it plain that this is Beloved, the girl, the way she builds up the character of this person, them knowing nothing about her. And the way she wants to hear stories of Sethe's past, it's like she's trying to catch up.

Alex: Barbara gave us this quote to look at. 'Many waters cannot quench love, neither can floods drown it'.[4] It comes from the 'Song of Solomon'. Morrison uses religious quotations from the bible quite often. It's sort of saying that you can't really suppress love but you also can't ever quench the desire for it. You always want it and you always want that person. And also you can never suppress the love for that person either.

---

4. I gave each group a relevant quotation as a prompt for the students to use as they wished.

Student responses to *Beloved*

I interviewed my students about studying *Beloved* one term after we had finished work on the text, so that there was a degree of distance from the immediate involvement in it. This was the first time that we had stepped back from the text in this way, to consider it in relation to other texts studied on the course. The extracts that follow are taken from the discussion.[5]

Ava: It was a completely different experience doing *Beloved* to the others. It was just much more intense, more involving.

Ozan: It was much richer and so complicated. It's got so much imagery and stuff in there that you need to analyse.

Joe: To start off it was really hard – the first couple of chapters you had to read a couple of times just to get into how the book was written, because it was quite different but once you got into it....

Kieren: It went backward and forwards all the time. That's what started off being confusing but once you got the hang of that and how it works, then when you started reading the rest of the book it was alright.

Nasreen: You get more out of it because it's a difficult text. You're learning about all these different things and you can use that for the other unknown texts that you get. You can apply that stuff that you learned.

Jean: In a book that's easier you can miss a lot because you might not be concentrating so much but with this you had to look really closely. So now when you look at the next text you're still doing that. You're still looking for tiny little details all of the time.

Nasreen: I wouldn't have chosen it to read on my own. I would have read the first two pages and then have thought, 'no, it's not for me.'

Ava: It encourages you doesn't it? Usually you wouldn't approach it because you'd think it's too intellectual for me, I won't be able to... but we found out that we could.

Ozan: It encourages you to go for similar kinds of texts because you know that you can handle it. If you can tackle that book you can tackle anything really.

Nasreen: It's a really good book because of how it's structured, so you can see that it's got more to it, so you get more out of it as well. So maybe with another book you think, well you'll get more out of that as well.

Cat: And I think they are easier to do for exams because there's more to write. Like with an easy text you need so many points to do an essay and you just end up waffling in the end because you've just got nothing else to write but

---

5. Talking to the students explicitly about the nature and quality of their learning was always an important part of my teaching style, not only at A Level but also with younger students. We had serious conversations about what they thought they had got out of a topic or text, and the implications for future study (both for them and me). This taught me more about how to approach teaching them. I have witnessed this since, in classrooms of all kinds, most strikingly in a KS3 Maths lesson, where the teacher ended the lesson asking what had been most helpful to the students in explaining a difficult concept. This is education as a collaborative enterprise.

with this there's so much to write that you really can do a good essay on just a few chapters of the book.

Ava: The second time you read *Beloved*, so many things come up that you hadn't even noticed before and I think if you read it again more stuff would come up because it's not shallow – there are so many different layers to it.

Jean: I went into it with a good attitude. People said how brilliant it was, so when you start off you think, 'I'm going to try really hard,' and I think if you put effort into it you really get a lot out of it.

Alex: It's worth putting the effort into it.

Barbara: If you know from the start that it's a difficult text then you know that it's not your problem whereas if you start thinking, 'Why on earth don't *I* understand this, what's wrong with *me?*' then you don't go into it with so much confidence.

Ava: And you did warn us.

Barbara: Yes, warning that if you don't understand it it's not your fault.

Ava: I was talking to someone who read it over the summer on their own before starting to study it. They were shocked that we hadn't because they thought they'd be more prepared but I think it actually benefitted us more. They had a negative outlook.

Jean: Because some people read it on their own and thought, 'Oh God, I don't want to study that. It will be too difficult,' but we just started.

Joe: And you also have to understand what's happening once you get into the second sections. You have to have understood how it was written to appreciate them.

Alex: It's the time shift in the different chapters – you're moving from the past to the future all the time. That's actually quite hard to understand, if you just picked up the book and started reading.

Ozan: If you can understand how the book works in the first place then you can understand how it works throughout really.

Alex: It's also really refreshing as a book because all the stuff we get nowadays, like Shakespeare – I'm not saying we shouldn't do Shakespeare – but it's quite repetitive and then you get *Beloved* coming in and you get a different culture, a different perspective and that's really good.

Writing about *Beloved*

Student writing on the text bears out the view that narratives that draw attention to their textuality by using unconventional structures and uses of language, elicit greater awareness of the 'constructedness' of texts.

Kieran's first year essays consistently failed to go beyond retellings of the story and character sketches. Keeping him focused on the nature of the writing and deeper levels of meaning was difficult. In an essay title beginning, 'How does the writer.....', the 'how' and 'the writer' were entirely absent. However, by the end of studying *Beloved*, there was a sudden and dramatic shift, which has established itself firmly in his writing on other texts. This extract from an essay on *Beloved* by Kieren shows something of this. It was an analysis of two different tellings of the birth of Denver, written as an interim essay in the course of reading the novel.

> *The second telling is provoked by Beloved's constant questioning of Denver, 'Tell me how Sethe made you in the boat?' It seems to me that since the character of Beloved has entered the novel she has not stopped dragging up the past for both Denver and Sethe, as if she wanted to be added to it, and not be left out, as if she had a part in the past with both of them.*
>
> *The first telling of the birth is told fairly briefly by Denver stepping into the story of the birth, which in this first part is told mainly about how Amy found Sethe and how Amy massages Sethe's swollen feet and tells her that, 'Anything coming back to life hurts.'.........*
>
> *Each of the tellings of the story focused on different aspects of Amy. The first being Amy's voice, that when she talked, in the first telling it said that it was Amy's voice what made her baby sleep, the baby which was hurting Sethe so, the baby which had been described as being like an antelope inside her belly. Amy's hands played a big part in the second telling of the birth as these were the hands that brought Denver into the world. Amy is called 'the bringer of life', by bringing Denver into the world. Denver told Beloved that 'They did it appropriately and well.' With this second telling of the story there is a lot more detail involved in it, it seems like the second instalment of a story but this second part has more detail and better description of surroundings than the first. With the story changing so does the audience. In the first telling Denver is telling the story to herself, but in the second she has a real audience, so she has to tell the audience the story with detail, to make Beloved more interested than she already is.*

In different ways, many of the students have produced their best essays on *Beloved*. This opening section from an essay by Jean was written at the end of studying the novel and shows her powerful grasp on the way in which narrative structure and technique are integral to Morrison's representation of slavery. The story and characters are explored analytically rather than merely descriptively. One can see her beginning to develop some quite sophisticated understandings of how texts work and how readers engage with them.

In 'Beloved' Toni Morrison uses a very effective way of writing about slavery which is very different to that found in other novels on the same subject. Her structure, style and use of language are linked throughout to the themes and ideas of the novel. She shows us how slavery distorted everything about the lives of black people and she goes deep into the emotions of her characters, showing how the effects of slavery continued long after it ended and how for black slaves freedom did not bring an end to the suffering.

The structure of 'Beloved' is very fragmented. Morrison has written the book in this way to symbolise the chaotic, fragmented lives of the slaves. Under slavery, family and community no longer existed for black people and Morrison writes about how this lack of structure and normality in life affected the slaves, not just during slavery but later on in life. For example, we hear of how Sethe struggled as a mother. She says, 'I wish I'd known more', but because she'd never been mothered herself and, 'there wasn't nobody to talk to,' motherhood was something very difficult for her.

Morrison's style of beginning stories and then returning to them later – an important example of this would be the killing of the baby – reflects the way the characters' minds work. Often in 'Beloved', characters begin to remember something and then stop because, 'saying more might push them both to a place they couldn't get back from.' Later, as they are forced to deal with these pieces of their past, more is revealed to us. As she gradually pieces together the story of the lives of Sethe and her family, they are doing the same thing in order to find out who they are. This fragmentation is very important to the novel because she uses the idea that many of the problems the black community faced after slavery stemmed from having difficulty in knowing themselves and claiming their past because it was so broken. At one point in the novel Suggs asks, 'Could she sing?.... Could she have been a loving mother? A faithful wife?' Under slavery slaves could not find out about themselves because their lives were not controlled by themselves and they had no opportunity to develop as individuals.

Toni Morrison uses her characters to show us how difficult it was for them and other slaves to know what they were really like. She uses many other situations to illustrate this, such as Paul D. torturing himself as he wonders if he is really a man and asks, 'What would he have been anyway – before Sweet Home – without Garner?' She emphasises the fact that her characters need to take hold of their memories, make them their own and accept them in order to move on, yet shows us why this is so difficult by letting us enter the thoughts of the characters as they struggle to do so.

Teaching and learning from challenging texts

The students' spoken and written responses suggest a number of directions in which our thinking could go, in terms of teaching challenging texts to any age group:

1. In choosing texts for classes, we may worry too much about their instant 'appeal'. Often in our heads 'appealing' is coterminous with 'immediate pleasure'. In fact, pleasure is a rather more complicated and odd thing, that can come from a more gradual process of getting to know a text. This is reflected in Nasreen's observation that she would not have read *Beloved* on her own but enjoyed studying it in class. Texts to be studied do not necessarily have the same qualities as texts that we want to read for our own individual pleasure.

2. Texts that deal with huge and momentous issues, such as slavery or the holocaust, can open up in pupils a spring of emotional, intellectual and cultural excitement and energy that will change them and their ways of seeing. Finding out that books can do stuff to you is a powerful discovery.[6]

3. Texts which make readers work hard draw attention to themselves as texts much more than more straightforward realist texts. In doing so, they force the reader to get to grips with their textuality and this awareness is then more readily transferred to the reading of other texts. Nasreen's comment highlights this – 'you're learning about all these different things and you can use that for the other unknown texts that you get, you can apply that stuff that you learned...' Challenging texts teach pupils to become more sophisticated readers.

4. Real strides of learning take place when pupils go beyond their usual boundaries and repertoires, rather than always remaining safely within them and a level of risk-taking can be exciting rather than frightening. Even in a subject like English where everything appears to be part of a continuum of learning, pupils like to feel that they have taken on board something new, rather than only practising and refining existing skills.

5. Challenging texts can have the reverse effect to the one we most fear. They can give confidence rather than taking it away. (Ava: 'It encourages you, doesn't it?')

6. It is important to establish for students that the problems of reading a challenging text lie in the text itself, not the reader. Pupils need to know that they are about to meet a challenge and that the struggle for meaning is what everyone expects and is hoping for, rather than a reflection of their abilities. As Ava said, 'You warned us.'

---

6. EMC's more recent work on cultural literacy has these ideas at its heart. This is exemplified in publications such as *Diverse Shorts* and the EMC 'Critical Literacy Cards', which are published as part of *EMC Curriculum*[Plus] *Card Collection*.

7. The early stages of reading a challenging text are of critical importance. Left alone with the whole text there is too high a possibility of pupils foundering. A framework for reading can be introduced early on, which will shape the whole of the rest of the reading experience. As Ozan says, 'If you can understand how the book works in the first place then you can understand how it works throughout really.'[7]

8. We should be careful about pigeonholing or patronising our pupils. Of the students in my group, it was many of the weaker students who identified the most difficult texts as the ones that they had most enjoyed studying. This was not just a question of bravado or face-saving in the discussion. I could myself see that the qualitative shifts in their written work had emerged out of studying these very texts.

9. Difficulty doesn't only reside in pre-twentieth century texts. It is entirely false and abhorrent to assume that everything beyond the canon, and in particular, world literatures, are simpler and cruder texts than those within a narrowly defined 'literary heritage'. The government and world at large need to be persuaded that tackling a text like *Beloved* presents just as many, if not more demands on students' intellectual, linguistic and literary abilities as reading poems by John Donne or a play by Shakespeare and that it adds a different and vitally important dimension to students' cultural and literary understandings.

---

7. This is an early example of the approach taken in EMC's current work on teaching novels at KS3 and in our CPD on narrative texts at GCSE and A Level. Chapter 9 'Teaching a Novel at KS3 (page 154) and Postscript: Harold Rosen Lecture (page 187) outlines the approach in detail on a KS3 text, *In the Sea There Are Crocodiles*. For a fuller account of this project, including documentation, see the blog 'Teaching a Novel at KS3' on the EMC website.

2.5 Diversity in the English classroom

This book is imbued with the belief that diverse English classrooms should be full of diverse texts, approaches, ways of thinking and responding to what students bring with them from their own families, communities and cultures. This includes everything from the language they speak, and are taught, to the books they read, as well as the other cultural experiences they engage in, inside and outside the classroom, and the way their voices are heard. Given that this permeates the whole book, I thought long and hard about whether it needed a separate piece in its own right. I decided that it did; I want to make sure that its centrality to good English teaching cannot be missed.

What do we mean by the term diversity? In current discussion of classrooms and the curriculum, it is a catch-all phrase for what might previously have been called 'multiculturalism', in other words the recognition that students in modern Britain come from a very wide range of different cultures, speak many different mother tongues and may have differing starting-points, experiences and, perhaps, different needs too. It also includes other aspects of identity – disability, gender, sexual orientation and class. It is a broader term than 'multiculturalism', encompassing all the ways in which children might experience inclusion or exclusion on the grounds of difference. Richard Quarshie in a chapter on diversity in *Becoming a Reflective English Teacher* (ed. Andrew Green) argues that we need a view of diversity which 'doesn't limit itself to a focus just on gender or ethnicity or social class but allows a 'cross-hatching' of all three.' We might helpfully extend this cross-hatching to other cultural and social identities as well. Andrew McCallum's discussion of this, in his book *Creativity and Learning in Secondary English*, uses Derek Attridge's term 'idioculture' as a way of recognising the complexity of how each individual's cultural experience is built up of 'a changing array of interlocking, overlapping, and often contradictory cultural systems absorbed in the course of his or her previous experience...' (Attridge, 2004 in McCallum, 2012).

In terms of the curriculum, thinking about the educational offer from the perspective of diversity means considering the question of whether students are excluded, or feel excluded, by the choices made. Does the curriculum speak to them and their needs? Does it define itself so narrowly that their talents and identities are not valued? Does the curriculum itself lead them *not* to succeed, because what they bring is automatically defined as 'lacking'. It also means considering the *value* of diversity for English both as a subject discipline and in the classroom, for instance the contribution of English writers of different cultures, the rich range of varieties of English they offer, as well as their different perspectives, both on literature and on the world, that throw fresh light on the subject.

In the whole period that I have been involved in education, multiculturalism has been attacked for a multiplicity of reasons, some more well-intentioned than others. For instance, it has been derided for: downplaying, or even threatening, the mainstream culture and traditions of established white Britain; for failing to instil

British values; for patronising people of colour or of different cultures; for failing to offer 'disadvantaged' children canonical, high prestige knowledge that will allow them to be successful in education and beyond; for emphasising difference rather than commonality and therefore being divisive rather than diverse. In the early days, it was the *Daily Mail* and other tabloid newspapers who were at the forefront of critiques of multiculturalism (and gender-sensitive initiatives), often latching onto apocryphal stories of 'political correctness gone mad', such as teachers no longer putting on Nativity plays, or forcing white children to learn only about Hindu or Islamic festivals, or uproar about books for children presenting same sex relationships. These attacks have often seemed to be as much on the communities and their cultures as on the educationalists who wanted them to be valued. They have played into the fears and insecurities of a society that felt its identity to be under threat. Nowadays, some in the world of education itself (including those with a high degree of influence), are also among the voices questioning whether diverse, multicultural schools should be teaching children anything other than mainstream, high culture and anglo-centric understandings about the world. Their thinking may derive from more noble intentions than those of the *Daily Mail* but the effect, in my view, has been equally concerning.

The questioning of a 'diverse' educational offer to students has been channelled most recently through debates about 'cultural capital', where both government (Michael Gove when Secretary of State for Education) and OFSTED (in the 2019 Inspection Framework materials) argue that 'poor', 'disadvantaged' children must be offered the kind of knowledge that middle-class children have greater access to, in order to help them succeed in the world and reduce educational inequality. (These arguments are dealt with more fully in Chapter 3.5, page 72: 'Cultural capital – is it a useful term?'.) It is interesting how much of a shift there has been in the 'official' view from government and the inspectorate in recent times. The Swann Report (1985), with its full title 'Report of the Committee of Enquiry into the Education of Children from Ethnic Minority Groups', insisted upon the need for change in order to address the needs of all children:

> We believe it is essential to change fundamentally the terms of the debate about the educational response to today's multiracial society and to look ahead to educating all our children, from whatever ethnic group, to an understanding of the shared values of our society as a whole, as well as to an appreciation of the diversity of lifestyles and cultural, religious and linguistic backgrounds which make up the society and the wider world. (DfES 1985).

In 2009 Ofsted was arguing in *English at the Crossroads* that

> There is an increasing acceptance that 'one size does not fit all' and that the curriculum should be adapted to meet the particular needs of pupils in a school, as well as reaching out to those pupils who are not currently engaged by the subject.

The early incarnations of the National Curriculum and GCSE specifications recognised the importance of offering diverse texts. Poems by writers of 'other cultures' and later 'different cultures' were a requirement. There was argument about the terms – otherness and difference – but at least the textual variety was a requirement. In the current National Curriculum for KS3 'seminal world literature' is expected but this choice of language signals a very different set of intentions – to offer access to a more 'international', 'other' high prestige culture, rather than the culture of the diverse 'us' of modern Britain.

The effects of the promotion of this view, in recent government directives, alongside the urging from Ofsted in 2019 that schools rethink their KS3 curriculum, are becoming all too clear. There has been a spawning of culturally narrow educational curriculum offers, privileging knowledge of Greek myths, the Bible, canonical authors (often white, male and dead), over all other forms of culture, both contemporary and culturally diverse.

Now there are many reasons why this is troubling. One reason is that it is based on a deficit model of what students bring from their own experiences, families and communities, which suggests either that they have 'no' culture, or alternatively that, if they do, it is inferior to the dominant one. Not different, not interesting, not vigorous and thriving, not an addition to our cultural understanding but rather, less valuable.[1] Even if this view recognises that there *is* another set of cultural experiences, rather than none at all, it devalues it, or even seeks to eliminate it, rather than capitalising on it. It does not regard it as valuable knowledge for *all* students, not just those fortunate enough to be immersed in it. Opportunities are lost for one culture to be seen through the lens of another, and, in English, for literary ideas, themes, genres or tropes to be explored across cultures. Teachers who know little, for instance, about myths across cultures, may be entirely unaware of the opportunities afforded by looking at them comparatively. So, for instance, if one is looking at literary depictions of seasonal change and renewal and common ways of representing these ideas through myth and allegory, why look just at the Greek myth of Persephone? Why not also look at whether there are common patterns in Native American, Slavic or Chinese mythology? Chinese or Polish students in the classroom might either know something about these, or enjoy finding out more from family or other community-based sources and this broader look at myth and allegory could be illuminating and enriching for all students.

Another concern about lack of diversity in the curriculum is what it does to students' sense of their own identity and how this connects with their educational experience. Christopher Emdin's work in the USA on 'neo-indigenous' students (urban African American or Latino students) in *For White Folks Who Teach in the Hood* does not wholly translate to a UK context but the underlying premise is very relevant – that schools ignoring and not learning from students' own cultural experiences is detrimental to their sense of self, their well-being and their ability to make educational progress without tearing them away from their own identity and community. If schools only value that which is not part of who you are, then you

---

1. This 'deficit' view applies equally to students' first languages, which are often ignored entirely, or regarded as less valuable than the modern foreign languages taught to all students as school subjects. It seems perverse not to regard students who are fluent in Polish or Sylheti or Somali as having valuable, additional linguistic skills and knowledge that they can bring to bear in all their educational experiences and share with others who do not have this additional expertise.

either deny that part of yourself, to your harm, or you find yourself not succeeding under the terms set by the school. This view is reinforced in the current work of linguists like Rob Drummond and Ian Cushing and others, who point to the ways in which the denigration and policing of young people's language acts as a barrier, rather than an aid, to their educational development.[2]

One additional concern – and an extremely important one for me – is that a failure to embrace diversity leads to a narrowing of the curricular conversations for all. Whether one teaches in a multicultural inner-city school, or a rural school populated largely by the children of families who have lived in that area for centuries, a diverse cultural offer enriches and opens minds. This is not simply a wishful, idealistic and flabby idea. It is the opposite of 'dumbing down'; it is not just about making education 'relatable'. If you talk to academics leading their fields in UK universities, say about the teaching of Shakespeare, you find that their teaching incorporates the ways in which Shakespeare is received and performed in different contexts (cross-culturally as well as over time), to throw light on the text and the writer. Andrew Dickson's book *World's Elsewhere: Journeys Around Shakespeare's Globe*, for instance, a critical book about Shakespeare's global influence, is described by Shakespeare experts like Stanley Wells as 'a revelatory journey of cultural exploration', while writer Margaret Drabble describes the 'cross-cultural insights' into Shakespeare's plays as 'remarkable.' In reviews of the book, words like 'revelatory', 'eye-opening' and 'insightful' abound. And, of course, what Dickson reveals is how Shakespeare is what one critic describes as 'defiantly plural'. So even here, with Britain's most iconic writer, recognising plurality within the text and plurality of responses in different cultures is to treat the work with the kind of respect that it properly deserves. A dry and dusty, mono-cultural reading of Shakespeare does not do justice to that.

This is just one example. Everything we teach can benefit from both looking at it from *within* and from *without*, with the fresh insights that this can offer. This was demonstrated clearly to me by the choice to juxtapose *In the Sea There Are Crocodiles* and *Great Expectations* in the Year 9 curriculum in the school where we did our novel project. Pairing two such different 'rites of passage' novels threw light on both. Similar, fruitful, cross-cultural possibilities abound. Why not teach a little bit of Homer alongside an extract from Derek Walcott's epic text *Omeros*, which translates the Odyssey into a contemporary Caribbean context? How about adding in Akala's hip-hop response to the Homer, a contemporary re-write from the perspective of the women, such as Pat Barker's *The Silence of the Girls*, or Madeline Miller's *The Song of Achilles*, which brings to the fore the possibility of sexual love in the relationship between Achilles and Patroclus? Creating literature, reading and studying literature are all about responding to other texts and making them speak to different readers, in different times.

---

2. See Chapter 12 for more on diversity, accent, dialect, Standard English and students' own uses of language.

This is not about offering *less* knowledge. That view is itself a diminution of what different cultures offer. Bansi Kara, a Deputy Headteacher, in an Opinion piece for the online journal *Schools Week* in 2017, reports on a conference talk she did on an inclusive curriculum, saying:

> My argument was for the inclusion of more knowledge, not less, for the sole purpose that our students deserve to be able to do more than fit into the culture of one country. They might, if we find space to colour in the black and white, learn the interconnectedness of the world they live in.
>
> This is not about diversity for the sake of audits or political correctness. It helps students to be part of the narrative of now – not just the narrative of the colonial past.

Arthur Applebee's take on this, in his book *Curriculum as Conversation*, sums it up very well for me. He says,

> Literature offers both contact zones and safe houses. When we read within familiar traditions, we experience the comfort of the predictable. When we read in alternative traditions, we are asked to step into another perspective, to view the world from an unfamiliar tradition of knowing and doing. In so doing we broaden the 'great conversations' about literature and the wisdom of the cultures that comprise it.

Applebee's metaphor of contact zones and safe houses is a helpful one. Another that has resonated with me, and with staff at EMC, is Rudine Sims Bishop's metaphor of the window, mirror and the sliding door. This metaphor is particularly valuable in thinking about diversity from the angle of students whose life experiences are not broadly those one might think of as being within the mainstream – people of colour, people with disabilities or those whose sexual preferences or gender choices make them more liable to be excluded in some way from the experiences of learning in schools and classrooms. Sims Bishop's work (1990) is most closely focused on books, the heart of the English curriculum.

> Books are sometimes windows, offering views of worlds that may be real or imagined, familiar or strange. These windows are also sliding glass doors, and readers have only to walk through in imagination to become part of whatever world has been created and recreated by the author. When lighting conditions are just right, however, a window can also be a mirror. Literature transforms human experience and reflects it back to us, and in that reflection we can see our own lives and experiences as part of the larger human experience. Reading, then, becomes a means of self-affirmation, and readers often seek their mirrors in books.

Sims Bishop lectured at the University of Massachusetts-Amherst, and then later at the Ohio State University. She said that her own childhood gave her few experiences of windows, sliding doors and mirrors. Her work has had a significant influence on the development of African American writing for children and on understandings about the kind of messages sent out to children by the texts that they are given to read in school.

If I look back on my time in the classroom, I think of the students I taught for whom mirrors *did* become windows and then sliding doors. I think of Nasreen, whom I taught for A Level. She was a high-attaining girl who was, nevertheless, silent, often ungiving in class discussion, unwilling to participate in group talk, uncommunicative in her demeanour, both towards me and other students. Early in the second year of the course, I chose as a set text *Reef* by Romesh Gunesekera, a novel that moves between Sri Lanka and London, exploring the experiences of a young man who migrates to the UK. (I subsequently co-wrote a resource for EMC on *Reef, Beloved* and Irish writer Seamus Deane's *Reading in the Dark*.) Nasreen chose to come and talk to me at the end of our time studying *Reef*. She wanted to tell me that this was the first book she had ever studied in school that spoke to her own experiences, that was about someone like her. The course came alive for her at that moment and her relationship with me changed.[3]

I think too of the powerful effect on students (discussed in other chapters) of reading other young people's published stories, or books like Mildred Taylor's *Roll of Thunder Hear My Cry, Friedrich* by Hans Peter Richter, Farrukh Dhondy's collection of short stories, *East End at Your Feet*, poems by Linton Kwesi Johnson, or later in GCSE specifications Grace Nichols, John Agard and Moniza Alvi. I think of the *emagazine* conferences where students are visibly enthused and energised by sessions led by Akala, Patience Agbabi, Sarah Howe, Raymond Antrobus and other writers of colour. In today's world of Young Adult publishing, there are many brilliant books and superb writers whose age-appropriate work can act as mirrors and windows for our students, by people like Sita Brahmachari, Alex Wheatle and others. Andrew McCallum's blog for EMC 'Mirrors, Windows and Sliding Glass Doors' offers a book list for older readers; EMC's regular summer and Christmas book choices always include new ideas for diverse texts for the classroom and as recommendations for wider reading. EMC's publication *Diverse Shorts* gives a taste of many such texts and suggests ways of exploring the issues that they raise. All of the Awarding Bodies offer texts that *could* make GCSE more diverse – Edexcel has recently had a special initiative on this. Yet these texts are rarely taken up by teachers; they have not been adopted with the kind of excitement and enthusiasm that a book like *Roll of Thunder* generated in earlier times. This may well be because of the climate in which high prestige, canonical texts seem to be so strongly favoured that teachers feel uncertain about the validity of including such texts. With the best of intentions, some teachers may fear depriving their students of high-value cultural experiences.

To come back round to the central argument of this piece, I would stress that it is not a question of either/or, it is both. Diversity is inclusive; it includes experiences of the canon, as well as the non-canonical. Windows (that are also mirrors) open doors and those doors should have no locks on them. They should lead into big rooms, and from big rooms out into wide open spaces, and from wide open spaces into other places and other worlds.

---

3. The piece about the teaching of *Beloved* on page 36 ('Challenge and text choice – walking the tightrope') also shows the ways in which 'decolonising' the English curriculum can provide powerful, life-changing educational experiences for students with diverse cultural backgrounds.

So, to sum up, it seems to me that we need to look at culture and curriculum in the following ways.

- We need to talk about cultures, not culture.

- We need to question why certain texts or cultural products are regarded as high prestige and be open to the idea that more than one culture can offer high quality texts that are worthy of study.

- We need to value what our students bring to the classroom, have respect for it, and show a willingness to look at the ways in which it relates to, and intersects with, literature and knowledge from mainstream traditions.

- We need to look for opportunities to broaden the conversations to incorporate the 'wisdoms' of different traditions, recognising that all students benefit from seeing literature both from within and from without.

- We need to recognise that students from diverse cultures, with diverse experiences, need to find themselves reflected in some of the books they read, if they are to become windows or sliding-doors onto the world and allow them to engage in a wider cultural world.

References for Chapter 2

Applebee, A.N. 1996. *Curriculum as Conversation: Transforming Traditions of Teaching and Learning*. Chicago: University of Chicago Press.

Attridge, D. 2004. *The Singularity of Literature*. In McCallum, A. 2012. *Creativity and Learning in Secondary English*. Abingdon: Routledge.

Barry, P. 2007. *Literature in Contexts*. Manchester: Manchester University Press.

Bleiman, B. 'It's good to talk – working on a novel at KS3' report. EMC blog www.englishandmedia.co.uk

DES. 1989. *English for Ages 5 to 16 (The Cox Report)*. London: DES and Welsh Office.

Dickson, A. 2015. *World's Elsewhere: Journeys Around Shakespeare's Globe*. London: Bodley Head.

Dixon, J. 1966. 'A method of definition'. In *Growth through English: A Report Based on the Dartmouth Seminar*.

Drummond, R. 2018. *Researching Urban Youth Language and Identity*. London: Palgrave MacMillan.

Eaglestone, R. 2017. [4th ed.] *Doing English: A Guide for Literature Students*. Abingdon: Routledge.

Emdin, C. 2017. *For White Folks Who Teach in the Hood…And The Rest of Y'all Too: Reality Pedagogy and Urban Education*. Boston MA: Beacon Press.

Freire, P. 2017 [1972]. *Pedagogy of the Oppressed*. Harmondsworth: Penguin.

Gibbons, S. 2017. *English and Its Teachers: A History of Policy, Pedagogy and Practice* (NATE). Abingdon: Routledge.

Halliday, M.A.K. 1985 [new edition 2014]. *An Introduction to Functional Grammar*. Abingdon: Routledge

Kara, B. 2017. 'Colouring in the curriculum'. In *Schools Week* 17th June 2017.

McCallum, A. 2019. 'What makes a KS3 novel challenging?'.
EMC blog www.englishandmedia.co.uk

Morrison, T. 1987. *Beloved*. London: Vintage.

Ofsted. 2019. School Inspection Handbook. Gov.UK/government/publications No 1900017.

Ofsted. 2009. *English at the Crossroads*. London: HMSO.

Quarshie, R. 2011. 'English and diversity'. In ed. Green, A. 2011. *Becoming a Reflective English Teacher*. Milton Keynes: Oxford University Press.

Sims Bishop, R. 1990. 'Windows, mirrors and sliding glass doors'. In *Perspectives: Choosing and Using Books for the Classroom* 6 (3).

Spielman, A. 2017. Speech at the Festival of Education,
www.gov.uk/government/speeches/amanda-spielmans-speech-at-the-festival-of-education

The Swann Report. 1985. 'Report of the Committee of Enquiry into the Education of Children from Ethnic Minority Groups'.

Vygotsky, L. 1986 [1934]. *Thought and Language*. Cambridge MA: MIT Press.

Wolsey, T.D., Lapp, D. and Fisher, D. 'Students' and teachers' perceptions: an inquiry into academic writing' in *Journal of Adolescent & Adult Literacy*, Vol. 55, No. 8 (May 2012), pp. 714-724. Wiley on behalf of the International Literacy Association.

The Use of English. 2018. 69 (3). The English Association.

3. Knowledge in English

This section consists of several pieces on the question of what we mean by knowledge, a central concern for all English teachers, at the heart of what goes on in individual classrooms. It is also fundamental to the shaping of the whole school curriculum, the system of examining and broader thinking by policymakers and regulators. Ideas about knowledge have been debated and contested for as long as school curricula have existed. Arguments and debates about knowledge in subject English have been equally fierce, both in schools and at university level.

3.1 Why aren't we talking about Applebee?

Arthur Applebee was an American educationalist specialising in English and literacy. While his output was prolific and highly influential in the United States, he is surprisingly rarely referenced in UK publications. This blog, written in May 2017, makes a case for the importance of his work, suggesting that it can help us to think about the learning that goes on in English classrooms in far more sophisticated and purposeful ways than is offered by other writers who currently have more influence, such as E.D. Hirsch. Applebee's social construction of knowledge owes much to the work of thinkers like Vygotsky and educationalists like Harold Rosen (whose PhD student he was in the 1970s) but he builds too on ideas about subject disciplines, how knowledge operates within them and how students become members of those subject communities.

Why knowledge matters... but Hirsch doesn't convince me

In working on EMC's group work project *It's Good to Talk* I decided to spend time reading E.D. Hirsch's *Why Knowledge Matters* – not just a quick skim-read but a careful, thorough, 'note-taking' read. I wanted to do justice to a book and writer who has been proving so influential. I imagined that I might disagree with some aspects but take others on board, and be, in some way, challenged and impressed. However, I was deeply disappointed on all counts – by its polemical rather than academically rigorous style, its lack of a thorough evidential basis and the gaping holes in some of the key arguments. The discussion in the book relates particularly to 'the language arts' (English and literacy, in UK terms), so I was especially interested in what Hirsch had to say.

One central idea is that vocabulary and knowledge should trump everything else in the teaching of 'language arts' and development of literacy. The reason given is that students' scores on reading tests in the US fall off in Middle to High school English and Hirsch suggests that it's because a.) poor vocabulary and lack of content teaching make students less effective readers than they should be and b.) the reading tests themselves are based on previously unknown material, on any random subject. He attacks the tests, saying they're not good reading tests if they're not testing topics where the vocabulary and knowledge have already been taught. These two arguments, put together, seem to me to be deeply flawed and mutually incompatible. A reading test is, by its very nature, supposed to test how well someone manages with a text that is *not* familiar, with vocabulary and content that is not necessarily known. The point of a reading test is to say to the world that this person is competent enough to grapple with unknown material of a certain level of challenge and make something of it. If the knowledge and vocabulary have been taught in advance, then it's not a reading test; it's a test of subject knowledge, of the kind that is done perfectly justifiably in many other subjects within the curriculum, whether it be History, Geography, RE or Biology. The overriding emphasis on vocabulary and knowledge also leads to an assertion by Hirsch that the best way of pupils acquiring these is by teachers explicitly teaching these to them in a well-ordered sequence. This is superficially appealing. Teach vocabulary, learn topics, be tested on topics, prove that you know more and can read more. But we know from research that the best indicator for pupils' future educational attainment overall is how much they read, and how much they read for pleasure.[1]

This is just one of many deep reservations. I could talk about what Hirsch makes of France and its appalling failures in literacy as a result of progressive policies (or not, if you choose to read different reports from the ones he quotes!), or his understanding of what knowledge is, which seems fixed, static, derived from historical versions of subject domains, rather than the living ones of current academic practice, and based on a model of pouring information in and finding ways of ensuring that not too much leaks out. Information and recall of information dominate.

In comes Applebee

At the same time as reading Hirsch, in my search for interesting research on group talk, I came across an article by someone called Arthur N. Applebee. Since reading it, I have been on an Applebee trail, ordering copies of his books and downloading articles from Jstor. I have been captivated by everything I have read, not just by the thoroughness of the research and the persuasiveness of the arguments but also the clarity of thought and expression. In groups of teachers and educationalists, like a latterday Ancient Mariner, I've been returning again and again to my latest obsession, asking, 'Who's heard of Applebee?' Silence every time. Most teachers and educationalists nowadays have heard of Hirsch, so why has no-one in the UK (including me, until recently) heard of Applebee? Like Hirsch, Applebee (who died in September 2015) was an American educationalist. Associated with the Center on English Learning and Achievement (CELA), established in 1987, he collaborated with many other academics, including Judith A. Langer, Martin Nystrand and Adam Gamoran. There is a substantial body of work by these educationalists on the 'language arts', from books on reading and studies on what

---

1. The DfE report *Research on Reading for Pleasure* (May 2012) sets out in its introductory section the evidence of the benefits of reading for pleasure, drawing on widespread research by OECD, PIRLS, PISA, Clark & Rumbold and others. Subsequent research continues to show the correlation between reading for pleasure and attainment. For instance, Alice Sullivan and Matt Brown's 2014 study on 'Reading for pleasure, and attainment in maths, vocabulary and spelling' showed that reading for pleasure in children between ages 10-16 made a difference four times greater than having a parent with a degree. Reading itself teaches pupils far more knowledge and vocabulary than could ever be explicitly taught, in however systematic a programme of teaching. You read in order to learn knowledge and vocabulary, as well as learning knowledge and vocabulary in order to read.

effective schools are doing in the disciplines of English, to the significant impact of discussion-based classrooms on pupil achievement. In a particularly substantial piece of research (2003) they analysed 64 classes, with 1,412 students and drew the conclusion that:

> The approaches that contributed most to student performance on the complex literacy tasks that we administered were those that used discussion to develop comprehensive understanding, encouraging exploration and multiple perspectives rather than focusing on correct interpretations and predetermined conclusions.

This built on the many previous research studies that they quote in the research survey that precedes their own study (Applebee, Langer, Nystrand, Gamoran, 2013).

One of Applebee's most important books, written in 1996, is called *Curriculum as Conversation*. It makes for compelling reading. In a short piece, I can only hope to flag up a few major points on how it speaks to me, where Hirsch doesn't.

First, Applebee sees knowledge as, what he calls, 'knowledge-in-action'. This contrasts with knowledge purely as a past tradition that you look back to and learn about. 'Knowledge-in-action' is learning about doing the discipline and involves taking thinking forward into the present and future. He says that what young people talk about in school may be 'at some remove' from what graduate students discuss in seminars but the discussions are 'nonetheless part of an exploration of the same culturally significant domain for conversation.' For Applebee,

> In learning to do school, students are in fact learning to enter into culturally significant traditions of knowing and doing. [...] The words that are used, what counts as knowing and doing, are shaped by what other individuals have said and done, by the conversations that have gone before. This is the irreducible nature of tradition, which constitutes the present matrix out of which we act.

This strikes a chord for me in everything we do at EMC and it also strikes a chord with all that we discover through our close relationships with colleagues in Higher Education and with developments in the subject English in the academic world. Take, for instance, Robert Eaglestone's book *Doing English*. Addressed directly to students, both at A Level and undergraduate level, it seeks to establish the cornerstones of what it means to study the subject English. Eaglestone's account of knowledge in the discipline of English is in close accord with Applebee's description of knowledge in English classrooms. Here's an extract from Eaglestone's introduction:

> English is like a long conversation through time. Like any conversation, it moves over various linked themes; it has quarrels and agreements; people talk at the same time, struggle to be heard or shout louder and louder to dominate the debate; people suggest fresh ideas ('what about this?') or respond to earlier ones ('can we just go back to…?'); there are newer and older participants; like all proper conversations, part of it concerns the point of the conversation itself ('can we please focus on why are we discussing this?'); and now you, doing English, have joined this conversation and will change what's said next.

For Eaglestone, and Applebee, knowledge is not just facts and ideas as inert material to be learned, but rather it is living and changing, a process of learning how the discipline operates, what its practices are, what is significant within it, how to 'do' what others within its traditions have done and continue to do.

Should we not be looking to the academic traditions of our own subject, as represented by its most eminent living practitioners, to determine how we define knowledge within it? If so, we come to rather different conclusions about what and how we should teach our subject than those provided by Hirsch.

Applebee is also very interesting on the idea of the curriculum as a fixed and highly-structured 'catalogue' of items to be covered. He explicitly references Hirsch on this and suggests that the seemingly ordered and disciplined sequences of learning that emerge from a 'catalogue' structure for the curriculum, actually prove to be deadly and singularly fail to fulfil the task of teaching students to think within subject disciplines. Instead, Applebee argues for the curriculum as conversation. He says,

> If we do not structure the curricular domain so that students can actively enter the discourse, the knowledge they gain will remain decontextualised and unproductive. They may succeed on a limited spectrum of school tasks that require knowledge-out-of-context, but they will not gain the knowledge-in-action that will allow them to become active participants in the discourse of the field.

Applebee does not shy away from acknowledging that advocates of 'progressive theories' of knowledge have themselves sometimes lacked the kind of rigour and efficiency that is required and have relied too heavily on gifted teachers and isolated examples – 'vignettes' he calls them – of great work, in place of 'well-articulated procedures of curriculum and instruction'. He says that there are some 'well-justified criticisms of progressive theories' which have allowed students to 'wallow in their own ignorance' or have a 'long recapitulation of previous discoveries.' Applebee is no zealous proponent of 'progressivism' right or wrong. And don't we all agree with that view? None of us wishes to be an apologist for poor practice. But he does argue that curricular 'conversations' can be structured around big areas of cultural significance and that these alone can offer the real deal for students in terms of serious learning in subject domains. He says,

> schooling should be organised to help students enter into culturally significant domains for conversation, themselves representative of broader cultural traditions of knowing and doing. By placing the emphasis on entry into such conversations, I seek to ensure that students will emerge with knowledge-in-action rather than knowledge-out-of-context. By stressing culturally significant domains, I seek to ensure that education is organised around living traditions that look to the present and future as well as the past. And by stressing domains for conversation, I seek to ensure that there is an emphasis on the structure and interrelatedness of ideas and experiences within a domain.

I'm still reading Applebee, and I'm also getting new leads and following up the work of Langer, Nystrand and others who have collaborated with him over the years. Langer's work on reading as 'envisionment', for instance, is fascinating and also has much to offer us in thinking seriously about the complexity of the process itself and how to teach it.

This blog is itself the start of a conversation – a conversation about knowledge of the kind that Applebee advocates so cogently. And the conversation with teachers and educators of English might continue, using the question I started with. Why on earth aren't we talking about Applebee?

3.2 What is significant knowledge at KS3?

Written in August 2014, this blog was a response to a sudden upsurge of interest in knowledge in English, itself responding to an increasingly narrow focus on exam achievement, the development of exam techniques, and a sense among some in the profession that students were being offered a curriculum based on 'decontextualised skills' divorced from content. This justifiable set of concerns, however, has led to a swing the other way towards equally de-contextualised notions of knowledge – the idea that information, content, facts are what matter most, not what you do with them. The concept of 'mastery' as a way of defining knowledge has been advocated by some. It is possible to see online numerous accounts of knowledge that seem to me to shrink it down to a collection of facts about a text that barely scratch the surface of the kind of highly developed thinking that students might need for future study both at KS4 and beyond. The false separation of knowledge and skills and the downgrading of skills is at least as unhelpful as the sole focus on skills. In this blog, I explore these debates by starting with a practical example using *Great Expectations*, a familiar text, and by thinking about what significant knowledge about this text might be.[2]

Great Expectations

1. Dickens was writing in the nineteenth century.

2. Pip's sister was called Mrs Joe Gargery.

3. Dickens wrote his novels in instalments as weekly serials. You can see that in the way the chapters are structured and the points of suspense that make you want to read the next instalment.

4. *Great Expectations* is a rites of passage novel – a novel showing the development of a character from childhood to adulthood. Rites of passage novels are often stories of children learning hard lessons from their experiences.

5. Dickens is particularly well known for his ability to create characters who are larger than life, exaggerated figures (called caricatures), as well as more realistic characters.

6. Dickens' novels were often read aloud, rather than read silently. That influences the style of writing, including the sentence structure and the amount of dialogue.

7. Dickens is well known for his descriptions of London life, particularly the criminal or dark sides of life. He wanted to use storytelling to tell people about life for the poor, the downtrodden and people on the edges of society.

---

2. There are many examples of lessons or schemes based on the idea of 'mastery' on the internet, shared on blogs or via Twitter. The most high-profile current example is the Ark English Mastery curriculum outline, which is currently being trialled by EEF and sold to schools as a complete curriculum package. Their curriculum map for KS3 and a sample lesson are available online. EMC's own flexible curriculum maps, based on our KS3 resources, are markedly different, both in content and understanding of what knowledge is.

8. Dickens' characters are often thought to be the most important and successful element in his novels. Claire Tomalin has described him as the greatest creator of character of all time. However, some critics, including very famous writers like Virginia Woolf and Oscar Wilde accused Dickens of being too sentimental and presenting people unrealistically, as villains or angels. Another very famous novelist, Henry James, called his novels 'loose baggy monsters.' Which of these critics do you agree with most?

9. Pip ended up discovering that his good fortune came from the criminal Magwitch.

10. Dickens was the most popular novelist of his time and was hugely famous. He did readings in public.

All of these ten pieces of information are 'knowledge'. All contain facts. All are about Dickens, a novelist often regarded as vital for instilling knowledge of the 'classics' or the 'canon', a highly favoured writer for those who believe in imparting significant cultural capital to all pupils. Assuming that teaching Dickens is a valuable thing to do (as few would dispute, whether crudely labelled as 'traditionalists' or 'progressives'), the question is, what knowledge and facts about Dickens are useful to teach? Is all knowledge of equal value in an English curriculum?

I would argue that some of these bits of knowledge are hugely more significant and useful than others. They teach students about Dickens' distinctiveness as a novelist, teach significant 'knowledge' about how narratives work, about character and characterisation, about how Dickens' texts were produced and what difference this made to the writing, how they fit within their generic and cultural context. Other bits of 'knowledge' are disconnected 'facts' that don't open up the door to wider knowledge, that can't be used to consider new texts or other authors, that don't form a web of knowledge that can be used and adapted or build a sense of how literature works. Some of the ten pieces of knowledge encourage thought, reflection, understanding; others are more like Trivial Pursuits – a thing you know and could answer a question on in *Mastermind*, or *University Challenge*, or a pub quiz, but which you couldn't build upon. The 'door opening' knowledge, of course, isn't just pure knowledge. It quickly blurs into something that could also be called 'skills'. Because this kind of knowledge is about how texts work, and about the key questions that literary studies is interested in asking and answering, it becomes a skill for future study. If you know that Dickens creates characters who are caricatures and you understand what that means, then when you read about Mrs Bennet in *Pride and Prejudice*, or you weigh up the ways in which Charlotte Brontë presents Mrs Reed in *Jane Eyre*, you are able to make use of that knowledge. It is neither solely skill, nor solely knowledge, to decide that there are elements of caricature in these characterisations – it is both. Equally, if you've thought about character and caricature, you may be able to try out some of the techniques you've learned about in your own story writing, again a blend of knowledge and skill.

Knowledge of the social and historical context of the times may be needed to allow students to engage with the world of the novel but this is not important

'English' knowledge in its own right, only valuable for how it can be applied in an illuminating way to the text itself. Even at KS3, keeping the text at the centre of discussions of context seems crucial, as does a recognition that the text itself often provides much of its own context. This avoids the risk of English becoming mistaken for history, with that history, at worst, becoming a grossly generalised and watered down version. An approach to contextual knowledge at KS3 that keeps the text at the centre of the discussion will be of immense benefit in teaching pupils an approach to contextual knowledge that avoids all the problems endlessly reported by examiners at GCSE and A Level. So, to continue with the *Great Expectations* example, it might be that taking an extract from an episode that introduces Magwitch, asking pupils to choose one of three or four bits of contextual information or images that seem to illuminate that extract and justify their choice is a better approach than a stand-alone lesson all about poverty, wealth and criminality in Victorian England. That's history!

In the debates about knowledge versus skills, or the drive towards a knowledge curriculum, there seems to have been a surprising lack of discussion about what exactly we mean by valuable knowledge in an English curriculum. In terms of Literature, as the *Great Expectations* example hopefully reveals, some kinds of knowledge are much more important than others:

- Knowledge about how literary texts 'work'. This means that English shouldn't be pretending to be another subject, like History, or Sociology and doing it badly. English knowledge has to be about the nature of literary texts, so needs to focus on ideas like characterisation, how narrative works (or how non-fiction, poetry or drama work).

- Knowledge about how texts were received in their own period, as well as in our own times. (Why Dickens was popular in his own times, why he has the reputation he has now.)

- Knowledge about how different readers approach the texts. Why do highly respected writers like Virginia Woolf , Henry James and Claire Tomalin take such radically different views of the same writer and his craft? How might individuals read texts in different but equally valid ways?

- Knowledge of the historical or literary context of a text that genuinely throws light upon the text itself.

- Knowledge of what questions and ideas are central to English studies at school and beyond, of what it means to study a text. This knowledge allows pupils to learn how to read, think and write critically and with independence, and discover what it means to be a student of English.

These kinds of knowledge are also genuinely part of a curriculum that shows progression – the development of a set of skills and knowledge that will lead students seamlessly from KS3 into KS4, on into A Level and potentially beyond into English studies in Higher Education. Tell any university lecturer in English Literature that your students understand about caricature and that will seem like a recognisable bit of literary knowledge. Tell them that they know the name of Pip's sister, or what happened to Magwitch and they'll, quite rightly, think that you've got the wrong end of the educational stick.

I would argue that *Great Expectations* can be taught at KS3. I'd argue that knowledge is important. But I'd also argue that a supposedly knowledge-based curriculum that takes a Trivial Pursuits approach to facts fails to engage with what's distinctive and important about English literary study. Pupils at KS3 are perfectly capable of grappling with the deeper, more significant aspects of the subject. That's what we should be encouraging them to do.

3.3 Setting the agenda

The term 'knowledge organiser' emerged around 2016-17. I saw a lot of examples online and felt concerned that in the subject of English, rather than increasing knowledge, extending its limits and making students genuinely more knowledgeable about texts, they ran the risk of limiting and containing it, making it seem simpler and less complicated than it really is. The very process of simplification involved in a knowledge organiser might deny students the chance to think about the most interesting aspects of knowledge in the subject – its debates and discussions, its disagreements and uncertainties and its links out beyond the text. There is a distinction to be made between simple facts about texts and significant knowledge to take forward into future study. Another way of thinking about this practically, in classroom work, I suggest, is the idea of an 'agenda' for the study of a text. This is something that teachers might use as a way of introducing knowledge. Unlike a knowledge organiser, it is expandable and adaptable, with scope to be changed and developed by students themselves, to keep track both of growing content knowledge and understanding. This is the context in which this blog was written, in September 2017.

There is a major focus on knowledge in discussions of the curriculum at the moment. However, it's much harder to define what that knowledge should be. Knowledge is boundless, so choices have to be made. What those choices should be is open to debate. Should knowledge look outwards towards the world, and what's useful, in adult, working life? Should it mirror or prepare for academia, following the structures of knowledge that apply in the academic study of the subject? Should it aim to provide a broad, liberal education, offering the kind of cultural awareness that fulfils expectations of a well-educated citizen? Is knowledge of any kind a 'good', a way of inculcating a thirst for learning that will continue into adult life. In other words is what you know less important than the fact of knowing more in any field? Whatever one's view on these ideas about knowledge, it's difficult, in a subject like English in particular, to delineate basic minimum knowledge without setting up unnecessary limits, or suggesting that the knowledge, of whatever kind, is simple, tidy and clear-cut, as opposed to complex, open-ended, wide-ranging and sometimes messy at the edges.

Without wishing to repeat earlier arguments from earlier blogs, I'll simply restate my view that knowledge, whatever its content-base, should be a synthesis of information, conceptual understanding and skill. The three are intimately related. Knowledge involves bringing new information into your existing conceptual framework and changing that framework in the light of the new material. It involves changing and developing thought processes and ways of seeing, so that you apply new thinking to fresh situations. Fact retention is part of this process, but just the starting point rather than the ultimate aim. It takes information, skill and understanding combined, what Arthur N. Applebee calls 'knowledge-in-action', to make use of new information, turn it into insights and apply them in fresh contexts. If you can't do that, your knowledge is of limited use. Understanding and skill are needed to make information work for you.

Understanding what's significant and what isn't

I want to consider one key aspect of this in relation to English Literature, to show how information, on its own, isn't enough, even in the narrowest terms of knowledge for examination success. A key element in what students are required to do, in order to get high grades at GCSE and A Level, is to make judgements about what is significant or not. The words 'significant' and 'judicious' crop up again and again in specifications and in Examiners' Reports. The examiners are looking for students to make good decisions about what is worth focusing on in their essays. Points made have to be well chosen ones. This is no faddish requirement that comes and goes. It is at the heart of what it means to have genuine knowledge in the subject. If students latch on to insignificant aspects of a text, in an unseen response, or in an essay on their set text, they will have failed to recognise what matters, in other words the essential aspects that make this text special, that make it stand out from others, or fall within a tradition or set of conventions. Understanding about what is significant is… hugely significant.

This is something that at EMC we have been addressing on A Level and GCSE CPD courses for many years. We come back to it frequently with teachers whose results haven't been as good as hoped for, and who worry that poor writing skills are responsible for this. We have discovered, through our work with schools, that when students' results are disappointing, it is often not so much to do with their poor writing, their lack of structure, poor punctuation, inadequate paragraphing, inability to write a good opening paragraph or embed quotations, to follow up on evidence with a sentence of analysis, or any of the other elements of writing that we have become so obsessed with in recent years. The truth is that the P (the point being made) in PEE, or PEEL, or PETAL or any other formula, has been sadly neglected. Points are what essays hinge on – having good, relevant and significant ideas to put across. Any old point won't do, for instance a comment on a tiny bit of alliteration in a poem, or a point that makes a big deal out of the use of caesura, stichomythia, iambic pentameter, enjambment when there are much more significant features leaping out at an expert reader. Latinate terms that are only used to prove that you know Latinate terms are worse than useless. The same is true of syntactic patterns and structures, whether it's a tricolon, or asyndeton. An exaggerated focus on the terms makes it highly likely that students will want to make sure they get them in, and end up talking about them regardless of whether they are significant, often with no real thought about effect. It's topsy-turvy. Observe something important and make a good point about it. Don't remember lots of terms and then search for examples in the text to show that you know the label. If a term helps you to explain what you've observed, then brilliant! Terms, including Latinate ones, can be learned along the way, as a shorthand, to act in the service of ideas. In a nutshell, knowledge of terms and drilling in essay technique are irrelevant if students don't understand what is significant about a text.

Can a knowledge organiser help define significant knowledge?

In theory, knowledge organisers could be a great way of providing a summary of significant knowledge about texts or topics, so long as it's just a summary – the bare bones of a much richer set of discussions. I have no fundamental objection to knowledge organisers. In fact, I think they could be very useful in helping students understand what's most important to know about a text. But I sometimes find those posted online disappointingly thin and random in the knowledge they identify.[1] They don't seem to capture the most significant aspects of the texts or topics they cover. There's often a mismatch between what's important in the text and background knowledge needed to read it which, once known, is not really part of developing subject knowledge. This can lead to some oddities and confusions, for instance the foregrounding and testing of students' knowledge of aspects of Victorian society rather than their understandings about the text itself and how it works. The problem of defining what is significant knowledge is at the heart of whether knowledge organisers are helpful or not. We can't assume that because there's stuff written on a neat looking grid, it has automatically captured what's most important about the text or topic.

I've been asking myself, 'what would a good knowledge organiser look like?' and realise that, in fact, EMC has, in a way, been advocating a particular form of knowledge organiser for many years, not with that name, and with some major differences, but nevertheless having many of the same features and possible benefits.

An agenda for the study of a text

Over many years, we have advocated a number of approaches to help students recognise what's most significant and interesting in a text. These have been designed to teach students how to make judgements, sift knowledge and decide what to apply to any given text or topic. One of the most powerful of these approaches has been the idea of an 'agenda' for the study of texts.[2]

The agenda is a working document, not a definitive, final summary of key aspects but something to be added to and developed over the course of study, with students contributing to its development. It is introduced early in the study of a text, put up on the wall, on a flipchart, or made readily available on a whiteboard, as a shared set of understandings or ideas for the whole class to refer to in the course of studying the text. It starts with some initial observations, perhaps with the identification of emerging themes and stylistic traits, on the basis of a shared reading of the first chapter, or after reading short fragments from the text. The teacher can, at this early stage, tease out significant elements that students might look out for, think about and be alert to as they're reading the text. It makes the first reading an active one, in which the students are aware of what is especially

---

1. This is equally true of the quizzes and some other forms of 'retrieval practice' one sees proliferating on Twitter at the moment, for instance asking 100 questions on a Shakespeare text that make no distinction between small factual details and big concepts and issues.

2. The idea of the 'agenda' was at the heart of our work in the 'Teaching a Novel at KS3' element of our project *It's Good to Talk*, the results of which are available online on EMC's blog.

interesting about this text, in relation to others. As time goes on, in the course of reading and study, more key elements emerge and are elaborated upon. So for a novel this might include the key themes, aspects of style, narrative techniques, voice, methods of characterisation, symbolism and so forth. The 'agenda' gradually fills out, and gaps are filled in, so that by the time students do their exams, they have a great, succinct overview of what is important to 'know' about that text. Usually the agenda is no more than one to two sides of A4 of headings but behind that is a huge amount of discussion and reference to the text that has led to this synopsis of key ideas.

You could definitely say that the agenda is a form of knowledge organiser. It itemises aspects of a text that are worthy of consideration. But it has some important elements that differ from some of the knowledge organisers currently being shared on the internet.

First, it is provisional, not fixed. It is clear from the start that it will develop and that students will contribute to that development, adding to it, making it more sophisticated and subtle, questioning the ideas raised and refining them. There is scope for students to change the agenda, and for teachers themselves to discover new things, whether through class discussion, their own secondary reading or conversation with other teachers, and add these to the agenda. It opens up possibilities rather than narrowing them down to a fixed list. It allows for higher than anticipated expectations being fulfilled.[3]

Second, its stated aim is to focus on what's significant in the text itself, rather than muddling that up with what students should be learning through the study of a text. Knowledge organisers on texts tend to be more along the lines of 'here's what I think students should learn while studying this text', rather than 'here's what's significant to know about this text.' It may seem like a subtle difference but I think it's an important one. The first is the teacher's agenda for what they want students to learn. The second identifies what's of key interest in the text itself. For example, in an agenda on *Jane Eyre* for A Level you might start with the identification of the overriding narrative voice – a first-person retrospective voice. By the end of the study of the text, this bald idea will undoubtedly have expanded, to include subtle shifts at different points in the novel. The aim isn't to learn the term 'first-person retrospective voice' but rather to discover what's distinctive about the voice of this novel. It allows you to reject the idea of retrospection if it no longer applies at key moments in the novel, when the voice becomes more immediate and direct, as if recounting something happening in the moment, or to take into account the way the voice seems to vanish and become almost like a third-person narrative at times, with most of the story told through dialogue. The agenda needs to develop and take these shifts into account, in classroom discussion and in the course of reading and reflecting on the text. Students using an agenda like this will think critically about the text, rather than simply using a label like first-person retrospective voice and thinking 'job done' because they've used the right label. Labelling isn't what we want students to do in English.

---

3. See page 205 for an example of an agenda on *Strange Case of Dr Jekyll and Mr Hyde*, created by teacher Lucy Hinchliffe and her class in her first lesson on the text.

Finally, and most importantly, the agenda places the emphasis fairly and squarely on significant knowledge about a text. It's not based on facts – the names of the characters, or the plot – who does what, when and how, nor on the life of the author, nor on broad, sweeping statements about the times in which they lived. It doesn't set out facts, in other words. Knowledge of these facts is assumed. Expectations are high, with an assumption that students will know the names of key characters and what happens in the plot. These facts are just the starting-point, the most limited kind of information, upon which really rich knowledge is based. Having a knowledge organiser that is predominantly about the facts of the text seems to set the bar way too low. It's nothing like challenging enough for most students.

So, knowledge organisers (or agendas)? Yes, definitely. But let's make sure they really are about knowledge in its richest, deepest sense rather than a limiting, thin accumulation of facts that, in the end, are really not that significant.

3.4 Literature – the walk, not the map

Ofsted's materials for its 2019 new Education Inspection Framework trumpeted the notion that students require significant quantities of prior knowledge (vocabulary and contextual knowledge) in order to be able to access texts. This view of reading is based largely on the work of E.D. Hirsch, the American educationalist, whose book *Why Knowledge Matters* has been a major influence not only on some teachers and educators in the UK but also on government ministers. My blog, written in January 2019, challenges assumptions about what young people need to be taught before they can fully engage with a text, suggesting that texts often provide much of their own context, that students often bring to texts more than teachers recognise (and draw on), and that too much contextual material can get in the way of students' authentic responses to texts and discoveries about how texts work as literary constructs.

In an article in the *TES* on 18th January 2019, entitled 'Is this presumed knowledge which I see before me?', the author Josie Stacks argues that students need to be taught a substantial amount of prior knowledge before being able to successfully read and understand literary texts. There are key concepts, ideas and background information, she argues, a body of 'precise knowledge' that they are lacking.

This belief in the need for prior knowledge before reading texts is being aired with growing frequency, and forms the basis of some of the workshop materials shared by Ofsted in their recent presentations on knowledge and the curriculum (Ofsted, 2019).

For me, it raises a number of significant issues and problems. It seems to be founded on some fundamental misunderstandings about literature, the nature of literary study and the knowledge required to read and interpret literary texts, both as experienced readers and critics, and for those learning how to do this.

First, I would take issue with the assumption that there is a defined, easily agreed and limited body of knowledge out there, distinct and separate from the text itself, that can be identified and applied to an individual text in a simple and straightforward way. It seems to me that the knowledge you need depends on what questions you are going to ask about the text, how the study is angled and what you and your students decide to focus on. Choices have to be made, otherwise English would become 'the study of everything you need to know before studying texts', rather than studying texts!

In his new book, *Literature – Why It Matters* (2019), Robert Eaglestone tries to get to the heart of what is special about literature and literary studies. He says,

Knowing about a work of literature is about experiencing it as a process, not – although it can sometimes feel like this – as a collection of answers for a quiz or exam: literature's the walk not the map. Knowing the chemical make-up of water is not the same as knowing what it's like to get soaked in a sudden summer storm.

If we could know about a text by being given background information, or by explaining its thematic concerns in advance, by focusing on the associated vocabulary as a requirement before reading, we would never have that walk in the rain, or we would at the very least delay it considerably, abbreviate it by spending most of our time putting on our walking gear, and perhaps end up finally doing it so wrapped up in waterproofs that we barely notice the rain.

Second, it seems to me that the development of students as readers of literary texts does not happen through an accumulation of knowledge applied in a simple transactional act of learning knowledge and then applying it to texts. The educationalist Arthur Applebee describes the study of English as entering into a series of significant disciplinary conversations that have taken place over time. In terms of the classroom (where he and colleagues Langer, Nystrand and others did large amounts of fascinating, but rarely quoted, research), he describes the most effective English teaching as being that in which the conversations that happen (in speech or in writing) are of the kind that could take place at any level from primary to postgraduate, and be recognisably the same kinds of conversation. So, in terms of a play like *Macbeth*, discussions around dramatic irony, or comic relief, or the dependence of drama on conflict, or what we mean by tragedy (along with many more) would be identifiable as 'English' questions. Equally, Applebee argues that classrooms where these conversations are developed and continue over time (through connections being made between one text or topic and the next) produce the most effective and powerful experiences of learning in the subject. In practical terms, this means developing a curriculum where links are made, where questions asked in relation to one text are picked up on in another text and so on. The questions asked of a particular text may vary, according to what comes before and after, so that ideas are picked up again in new texts and contexts. In terms of current thinking about learning being all about committing knowledge to memory, this kind of ongoing conversation is much more convincing to me than the idea of committing factual information to memory. If you have learned something about different kinds of narrative voice in one novel, then what matters is being able to apply it to the next novel you study, drawing on your understanding in the previous text to gain fresh insight into the new one and consolidate and build on that knowledge.

Third, there is a very important question to ask of the 'chicken and egg' kind. Do you need to know a lot of specific things in order to study a literary text, or does the text itself teach you much of what you need to know? I would argue that texts usually provide much of their own knowledge. This question presented itself starkly to me and my colleagues when we looked at the slides and presentations from Ofsted's workshops on the curriculum in 2019[1]. A text by Robert Macfarlane was introduced. It was an extract from his non-fiction book *Mountains of the Mind*. The presentation made the case for this same 'knowledge-absent, knowledge-needed, knowledge-offered-before-reading' approach to literary study. So, in answering the question, 'What do you need to know to be able to understand this extract from

1. These were training materials released during the consultation period for the new Education Inspection Framework.

the Macfarlane's book?' all kinds of things were suggested, from knowledge about mountains, to the biology of the body's response to cold. The fact is, this bestseller would never be read by *anyone* apart from experts in anatomy or mountaineers if readers needed this kind of knowledge to read it. The book provides its own knowledge. People read it to find out more about mountains and the writer's understanding of them, which is really what the book is about – human beings' fascination with them and relationship to them, as much as mountains themselves.

This applies equally to texts in the classroom. There are, of course, some things that it's helpful for students to know if they don't know them already – and it is the teacher's role to bring these in, to enrich and deepen understanding. But often these things can be taught along the way, as they crop up. Occasionally something is so important – and so unexplained in the text itself – that it might need addressing before reading. But in general, I'd argue that the text can do its own talking, provide much of its own context and the significant *literary* issues are those that come from reading and talking about it – in other words, getting soaked in the rain, as Eaglestone puts it.

As I've suggested, there's a body of work in English in education, drawing on work on the subject discipline in the academic world, that corroborates this view.[2] There's also the experience of teaching texts, or working with teachers, and discovering that far too much time is sometimes spent on extra-textual study, historical or biographical context, extraneous facts, and not enough on the text itself. (The English Examiners' Reports for GCSE and A Level have also recognised this as a serious problem.) But now, there's some new evidence I feel able to draw on, from some recent research I've been involved with at EMC.

In Autumn 2018, I worked on a research project with a colleague, Lucy Hinchliffe, in her school in outer London. (She works part time at EMC and part time in school.) We constructed a piece of research on teaching a class novel in Year 9, with half of the cohort following the department's scheme of work, and the other half following one devised by the two of us at EMC. This gave us scope to compare the work of the two along the way, as well as the written outcomes in their exercise books and final assessments. We did student and teacher questionnaires, and held a department meeting at the end of the project to share the findings. The text was *In the Sea there Are Crocodiles*, a novel by the Italian journalist Fabio Geda, based on his interviews with Enaiatollah, a boy migrant from Afghanistan. The book is Enaiatollah's story. A key element of the EMC scheme was the development of knowledge about texts in the form of an ongoing conversation. Important concepts were developed in dialogue (both whole class and small group), students were encouraged to think hard for themselves about the nature of the text as a narrative, and to reflect on what was most interesting and characteristic about the writer's style and approach to his subject matter. This way of studying was very much in line with the Eaglestone and Applebee view of what it means to study literary texts – the students took the walk through the novel.

---

2. In her book *Envisioning Literature: Literary Understanding and Literature Instruction* 2nd Edition, Judith A. Langer's concept of 'envisionment' and research in classrooms in the US provides valuable theoretical underpinning and classroom exemplification of this.

In the original scheme of work, followed by half the cohort, the students spent the first few lessons being given information about Afghanistan, the Hazara and Pashtun peoples and the migrant 'crisis' in Europe. They explored images of Afghanistan and its people and they did research. In other words, they were provided with a lot of prior knowledge that the teachers believed they needed in order to study the text. The 'EMC group', by contrast, jumped straight into the book, working initially on fragments from the text to develop some initial ideas about what would be significant in the text. Their first lessons were all about the text as a work of literature, raising issues about whether it was fiction or non-fiction, its genre, its rites-of-passage structure, the nature of its voice, unusual aspects of its style and ways of telling and the impact on them as readers, including their response to some quite emotional and highly charged events in the first chapter. There was a discovery that the students themselves had quite a lot of knowledge that they could bring to bear about Afghanistan, Pashtuns and Hazara and the migrant 'crisis' in Europe, and, even if they hadn't had that, most of what they needed to know was there in the first chapters of the book.

The focus of the lessons was on developing understandings about the text that were 'literary' knowledge that could be built on and developed in future learning about other narrative texts. So, for instance, students were encouraged to think about what was 'characteristic' of this text, as compared with others they might have read in the past. The study of the text would start a 'conversation' that would develop over the course of Year 9, and extend into KS4 and beyond. In the writing of the 'EMC groups' that we collected during the project, one can see students confidently talking about narrative voice, the nature of fact and fiction, rites of passage novels, narrative structure, symbolism, unusual shifts in perspective and more. They make valid and authentic points about the text and write at considerable length. It is clear that they have done the walk, and been soaked in the rain. Interestingly, now they have moved onto the study of another novel, *Great Expectations* – a rather well-chosen text in continuing the literary conversations they have begun – the teachers are reporting that their students are making natural, unprompted and well-considered connections between the Geda novel and the Dickens. For instance, students have been remarking on a different rites of passage structure; while the Geda moved from dire circumstances, through ups and downs, towards better fortunes, the Dickens seemed to follow a different kind of trajectory.

So, where does this leave us? It seems to me that knowledge in English has its own organising principles and its own special qualities. It isn't necessarily the same as in other subjects. Knowledge accumulates and develops across texts and over time (via a disciplinary set of conversations). Historical and other extraneous knowledge are often found within the texts themselves, or need to be offered in appropriate amounts along the way, not ladled out in advance in hefty portions. Texts need to be read and experienced, background information should be just that – background, not foreground – and students need to get well and truly soaked in a big range of texts that provide the literary context for each other.

3.5 'Cultural Capital' – is it a useful term?

From around 2013 on, the term 'cultural capital' started to be used with increasing frequency in debates about knowledge and how it should appear in the curriculum. Its use seemed to be rather different from the way it might be considered in the world at large, and from the more precise use of it by the originator of the term, Pierre Bourdieu. Those arguing for an emphasis on cultural capital in schools suggested that disadvantaged children, often defined as those who did not have a middle-class upbringing, were disadvantaged by not having the same 'cultural capital' as their more fortunate peers and that it was the role of the school to make up for this by providing them with cultural capital in spadesful. The term was, rather controversially, used by Ofsted in its 2019 Education Inspection Framework materials. One could see it being treated as a given in teachers' discussions of their curriculum, their text choices and their aims for their students. In practice this has meant teachers introducing into the curriculum more and more canonical texts, often pre-twentieth century ones, more and more western cultural background, such as Greek myths, and fewer and fewer contemporary texts, Young Adult fiction and texts from diverse cultures. In this blog, I argue that 'cultural capital' is a highly complex idea being applied much too simply and inappropriately in discussions about knowledge and the curriculum. I suggest that its impact in English may well not only be counterproductive but also sell students short in terms of genuine cultural and intellectual development.[1]

The phrase 'cultural capital' is everywhere these days. In 2013 the then Education Secretary Michael Gove said,

> The accumulation of cultural capital – the acquisition of knowledge – is the key to social mobility.

He went on to say that at private schools chosen by the wealthy,

> you will find children learning to read using traditional phonic methods, times tables and poetry learnt by heart, grammar and spelling rigorously policed, the narrative of British history properly taught. And on that foundation those children then move to schools like Eton and Westminster – where the medieval cloisters connect seamlessly to the corridors of power.[2]

It's interesting that in Gove's use of the term there is a conflation between the idea of cultural capital and a traditional education of the sort one might receive at the 'great' public schools. Cultural capital is, seemingly, intrinsically bound up with phonics, times tables, rigorous attention to language, chronological British history and so on.

The term has gone on to be used as shorthand for offering working-class children the kind of knowledge that will open doors for them. Often it is presented in terms of its absence, as a gap, a deficit, or something that teachers are failing to give to students. Usually, working-class children are perceived as 'lacking' it.

---

1. A shorter version of this blog was published in *Impact*, the Chartered College Journal, in September 2019.
2. From a speech to the Social Market Foundation, February 5th 2013, entitled 'The Progressive Betrayal'.

Now, in the new draft Inspection Handbook (2019) produced by Ofsted as part of its Education Inspection Framework, cultural capital is given a section of its own, with this statement:

> As part of making the judgement about the quality of education, inspectors will consider the extent to which schools are equipping pupils with the knowledge and cultural capital that they need to succeed in life. Ofsted's understanding of this knowledge and cultural capital matches that found in the aims of the National Curriculum.[3]

If it does match the National Curriculum aims, one has to ask oneself why Ofsted couldn't simply quote them, so that we all know exactly where we stand.[4] For cultural capital is a complex and slippery term, meaning different things to different people, and is harder to pin down in practice than to glibly pronounce on.

What follows are some thoughts about this complexity and slipperiness that I hope will make people (and Ofsted itself) think a bit harder about whether it really is a helpful concept upon which to base the inspection of our schools.

First, where did it come from? The sociologist, Pierre Bourdieu, himself of working-class origins, invented the term to describe all those advantages that accrue to people of a particular class that have nothing to do with money and everything to do with social status. *Social Theory Re-Wired* website at Routledgesoc.com has a very simple and succinct account of what cultural capital meant for Bourdieu (with the key passage identified by me in bold):

> While he didn't consider himself a Marxist sociologist, the theories of Karl Marx heavily influenced Bourdieu's thinking. Marx's influence is perhaps most evident in Bourdieu's theory of cultural capital. Like Marx, Bourdieu argued that capital formed the foundation of social life and dictated one's position within the social order. For Bourdieu and Marx both, the more capital one has, the more powerful a position one occupies in social life. However, Bourdieu extended Marx's idea of capital beyond the economic and into the more symbolic realm of culture.
>
> **Bourdieu's concept of cultural capital refers to the collection of symbolic elements such as skills, tastes, posture, clothing, mannerisms, material belongings, credentials, etc. that one acquires through being part of a particular social class. Sharing similar forms of cultural capital with others – the same taste in movies, for example, or a degree from an Ivy League School – creates a sense of collective identity and group position ('people like us'). But Bourdieu also points out that cultural capital is a major source of social inequality. Certain forms of cultural capital are valued over others, and can help or hinder one's social mobility just as much as income or wealth.**
>
> According to Bourdieu, cultural capital comes in three forms – embodied,

---

3. This formulation in the draft Inspection Handbook was adapted in the final version of the Handbook to read: 'It is essential knowledge that pupils need to be educated citizens, introducing them to the best that has been thought and said and helping to engender an appreciation of human creativity and achievement.' The change seems to have been made in response to arguments and debates such as those raised in this blog.

4. It seems that Ofsted took this on board and did quote the National Curriculum in the final version.

objectified, and institutionalised. One's accent or dialect is an example of embodied cultural capital, while a luxury car or record collection are examples of cultural capital in its objectified state. In its institutionalised form, cultural capital refers to credentials and qualifications such as degrees or titles that symbolise cultural competence and authority.

So for Bourdieu, cultural capital is everything that you learn that signifies for others that you are of a particular class. We know how important this panoply of signifiers is, when we hear about students attending Oxbridge interviews and feeling alienated, out of their depth, unsure of themselves and their entitlement to even be there. But often that is more to do with those social aspects like dress, accent and confidence in particular social situations (as identified by Bourdieu above), and less to do with their curricular subject knowledge and certainly not to do with whether they have learned to read using phonics or not, or can recite their times tables.

One can ask the question of whether the narrower definition of cultural capital that has emerged in a post-Goveian era encapsulates the kind of thing that really does disadvantage students. And then, even if one assumes that there are elements of 'knowledge' that furnish one with cultural capital, it still remains to ask which kinds of 'knowledge-lack' genuinely put people at a disadvantage and which are of less significance in terms of social mobility. And finally, even if we can agree that some things are so important that they are indispensable and must be taught, one can go on to ask the question about how best to teach them, and in what quantity and at what point.

So here are a few more thoughts on those three inter-related questions.

The first – does the narrow 'knowledge' definition of cultural capital really get to the heart of what disadvantages some students? University interviews are a crunch moment when students' supposed cultural capital is often thought to be put to the test. It is the culmination of students' education in a school setting. Here's what the Cambridge University website says in 2018/19 about its interviews:

What will I be asked?
Interviews are discussion-based, predominantly academic and subject-related, so you'll be asked questions:
- Relevant to the course you've applied for
- About the information you provided in your written application

In all subjects, we're looking for informed enthusiasm and an ability to think independently about your subject.

You'll probably find some of the questions quite challenging. They're designed to encourage you to think for yourself and develop an argument or tackle a problem. Don't panic if you don't immediately have an answer to a question.

Remember:
- Interviewers want to find out how you think and apply your current knowledge, how well you can expand on and apply your existing knowledge to unfamiliar problems rather than how much you know.

- Very often there are no right or wrong answers to the questions asked. It's the process of reaching your answer that's generally of more significance than the answer itself.

- Don't be afraid to consider new ideas but if you don't understand something, say so and feel free to ask for clarification at any point if you need it.

- Answer the questions in your own way, the interviewers want to hear what you have to say about your subject; don't just say what you think the interviewers want you to say or what your teachers or others would want you to say.

The emphasis here is not on 'what you know' but rather on quality of thinking, confidence and approach to knowledge, a kind of proof of 'know-how' in the subject rather than of any specific content. Here, as in other university interviews, your cultural capital comes from your confident ability to engage in academic enquiry and discussion. On this basis, developing all students' cultural capital should involve masses of opportunities for discussion, debate, exploration of ideas, independent responses to new material, individual research and development of one's own lines of enquiry and so on – a very different kind of emphasis to that which foregrounds particular items of knowledge as being of overriding value.

Second, if there were some knowledge without which you might be at a disadvantage, what might that be? Well, in the world out there, as an adult, it seems reasonably uncontroversial to say that, for British-educated people, never having read or seen a single play by Shakespeare would make you seem poorly educated. Shakespeare's position in our national cultural life is beyond dispute. In all the time I've been teaching, no English teacher I've come across has ever suggested not teaching at least one Shakespeare play. Shakespeare, however, is the one writer for whom this seems to be the case and whose place in the National Curriculum is assured. We might all agree about a broad and rich range of other reading in English, but I think we'd be hard pressed to agree that there are any other particular writers who *must* be studied over and above any others. If you've read poems by Milton but not Blake, or Blake but not Keats, or Browning but not Tennyson, everyone will understand that choices have been made. Even at degree level there isn't time to do everything. I studied Middle English Romances but not Milton, American literature but not Old Norse. Equally, I would argue, if you've read only the poets listed above but no contemporary poets, if you've never heard of Derek Walcott, or Sharon Olds or Billy Collins, if you never choose to read or listen to poetry yourself, if National Poetry Day and the Forward Poetry Prize pass you by and you don't know who Kate Tempest or Benjamin Zephaniah are, that might put you at a different, but possibly equal disadvantage, though that too is debatable. As adults, we can make our way in the world through our popular cultural interests as much as our high culture ones, by sharing a passion for the same football team or by our obsession with *Strictly Come Dancing*. Interestingly, again, coming back to the question of the university interview, John Mullan, professor of English in the highly prestigious department at UCL, always advises students at our *emagazine* conferences that evidence of reading widely and with commitment is what they are looking for, rather than simply following a teacher's prescriptions. It's less important what you're reading than the fact that you're making interesting choices and that you're a keen reader.

In terms of English, the case is often made that there are other forms of knowledge, a broader 'cultural capital' without which the study of literary texts is impossible, or at the very least impoverished. It is presented as being essential 'prior knowledge'. Someone arguing from this position would claim, for instance, that you can't read many literary texts without knowing the Bible, knowing something about Greek and Roman myths and ancient civilisations and having a strong chronological grip on British history. The problem with this is that prior knowledge is infinite and of uncertain benefit. A few examples might reveal this.

First, the Bible. What exactly are you going to teach if you believe that many literary texts require a knowledge of the Bible? The whole Bible? Selected famous stories? The Old Testament? The New? Famous 'gobbets'? You might teach all the famous stories but where would that leave you if you were teaching Chaucer's 'The Merchant's Tale' and might genuinely find it helpful to know something of the 'Song of Solomon'. And what about Christina Rossetti, where knowledge of a few Psalms might help. Or *The Grapes of Wrath*, where a bit of Exodus might come in handy. As someone who grew up with scant knowledge of the Bible, and the New Testament in particular, I got a good degree from Oxford, reading many writers whose work was either religious or rooted in biblical language or narrative, by doing what all sensible people do – identifying that there was something I needed to know more about, and reading as much as I needed to know at that point. With Emily Dickinson, it was understanding about the American Civil War, the divisions in the Church more than the Bible and the way a woman's writing was influenced by a woman's life at the time. With American writers, it was American history, rather than British kings and queens, that I needed to have roughly mapped out for myself. And truthfully, as students of English really need to be told time and time again, knowing about things beyond the text is only helpful if they illuminate the text itself, and often much of the knowledge you need is there in the text itself.

In relation to this view of cultural capital for academic success, the other glaring issue is the fact that many texts studied at all levels in subject English are not ones that are illuminated by these iconic cultural items of knowledge. Academic study is more inclusive of diverse cultures than we might realise. For instance, Oxford's undergraduate modules for 2018 include Postcolonial Literature, Writing Feminisms/Feminist Writing, Film Criticism and Afrofabulation. At Cambridge there is Postcolonial and Related Literatures and Contemporary Writing in English. At A Level, you might be studying *The Kite Runner, God of Small Things, The Great Gatsby, Revolutionary Road, Atonement, Small Island, The Lonely Londoners, In Cold Blood, Beloved, A Thousand Splendid Suns, A Doll's House, The Reluctant Fundamentalist, The Bloody Chamber*. None of these texts is highly dependent on knowledge of Victorian London, the Bible or Greek myths. A passing knowledge of the story of Rostam and Sohrab, a reading of a fairy tale by the Brothers Grimm, some awareness of the relationship between the Caribbean and UK, knowledge of the caste system or Hindu myths might be more helpful for one or more of these books.

So, to recap on this last point, I've argued that cultural knowledge is almost without limit, that you can't teach it all, that it depends on which texts you're studying, that it doesn't need to be exhaustive but just enough to illuminate the text, that many texts provide their own cultural knowledge – they are, in fact, the way in which students absorb that knowledge. If all of this is true, it has profound implications for how we teach this kind of knowledge. I'd advocate a 'when it's needed, along the way, light touch' approach, along with giving students the judgement and tools to know when (and how) to find out more.

I'm not arguing against knowledge, nor against a broad and varied curriculum that includes a range of encounters with texts that are, in one way or another, culturally significant. But, as I hope I've suggested, the term cultural capital doesn't seem to be a helpful one in deciding what these should be. Let's stick rather, with the more uncontroversial National Curriculum rather than bandying about a term loosely that raises more problems than it answers.

References for Chapter 3

Applebee, A., Langer, J., Nystrand, M. and Gamoran, A. 2003. 'Discussion-based approaches to developing understanding: classroom instruction and student performance in middle and high school English'. In *American Educational Research Journal* 40 (3). American Educational Research Association.

Applebee, A.N. 1996. *Curriculum as Conversation: Transforming Traditions of Teaching and Learning*. Chicago: University of Chicago Press.

DfE. 2012. Research Evidence on Reading for Pleasure.

Eaglestone, R. 2017. [4th ed.] *Doing English: A Guide for Literature Students*. Abingdon: Routledge.

Eaglestone, R. 2019. *Literature – Why it Matters*. Cambridge: Polity Press.

Geda, F. 2012. *In the Sea There Are Crocodiles*. London: Vintage.

Gove, M. 2013. 'The progressive betrayal'. Speech to the Social Market Foundation.

Hirsch, E.D. 2016. *Why Knowledge Matters – Rescuing our Children from Failed Educational Theories*. Cambridge MA: Harvard Education Press.

Langer, J.A. 2011. *Envisioning Literature: Literary Understanding and Literary Instruction*. New York: Teachers College Press.

Macfarlane, R. 2003. *Mountains of the Mind*. London: Granta.

Ofsted. 2019. Training videos https://www.gov.uk/government/publications/school-inspection-handbook-eif

Ofsted. 2019. *Inspection Handbook* (Draft for Consultation).

Ofsted. 2019. *Inspection Handbook* (Final Version).

Social Theory Re-wired website – Routledgesoc.com

Stacks, Josie. 2019. 'Is this presumed knowledge which I see before me?'. In *Times Educational Supplement* (18th January 2019).

Sullivan, A. and Brown, M. 2015. 'Reading for pleasure and progress in vocabulary and mathematics'. In *British Educational Research Journal*.

Recommended reading

Durst, R.K., Newell, G. E. and Marshall, J.D. 2017. *English Language Arts Research and Teaching: Revisiting and Extending Arthur Applebee's Contributions*. Abingdon: Routledge.

4. Vocabulary

In April 2018, a book was published by Alex Quigley called *Closing the Vocabulary Gap*. It caught the educational zeitgeist and has become a bestseller among teachers. Teachers were, understandably, looking for ways to address underachievement and meet the needs of the full spectrum of students, including those who seemed disadvantaged by their context and family background.

Work by the likes of of E.D. Hirsch seemed to offer Quigley and others a set of ideas about why these students found reading hard; it was because they didn't have as many words as their more advantaged peers, who encountered many more words in their early years and home environments. The idea of a 30 million word vocabulary gap (based on research in the mid 1990s in the USA by Hart and Risley), took hold, first in the USA and then in the UK. In the UK, many initiatives were set up to support the teaching of vocabulary in English and across the curriculum. Teaching vocabulary was seen as being of prime importance. The interest in vocabulary has continued to grow but there have been more voices of caution – not least my own – drawing attention to flaws in some of the research upon which the push for vocabulary teaching was based, questioning the methods by which vocabulary is best taught (and learned) and arguing for a broader focus on *all* aspects of language to help students develop both their reading and their writing. At various conferences, in CPD sessions, in blogs and in feature articles for the *TES* and others, I have presented the arguments. It is interesting to note that since raising these concerns there have been many other voices joining this side of the debate, asking similarly probing questions, with some resulting shifts in the dominant thinking.[1]

4.1 Over-emphasising the vocabulary challenge

What is the link between word knowledge and reading? And is the case for its importance sometimes overstated? Here I look at some of the arguments and explore them in relation to the opening of *A Christmas Carol*, to consider what makes it a challenging read for adult readers as well as school students, and what might help them understand this text and others like it. There are interesting connections between the idea of students needing word knowledge prior to reading and the belief that they need a lot of prior cultural, historical and other knowledge. This is dealt with in another piece on page 68, 'Literature – the walk not the map', where I look at what students really need to know before tackling a challenging text. The blog which follows on page 80 was published in March 2018.

---

1. Megan Dixon's blog for EEF 'When is a word not a word' (2nd October 2019) takes a more nuanced approach to the teaching of vocabulary and sets out a view of how children learn words that is more in keeping with my own than much that came earlier.

There has been a lot of interest recently in vocabulary and how it should be taught. For example, if you google 'the vocabulary gap' you get page after page of references to books and articles about the subject, originating largely in the USA but now spawning a lot of pedagogic advice and teaching material in the UK as well. For example, there's a new book by Alex Quigley coming out at the end of this month devoted to this subject, entitled *Closing the Vocabulary Gap*. The main idea behind all of this is that some children come into school with a very large vocabulary 'deficit' – they simply don't know as many words as other, more advantaged children. What follows from this, so the argument goes, is that this vocabulary gap makes reading more difficult and the answer is to teach them more words. It seems logical. If they encounter a text with too many words that they don't know, they'll struggle with it. So pre-teach the words to allow them to understand it better. The advocates of this approach are aware that closing the vocabulary gap by teaching individual words has some problems. How on earth do you teach enough words to make a difference? So they recommend being selective. They identify 'tiers' of words, from the everyday to the specialist and encourage teachers to identify which are the priority words. Nevertheless, the broad message is that it is, above all, lack of word knowledge that impedes confident reading and that creating confident readers entails teaching them more words.

Even from a commonsense perspective, it seems to me that this approach demonstrates a rather limited view of what confident reading entails, both for young learners and for adults. While I recognise that pupils' lack of understanding of words might inhibit their free and confident ability to read difficult texts and agree that work in the classroom undoubtedly needs to include some focus on vocabulary to support readers and develop their interest in words, I'm doubtful about the pre-eminence given to it above all other aspects of language. Equally I'm not convinced about some of what follows from this emphasis, such as substantial amounts of pre-teaching vocabulary before students read texts.

Some of my doubts stem from serious concerns about the basis upon which the claims for vocabulary are made[2]. On page 54 in the blog 'Why aren't we talking about Applebee' I examine some of E.D. Hirsch's assertions about reading tests, vocabulary and knowledge, raising questions about the premises upon which his views are based and the failure to distinguish between learning in subjects (concepts and terminology) and the ability to 'read' in broader terms.

Even Hirsch acknowledges that the way most words are learned most effectively is by 'massive immersion':

---

2. Jill Gilkerson and Dale Walker's research for the LENA Foundation (an *Education Week* article, April 21st 2015) questions the significance of quantity of words as compared with 'conversational turns' in adult/ child talk, as well as raising doubts about the Hart and Risley findings on lower income families consistently talking less to their children. Nelson Flores, Susan D. Blum and other American linguists, in 'Invited Forum: Bridging the Language Gap' (2015) have put up a strong set of arguments against the whole 'deficit model' applied to working-class children and children of colour from poor communities. In 'Nurturing a lexical legacy: reading experience is critical for the development of word reading skill', *Science of Learning* (2017) Kate Nation argues that reading is much the most significant way in which children learn new vocabulary. This is also one of the arguments in her article with Anne Castles and Kathy Rastle, 'Ending the reading wars: reading acquisition from novice to expert' (2018).

Most vocabulary growth results incidentally from massive immersion in the world of language and knowledge… It has long been known that the growth of word knowledge is slow and incremental, requiring multiple exposures to words. One doesn't just learn a word's meaning and then have the word. One gradually learns the word's denotations and connotations and its modes of use little by little over many, many language experiences.

Reading Comprehension Requires Knowledge – of Words and the World (2003)

EMC's Andrew McCallum and Kate Oliver have also written excellent blogs about vocabulary, exploring how understanding words in context is a very different thing from knowing how to define them, and showing how reading is a set of complex, interconnecting skills and knowledge. Kate Oliver also offers strategies for teaching vocabulary in its context.[3]

Here I want to take a slightly different approach, looking at the other ways in which texts can create difficulty for inexperienced readers, that have nothing to do with unfamiliar vocabulary, to question the case for a vocabulary-heavy pedagogy. I'd argue that we need to focus on these, as much as lexical knowledge, if we want to support our students in becoming more confident and fluent readers of texts. I'd also even argue that focusing too much on vocabulary runs the risk of damaging students' ability to read difficult texts.

What makes difficult texts difficult to read?

1. There is a serious argument that understanding texts is much more about being able to grasp the big picture, rather than understanding every word or even understanding every individual sentence. It's about recognising the bigger structures and distinguishing between what is significant and what is not, what point is being made, deciding whether it's just the preamble or a wider development of the most important point. This judgement comes not from an understanding of every item of vocabulary but rather from the ability to read quickly and broadly, with a strong sense of what leaps out as the line of argument, or as the most significant idea. In a way it's a 'summarising on the hoof' or 'summarising in your head'. You bring some information to the fore and let other items slip into the background, to make the process of reading manageable. Once you have an overall sense of what the text is doing, you can go back, if you want to, and fill in the gaps in terms of detail, understanding what role the detail is playing and whether it's worth exploring more fully. You can also often understand more about what individual words mean, because of the context surrounding them.

Linguist Katherine Perera (2006) is very interesting on this:

Even if the reader can understand all the technical vocabulary of the passage and has no difficulty at sentence level he may still not be able to make sense of the text as a whole. There are frequent instances of pupils understanding

---

3. These blogs were written not only as a sceptical response to vocabulary gap rhetoric but also to some of the resulting suggestions for classroom work on vocabulary. They provide some more practical angles on the teaching of vocabulary, drawing on the authors' reading of the current research. (Available at www.englishandmedia.co.uk/blog)

all the constituent sentences of a passage and yet not understanding the relationship between them i.e. not understanding the point that is being made. Pupils will frequently remember a dramatic or vivid example without having any idea of the generalisation it was intended to exemplify.

Getting a sense of the big picture – of a whole sentence, paragraph or bigger section – is particularly difficult for students who read slowly. By the time they've got to the end of a long sentence, they can't remember where it started. By the time they've reached the end of the paragraph, the beginning is a blur. So what's the answer to this? Slowing it down with lots of work on vocabulary? Or reading faster, in the first instance, to get the gist and see what the writer is wanting us to get from the writing?

2. Long sentences and complex syntax, often associated with writing from previous eras but also with much academic writing and non-fiction, are a significant challenge for inexperienced readers. The vocabulary of a specialist non-fiction text, written in a subject domain like geography or science, is obviously a barrier to understanding for a non-specialist reader. Learning the subject is learning its concepts and associated vocabulary. But equally, both in specialist texts, and in more general reading of demanding texts, it is often syntax more than vocabulary that can get in the way of comprehension. Again, the linguist Katherine Perera has done brilliant analyses of the sentence length and syntactic patterns of non-fiction texts compared with fictional ones, and demonstrated why it might be that students encountering non-fiction might struggle with it.

Perera says:

The average sentence length for 'general fiction' is fourteen words and for 'learned and scientific writings' twenty-four words. So, on average, sentences in textbooks can be expected to be roughly twice as long as sentences in fiction [...] Long sentences such as these with complex internal relationships place greater burdens on the reader's Short Term Memory and on his syntactic abilities.

Of course, when it comes to reading texts from the past, this is also a very significant issue. Mean sentence length is around 50% more for texts written 100 years ago and this will inevitably cause challenges for students reading a nineteenth-century novel and pre-twentieth-century non-fiction in GCSE specifications.

Perera argues that it is often complex syntax that creates the most difficulty regardless of sentence length. Speeding up reading (and showing them the benefits of reading aloud, under their breath, or in their head) can help students to get to the end of a main clause, and recognise the subsidiary importance of the relative clauses that provide the 'extra information' along the way.

3. For all that we talk about the detrimental impact of the 'vocabulary gap' on reading, it can be the simple words, used in idiomatic or unusual ways that can floor inexperienced readers, pulling the rug out from under their feet.

Floor? Rugs? That last sentence is just one example of potentially confusing language where the words themselves are perfectly simple, monosyllabic, everyday ones, yet they're being used in ways that might not be familiar. It might be no less difficult for a student to understand this idiomatic use of language than it would be for me to say, *'It can be the simple words that can be disconcerting, capable of disorientating inexperienced readers.'* Only seeing vocabulary as hard words misses out a much bigger aspect of what it means to understand a text.

We all know too, that some of the most complex texts we might read in the literary canon – the most difficult to comprehend – are made up of predominantly simple words, used in elliptical or unexpected ways. Think of William Carlos Williams, Samuel Beckett, Sylvia Plath or these lines from T.S. Eliot's *Four Quartets*:

Time present and time past
Are both perhaps present in time future
And time future contained in time past. [...]

What might have been and what has been
Point to one end, which is always present.

Exemplifying these views on reading in a commonly taught text

A Christmas Carol is often quoted an example of a text that is chock-a-block with words that will get in the way of students' comprehension of the text. Dickens uses a whole host of words that, I think we'd all agree, are not likely to be well-known to many students and could make reading the novel a challenging experience, especially if they feel that they need to understand all of them. You could decide that the answer is to focus on the vocabulary and pre-teach it before reading the text. However, it seems to me that the other demands and prerequisites for successfully reading, understanding and enjoying the text are just as important, if not more so, and therefore spending too much time on vocabulary, before and during reading, might actually be counterproductive.

To demonstrate this, take a look, yourself, at the opening of *A Christmas Carol*. Read it as you would the opening of any novel, then think about what you were doing as an experienced reader. Were you reading every sentence, slowly, to understand every word? What happened when you encountered something hard to follow (as I did as early as the third sentence)?

MARLEY was dead: to begin with. There is no doubt whatever about that. The register of his burial was signed by the clergyman, the clerk, the undertaker, and the chief mourner. Scrooge signed it: and Scrooge's name was good upon 'Change for anything he chose to put his hand to. Old Marley was as dead as a door-nail.

Mind! I don't mean to say that I know, of my own knowledge, what there is particularly dead about a door-nail. I might have been inclined, myself, to regard a coffin-nail as the deadest piece of ironmongery in the trade. But the wisdom of our ancestors is in the simile; and my unhallowed hands shall not disturb it, or the Country's done for. You will therefore permit me to repeat, emphatically, that Marley was as dead as a door-nail.

Scrooge knew he was dead? Of course he did. How could it be otherwise? Scrooge and he were partners for I don't know how many years. Scrooge was his sole executor, his sole administrator, his sole assign, his sole residuary legatee, his sole friend, and sole mourner. And even Scrooge was not so dreadfully cut up by the sad event, but that he was an excellent man of business on the very day of the funeral, and solemnised it with an undoubted bargain.

The mention of Marley's funeral brings me back to the point I started from. There is no doubt that Marley was dead. This must be distinctly understood, or nothing wonderful can come of the story I am going to relate. If we were not perfectly convinced that Hamlet's Father died before the play began, there would be nothing more remarkable in his taking a stroll at night, in an easterly wind, upon his own ramparts, than there would be in any other middle-aged gentleman rashly turning out after dark in a breezy spot – say Saint Paul's Churchyard for instance – literally to astonish his son's weak mind.

Scrooge never painted out Old Marley's name. There it stood, years afterwards, above the warehouse door: Scrooge and Marley. The firm was known as Scrooge and Marley. Sometimes people new to the business called Scrooge Scrooge, and sometimes Marley, but he answered to both names: it was all the same to him.

Oh! But he was a tight-fisted hand at the grindstone, Scrooge! a squeezing, wrenching, grasping, scraping, clutching, covetous, old sinner! Hard and sharp as flint, from which no steel had ever struck out generous fire; secret, and self-contained, and solitary as an oyster. The cold within him froze his old features, nipped his pointed nose, shrivelled his cheek, stiffened his gait; made his eyes red, his thin lips blue; and spoke out shrewdly in his grating voice. A frosty rime was on his head, and on his eyebrows, and his wiry chin. He carried his own low temperature always about with him; he iced his office in the dog-days; and didn't thaw it one degree at Christmas.

External heat and cold had little influence on Scrooge. No warmth could warm, no wintry weather chill him. No wind that blew was bitterer than he, no falling snow was more intent upon its purpose, no pelting rain less open to entreaty. Foul weather didn't know where to have him. The heaviest rain, and snow, and hail, and sleet, could boast of the advantage over him in only one respect. They often 'came down' handsomely, and Scrooge never did.

When you've read it and thought about your reading strategies and responses, look at mine to see how far they match up with yours.

1. I struggled with the phrase, 'Scrooge's name was good upon 'Change for anything he chose to put his hand to' but I just ignored that and read on.

2. I latched onto 'Old Marley was dead as a door-nail' as the first really certain, important thing. I thought it was a pretty unsentimental way of describing Marley's death.

3. In the paragraph starting 'Mind!' I recognised that the voice was playing with the idea of the door-nail metaphor, in quite a jokey way. By the time I

was two or three sentences in, I'd got that that was what he was doing and switched off a bit before tuning back in for the repeated 'Marley was dead as a door-nail.' I realised we were back from the digression about the door-nail metaphor. I didn't know – and still don't really know – what 'assign' or 'residuary legatee' mean but I got the gist from everything else and read on, rather than looking them up in a dictionary. Scrooge was his only friend and his partner at work, and the only person at his funeral – so bound together were they that people mistook one for the other. That was enough for me.

4. In the next paragraph, the narrator draws attention to himself and backtracks again. It seems to be more to do with giving me a sense of the narrator's voice than anything else. The reference to Hamlet and Hamlet's ghost is interesting, if you know the play, and possibly worth coming back to at a later stage, but not really essential at this point. It'll slow the reading down to spend too long working it out, so I don't bother but subliminally there's something about ghosts coming back to haunt you that has been implanted in my head.

5. Ah now! The paragraph about Scrooge and Marley is important. No tricky vocabulary at all, but it says so much and so well. Mentioning the two names together so often suggests that in life they were inseparable – a double act. It starts to make me wonder what about now, when Marley is dead – as a door-nail. What's going to happen to Scrooge? He hasn't painted Marley's name out. Why not?

6. And now we have a great long paragraph describing Scrooge. After all the preamble of the opening (which is basically telling us that Marley is dead, and that we have a very lively narrator who wants to both make us laugh and think a bit, but mainly laugh), we now have a fantastic description of the character Scrooge, the one who is still living. I recognise all the words here but there are a few that might cause particular difficulty for students, 'grindstone', 'covetous', 'gait', 'shrewdly'. I can get the general gist without knowing these – his hardness and sharpness, 'the cold within him', a frostiness that echoes the Christmas season are all clearly evoked.

7. The subsequent paragraph develops this further – brilliantly – with hardly any tricky vocabulary at all.

8. I've got to this point and am rather pleased I didn't over-worry about the beginning or spend too long on it because this is amazing stuff now. I'm getting a strong sense of the main character, with his dead partner, Marley, and the set-up and I'm raring to go.

9. After I've read the first chapter, I might go back to those paragraphs I read really quickly to remind myself of them and just check that I haven't missed something important. In fact, now that I do, I see it says, 'Marley was dead: to begin with.' Very odd, that 'to begin with'. Perhaps Marley and Scrooge aren't going to be separated after all, even though Marley is 'dead as a door-nail'. There are just six words in that first sentence – all of them easy,

monosyllabic ones apart from the name – and yet now I look back, I realise just how much they were telling me, if only I'd paid attention! Dickens's 'to begin with' seems far more important to me than 'assign' or 'residuary legatee'.

I'm not arguing that vocabulary isn't important. There will be times when knowing a particular word is vital. But there will be just as many times when other understandings about reading are employed, or when speed is more important than punctiliousness over word knowledge, to help students reach the end of a sentence or a paragraph and hold onto the meaning. Equally, there'll be lots of occasions when the meaning is quite opaque to students, despite the fact that every word is a common, everyday monosyllabic one. Let's teach vocabulary but recognise that it's not the fairy godmother of reading, waving the wand that opens up comprehension on every occasion. It's one of a complex array of reading and comprehension strategies that need to be taught alongside vocabulary.

4.2 Focusing on terms, missing meanings

What does it mean to use the language of the subject, and use it well? What is the place of literary terminology in student writing? How much is enough, how much too much? These questions have exercised English teachers for many decades, with debates about whether glossaries and word lists are a help or a hindrance, and whether Latinate rhetorical terms are worth teaching or not. The discussions have become increasingly heated and of ever more importance, in the light of some developments in English teaching. The most important are the references to 'terminology' in the assessment objectives both at GCSE and A Level. This has led to a lot of anxiety about how to interpret this, both for teachers and students. At the time of writing this blog, in May 2019, the Awarding Bodies had all been flagging up major concerns about the overuse and inappropriate use of terminology in students' writing. In this blog, I respond to some of the voices suggesting that teaching more sophisticated terminology will help students to write well about literary texts.

In May 2019 I got caught up in a rather extended debate on Twitter about the use of literary terminology by students, provoked by a *TES* piece 'Five Complex Terms Every Student Should Know', by English teacher and educational writer Mark Roberts. The gist of the piece was that teachers were wrong to shy away from teaching complex literary terminology and that they were doing so because of a false set of arguments being circulated about their value and impact. There was an acknowledgement that the views expressed in the article would probably not go down well with examiners. I think the piece is wrong about the first thing – teachers are in fact teaching a substantial amount of complex terminology – but absolutely right about the second, that examiners really will not thank anyone for suggesting that terminology is lacking and that specific terms should be taught.

Here are some quotations from the AQA GCSE Examiners' Report for Paper 2 Literature, 2017. (They are echoed in the comments in 2018 and 2019 too.)

> Students made huge efforts to use subject terminology and many did so with accuracy. However, at times students were more concerned with the use of technical terms than the effect. Students should remember that critical terms should be used judiciously and must always be linked to effect on the reader/audience.

> Students who dealt with AO2 most successfully were the ones who had not been too restricted by subject terminology.

> [...] students are rewarded for their appropriate use of the language of the subject in terms of how they use it to help them to craft a response to a literary text. In other words, what they say about the craft of the writer is far more significant than how many technical terms they include. The specific mention of subject terminology in the mark scheme is there to reflect that students are being assessed on their ability to deal with aspects of craft. A balanced and well-illustrated response to the question will eventually lead students to explore the methods used to present those ideas, feelings and attitudes. Subject terminology is not given any particular weight in isolation;

on the contrary, naming of parts can actively impede students, who are being rewarded for their focus on the how an element of writer's craft affects meaning.

This kind of comment isn't confined to GCSE. At A Level too, Awarding Body Examiners' Reports, for as far back as I can remember, have counselled against an over-emphasis on terminology. Use of terms, for their own sake, as mere window-dressing, appears regularly in the list of features of the least successful writing. Here are just a few examples from recent reports:

> To write impressively does not mean to flood writing with critical, tragic and comedic terminology, often using that terminology for its own sake and not really understanding it anyway. Some students unfortunately wrote in a style that was awkward and cluttered, sometimes making little sense.
> (AQA B Literature, 2017)

> As in Section A, the best responses indicated an understanding of the poems as autonomous creations rather than pegs on which to hang lists of technical terms and, for this section, contextual information. (Edexcel, 2017)

> Unless terminology is used accurately and as an economic means of making a point about meaning and impact it cannot be rewarded. This is a strand of AO1 which needs careful explanation to candidates who also need to be realistic and sensible about what can be achieved by alliteration, sibilance and the caesura. […] It is important candidates ask themselves 'what is the meaning here and how is it shaped?' Too many trawl through the lines, mining for rich pickings in terms of terminology, while missing the central meaning.
> (WJEC, 2017)

Now, you could decide to ignore this evidence. And, like the writer of the *TES* piece, you could suggest that the problem with poor exam performance by students is to do with 'sloppy' teaching of literary terminology, rather than with the terms themselves. You could argue that really brilliant teachers will be sure to introduce terms like zeugma, metonymy, epiphora or chremamorphism in relation to their effect and that, as a result students would then be able use them well. If so, you might think that, well used, Latin and Greek terms can only enhance the sophistication of students' responses.

But, for me, there are a number of problems with this.

1. It just isn't the case, from the evidence of the exam entries, that students are able to use an extensive range of esoteric Latinate and Greek terms successfully, even very able students being taught in very good schools by very good teachers. Quite the contrary. The examiners obviously see large numbers who simply don't, by comparison with an extremely small number who do. Where does that leave us? Thinking that most teachers do a terrible job? Or, rather, recognising that students are taking away the wrong messages about complex terminology being required to prove knowledge, seeing labelling as an alternative to thinking hard about texts, their meanings and effects and becoming focused on 'sounding' academic rather than genuinely 'being' academic.

What examiners often say is that they would love to see students using the basic language of the subject better instead, to analyse texts and work within its common practices, for example, using well words like 'explores', 'reveals', 'signals', 'develops', 'symbolises', 'reflects', 'shows features of', 'is characteristic of', 'is of significance' and so on.

In the wording of AO2 at GCSE the words 'relevant' and 'appropriate' are key and offer a good steer in deciding what's worth teaching in relation to the particular texts being studied. One should always ask:

- Is this a key concept or technique for this text and this writer?

- Will this term enable students to say something rich, important or interesting about the effect on the reader?

- Will this student be able to use this term appropriately and relevantly?

These questions offer a good rule of thumb, rather than having a fixed list of terms that all students should know.

2. At EMC, we don't see students using Latinate and Greek terms well either. We run two annual writing competitions for A Level, for *emagazine*, one on poetry, the other on the close reading of prose. Sadly, we also see a great deal of writing in which impressive sounding literary terms are used extensively, inaccurately and inappropriately, without enriching the argument or providing greater sophistication of thought. The students who are shortlisted, or come close to being shortlisted, tend to use common, important literary terms very well, use more complex, esoteric terms very sparingly if at all, and instead focus their attention on valid observations, interesting ideas about texts and insightful comment expressed with clarity and sophistication. Here's an extract from the 2019 Close Reading Competition winning writing[1], showing how excellent analysis doesn't have to be crammed with terms:

Joyce's textual idiosyncrasies initially seem due to childlike wonder, in the giddy, ungrammatical repetition and sweet-shop imagery in 'a long long chocolate train with cream facings', and wide-eyed taking in of the balletic movements of the guards 'opening, closing, locking, unlocking the doors … their keys ma[king] a quick music: click, click: click, click.' But it is these blissful observations, especially the one-word paragraphs, 'Lovely …' and 'Noises …', which give the dream away. 'Noises of welcome' become 'Noises …' become the 'noise of curtain-rings running back along the rods…' The connection of the 'noises' is ironic, even sadistic, as Joyce slowly twists joy into disappointment, and the differences are immediately apparent. The discomfort of Stephen's stocking's 'horrid rough feel' is far from the floating sensations of 'telegraph poles … passing, passing …' Less tangibly, he is now unloved: his former raptures of 'Holly and ivy for him and for Christmas' and cries of 'Welcome home, Stephen', are sharply contrasted with the reaction to the announcement that he's ill – '— Who is?' – and the barked 'Dedalus'. To the end, febrile and hallucinating, he must desperately fight his corner: 'He was not foxing. No, no: he was sick really.'

---

1. The full winning entry and those of the runners' up on the *emagazine* website are good examples of this.

Those students who think good writing has to be peppered with words like zeugma, metonymy, synecdoche and more, usually write very poorly. If it weren't for the fact that I feel squeamish about quoting examples in public, which seems rather unfair on the individual students, I could offer dozens of examples of poor use of terminology from the last few years of our competitions.

3. In academic writing more generally, you don't see extensive use of such terms either. In books on poetry, in articles in English journals, in critical pieces in broadsheets and journals, in university essays and dissertations, important terms like 'stream of consciousness', or' free indirect style', 'narrative voice' or 'metaphor' are, of course, constantly being used to good effect but not a whole swathe of Latin and Greek words for rhetorical tropes. It's very rare to see great academic writing swimming in such terms. We did an analysis of the close readings by academics in our *Doing Close Reading* publication and in *emagazine* articles and this was borne out there too.

4. In many of the debates about subject terminology, I find it strange how little sense there is of what's very important to know as underpinning concepts for the subject versus small word or sentence-level techniques that can be labelled but are not really worth spending valuable classroom time learning and memorising.

Here are the terms that appeared in the article in the *TES*, as ones all students should be taught, along with others mentioned along the way:

- Anagnorisis
- Synecdoche
- Paranomasia
- Anadiplosis
- Zeugma
- Liminal
- Metaphor
- Metonymy
- Chremamorphism
- Anaphora
- Epiphora
- Dysphemism

These terms seem to me to be qualitatively different, rather than being of equal value or importance. Anagnorisis and liminal stand out as being very different from the others. They are words that express complex literary concepts that are of particular use if you are studying either tragedy or Gothic texts. The concepts the words embody are important ones. The liminal, for example – states of being or physical things that are on boundaries or thresholds between one thing and another, neither entirely one thing nor the other – is a central feature of the Gothic genre. It is talked about by critics of Gothic and can be observed in texts in everything from settings and scenery to characters (human or abhuman, alive or dead, awake or asleep, corporeal or spiritual). As such the concept of the liminal, challenging though it is, is a very useful, if not an essential, one, if you are studying *Strange Case of Dr Jekyll and Mr Hyde* at GCSE for example, not just as a label but for what it offers conceptually in allowing you to explore the multiple ways in which borderlines may arise in the text and the reasons why.

Metaphor is an equally important, and pervasive idea in all texts at GCSE and A Level. You couldn't get very far with the study of literature without understanding the idea of metaphor, and being able to use it appropriately. It's a major, underpinning idea. It accrues meaning the more texts you read and the more you reflect on its multifarious uses. It is much more than just a label.

By contrast many of the other terms in the list above refer to small rhetorical devices – word, phrase or sentence-level techniques, which can be taken or left to a larger extent and for which there is often a very simple alternative form of explanation. The word 'paranomasia' for instance can be described more plainly as a pun, or as word play. In the context of, say, *The Handmaid's Tale*, I'd opt for word play to describe what Atwood is up to, largely because it's not just puns (paranomasia), nor is it just a small, easily observable and nameable rhetorical technique – it's something much more sustained and of greater significance than a one-off device. In using word play, Atwood is exploring the meanings of all kinds of things that we take for granted, flagging up for the reader the misogyny encoded in language choices, playing with ideas about identity, gender and knowledge in ways that make us question the very concepts. This is much more than simply a neat rhetorical gesture or flourish. It is taking words and metaphors that have become stale and unpicking their underlying meanings to look at the very nature of language and identity, or language and politics. It is wordplay as language and theme as well as style.

5. One of the dangers of teaching multiple small devices (and the terms for them) is that it encourages students to engage in labelling things, rather than observing things in the text that are significant and then looking for ways of describing them. So there may well be an example of zeugma, metonymy or andadiplosis in a text but how often is it really significant? If a small rhetorical trope forms an important pattern or stands out in a text (as for instance with oxymoron in *Romeo and Juliet*), then it may be worth spending time on. But often in the case of something like metonymy, it takes the form of 'dead' metaphors, not worthy of comment, for instance 'the crown' for the monarchy, or 'die by the sword' for dying by violent means. It is much rarer for this to be the freshly minted use by a writer for a particular effect that's worth spending time on, commenting on and learning the term for.

One further issue I have with the *TES* article list (liminality, anagnorisis and metaphor excepted) is the fact that the attention paid to naming small rhetorical devices sends students scuttling off to look at and think about small things, even where this is inappropriate. In a modern play, or a substantial narrative text, it is unlikely to be helpful to focus a lot of attention on word-level techniques, unless they are part of a sustained pattern. So symbolism is likely to be really useful (in a sustained pattern of imagery across a play or a novel), while a single example of zeugma or anadiplosis far less so. Teach symbolism as your more significant and helpful term – and spend lots of time reading examples of it, exploring its different uses and understanding what it contributes in different texts, rather than causing 'cognitive overload' by teaching endless difficult names for small devices.

This is nothing to do with dumbing down, low expectations or not wanting to teach high level thinking in the subject. The reverse. If you focus on noticing what's significant, engage in discussion that explores complexity and ambiguity rather than shutting it down, and encourage students to say what genuinely strikes them as interesting about texts, the language in which to express that can come much more naturally and convincingly. Here is just one example of student writing of this kind:

> The way that parenthesis is used is similar to the rest of the novel in some ways, as it keeps up the sense of a conversation. For example, Enaiat says 'I've already said – if I'm not mistaken' and he says 'and one of the most appropriate (so I believed).' This shows his uncertainty to his memories. Also it reminds us of the age that he is narrating and that it was long ago when it happened. It shows us the unreliability of his memories and it reminds us that the book is a work of fiction. Also it is a constant reminder that Enaiat is telling Geda about his experience.

This was written by a Year 9, in a class working on EMC's 'Teaching a Novel at KS3' project developed as part of our wider research project, *It's Good to Talk*.[2]

The emphasis in the classroom was on talking and thinking about significant ideas in the text – what were characteristic features of the narrative, how these related to the subject of the novel, what the students felt and thought about the events and the way the narrative was told. Words and concepts were there, floating in the classroom air, spoken as they seemed useful, brought in to illuminate and provide a means of expressing thoughts. There was no emphasis of any kind on 'using terminology'. But, hopefully, most people would agree that this 14 year old is, in fact, using the terms of the subject very well indeed. There are lessons for all of us in this.

One final caveat to what I have said, in response to the inevitable accusation that may come that this is 'anti-knowledge' or indeed 'anti-language'. It's not. There's nothing that makes my heart sing more than a brilliantly written student essay or article sent into *emagazine*, that makes you forget you're reading a student's work. But it's about judging what's most important, what's most useful, what's most appropriate, and what students being introduced to the world of literature and literary critical practices aged 11-19 are able to use with the greatest success. If I (and examiners) were seeing brilliantly insightful writing that used such terms as anadiplosis and zeugma to powerful effect, I might change my mind. If the literary critical writing I read – and I read a lot of it – were drawing on them extensively, I might change my mind. If I found myself using them, or needing them in my own writing or admiring them in the writing of my colleagues, I might change my mind. As things stand, a judicious approach concentrating on major concepts (and useful terms to describe them) along with discussion of what you notice and how you can describe and analyse it simply and clearly, seems like the best advice for students.

---

2. This is referred to in other sections of the book. In particular, see the Postscript: Harold Rosen Lecture, NATE Conference 2019.

References for Chapter 4

Bleiman B. and Webster, L. 2014. *Doing Close Reading*. London: English and Media Centre.

Blum, S.D. 2015. 'Wordism. Is there a teacher in the house?'. Invited Forum: 'Bridging the Language Gap'. In *Journal of Linguistic Anthropology* 25 (1). The American Anthropological Association.

Castles A., Nation, K. and Rastle, K. 2018. 'Ending the reading wars: reading acquisition from novice to expert'. In *Psychological Science in the Public Interest* 19 (1).

Drummond, R. 2018. *Researching Youth Language and Identity*. London: Palgrave Macmillan.

Hart, B., and Risley, T. R. 1995. *Meaningful Differences in the Everyday Experience of Young American Children*. Baltimore, MD: Paul H. Brookes Publishing Company.

Labov, W. 1969. *A Study of Non-Standard English*. ERIC Clearing House for Linguistics.

Hirsch, E.D. 2013. 'The vocabulary size of students is the best single index to their life chances and to school quality'. Interview with Michael F. Shaughnessy. In *Education News*.

Hirsch, E.D. 2003. 'Reading comprehension requires knowledge – of words and the world'. In *American Educator* 7 (1).

McCallum, A. 2016. 'The value of talk, or how we need to use new words to learn new words'. EMC blog www.englishandmedia.co.uk/blogs

Nation, K. 2017. 'Nurturing a lexical legacy: reading experience is critical for the development of word reading skill'. In *Science of Learning* 2 (1).

Oliver, K. 2016. 'How to teach vocabulary acquisition'. EMC blog www.englishandmedia.co.uk/blogs

Perera, K. 2006. 'The assessment of linguistic difficulty in reading material' in ed. Carter, R. *Linguistics and the Teacher*. Abingdon: Routledge.

Quigley, A. 2018. *Closing the Vocabulary Gap*. Abingdon: Routledge.

Gilkerson, J. and Walker, D. https://www.lena.org/achievement-gap/

Roberts, M. 2019. 'Five terms every GCSE student should know... and five reasons you're wrong if you don't think they should use complex terminology'. In *TES* (5.5.2019).

Rosa, J. and Flores, N. 2015. 'Hearing language gaps and reproducing social inequality'. Invited Forum: Bridging the Language Gap'. In *Journal of Linguistic Anthropology* 25 (1). The American Anthropological Association.

Rosen, H. 1972. 'Language and class'. In *Harold Rosen: Writings on Life, Language and Learning, 1958-2008*. ed. Richmond, J. 2017. London: UCL IOE Press.

Rosen, H. 1982. 'Language and the education of the working class'. In ed. Richmond, J. 2017. *Harold Rosen: Writings on Life, Language and Learning, 1958-2008*. London: UCL IOE Press.

5. Group Work and Talk in English Classrooms

This is a substantial section of the book. It reflects the work undertaken by EMC in *It's Good to Talk*, a self-funded project started in 2015. It will continue its work while there are still interesting aspects to explore. Though it might be easy to pigeonhole it as 'group work', in fact we have found that the project has tentacles reaching into all aspects of English, from the teaching of poetry or the novel, to ways of developing knowledge in English and more. Dialogic learning and the opportunity to talk to your peers in constructive ways are at the heart of English as a subject. Some of the pieces in this section argue for this view of English knowledge and pedagogy; others look in detail at aspects of learning in groups, exploding myths along the way.

5.1 Speaking up for group work

This is the earliest of several blogs on group work, setting out EMC's position and the rationale for group work in English. Though written in September 2015, the debates are still very current in 2020, the arguments continuing to burn fiercely on social media and in schools. Some schools still proudly assert that they never do group work, some teachers seeing it as a waste of valuable time. Here I set out some of the key ideas about group work – not simply as a context for learning but as a fundamental part of engaging with the subject discipline.

> When children bring language to bear on a problem within a small group their talk is often tentative, discursive, inexplicit, and uncertain of direction; the natural outcome of an encounter with unfamiliar ideas and material. The intimacy of the context allows all this to happen without any sense of strain. In an atmosphere of tolerance, of hesitant formulation and of co-operative effort the children can 'stretch' their language to accommodate their own second thoughts and the opinions of others. They can 'float' their notions without fear of having them dismissed. (10:12)
>
> *A Language for Life (The Bullock Report), 1975*

There's been a lot of discussion about group work recently in the blogosphere. David Didau's blog 'Why (the hell) should students work in groups?', with its deliberately provocative title, stirred up the waters.[1] The piece countered the views expressed by Neil Mercer and James Mannion in a *TES* article in February 2015 'Talk may be cheap but group work is priceless' where they argued that

> In not using group work, students are denied the chance to develop skills that can not only help them perform better in schools, but which are also vital for their future employment prospects – not to mention the realisation of a more fully participatory democracy.

---

1. This blog, published in 2015, was subsequently followed up by others that adopted a rather more measured tone but the essential argument that group work rarely pays its way remained the same.

For quite some time, a number of influential teachers, opinion-makers and others have also been extolling the virtues of direct instruction (lower case rather than upper case)[2], demanding more of a focus on knowledge, bewailing the vast holes in young people's cultural awareness and generally retreating from what they pose as a 'progressive' set of practices that have supposedly dominated and damaged children's education. Suddenly it seems that people are not only willing, but proud to challenge old certainties.

In some classrooms, as part of this new drive for a knowledge and instruction-based approach to learning, children are not encouraged to talk in exploratory ways but are expected to spend a lot more time listening to teachers and are handed down academic forms of language from a teacher who supposedly has a monopoly on knowledge.

Here at EMC, we have responded to some of these debates in our own blogs – one on knowledge, another on reading, a third on group work. We have tried to reassert some of the principles that have underpinned our work for over 40 years.

Much of what we do in terms of approaches to classroom resources and pedagogy is so long-standing, in such a continuous tradition, passed down from expert teacher (or teacher trainer) to expert teacher, that we don't necessarily spend enough time remembering the thinking that underpins it. Of course pragmatic questions about classroom activities (beyond the increasingly hollow 'does it work' refrain) are vitally important – how to do it well, how to make sure it's fully participatory for all pupils, how to structure it tightly, how to set up ground rules and so on. (Useful in trying to resolve some of these questions are all those very valuable strategies that we and many others promote, whether it be jigsawing, statement sorting or Socratic circles, or key pedagogical choices such as making individuals accountable for group activity, how to determine the optimum size of groups, creating lists of rules, or making decisions about ability or friendship grouping.) But beyond and behind the pragmatic questions it seems to us that there is a much deeper, more fundamental set of issues about the ways in which people learn. This set of issues should be at the heart of thinking about group work because it provides both the rationale for it and invaluable fuel for pragmatic thinking about it. It also provides a guiding light to help teachers find a path through the undergrowth of inevitably messy classroom interaction, to carve out the best route through for their students. In our recent experience of discussions about group work, we find some of this deeper thinking to be missing.

What are the theories and ideas underpinning this deeper thinking? At EMC, on one day in the summer of 2015, we held a training day for ourselves, to remind ourselves of their relationship to group work. We worked in small groups … productively. It was exciting, energising and inspiring. We all felt that we came out of it thinking differently, knowing more, having extended our knowledge.

---

2. There has been some confusion between Direction Instruction (upper case) and direct instruction (lower case). DI, a model for explicit teaching, was first developed by Siegfried Englemann in 1964 with a clear set of procedures and ways of working. Direct instruction (lower case) is often more simply used to mean more teacher talk, more teacher instruction and less student discussion, group work and so on.

Our central question was this: if all our materials and all our training with teachers involves such strong elements of group work, why is this? Why are we so wedded to it? Why are we so certain of its value? The session was led by me. To prepare for it I went back to Vygotsky (re-discovering his work on zones of proximal development and the social nature of thinking and language learning). I went back to the extraordinarily significant work of Douglas Barnes. I reminded myself of the work of The National Oracy Project and Alan Howe, and the work we've been doing over the past few years on literacy across the curriculum, including collaborating with Peter Campbell (Institute of Physics) on literacy in science. I re-read bits of Karen Littleton and Neil Mercer's *Interthinking*. I looked back at Chalkface Press's *Small Group Learning in the Classroom* (published in Britian by EMC). I went back through EMC's publications – everything from *The Island*, *Powerful Texts* and *School* to the more recent material, *Worldfriendly Books*, *Spotlight on Literacy* and *Strange Case of Dr Jekyll and Mr Hyde*. I also looked back at John Hattie's *Visible Learning*, blogs about group work, such as the one by David Didau quoted above, as well as new books on the subject by Val Coultas and others.

A few powerful ideas emerged from our discussions that we want to take further.[3] We are thinking of setting up a project on 'Productive Group Work', in the course of next year. It will be funded by us, out of other aspects of our work. We don't want to engage in a Randomised Control Trial experiment but rather in a developmental project with teachers that explores and develops our thinking and theirs, one that extends our collective thinking, practice, knowledge, confidence and understanding by trying out, observing, analysing, reflecting and adapting – in other words, using the approach that turns teachers into experts, capable of making subtle and telling judgements on behalf of their students. We want to fund it ourselves because we believe that it's a vitally important area for English teachers to continue to develop in their classrooms and get right.

And now, here are just a few those underlying ideas that you may have been waiting for patiently while reading this article, the ones that we'll be exploring more fully and exemplifying in our project.

1. That exploratory talk between people is a way of extending their knowledge and, most importantly, what they do with that knowledge. Talk changes thinking. It allows people to take in knowledge and then 'recode' that knowledge, so that they think differently. If we believe this, then it has to be an important part of what happens in classrooms.[4]

2. The idea that group work is good or bad is a gross over-simplification of the complexities of what happens in good classrooms. Group work of different

---

3. This was the impetus for *It's Good to Talk*, our project on group work that has been running since 2015.

4. This view is validated in numerous national reports. For instance *English at the Crossroads*, Ofsted's inspection report of June 2009, has as one of its key findings that 'The most effective schools used speaking and listening activities successfully to help pupils to think for themselves. Too few schools, however, planned systematically for these [...]' This report is well worth reading in its entirety for its many wise and insightful descriptions of high quality teaching and learning. Debra Myhill's work, in *Talk, Talk, Talk: Teaching and Learning in Whole Class Discourse* makes strong arguments for the most effective forms of talk in groups being 'exploratory in nature', because they make 'higher order demands on participants'.

kinds serves different purposes. One size doesn't fit all. Tight versus loose structure, friendship versus ability groups and all the other pragmatic decisions, need to be closely allied to purposes and contexts. A list of strategies is only a starting-point for a really skilled teacher – a repertoire or aide-memoire. There's a huge amount more to be done in exploring a range of purposes, different kinds of classes, the age of pupils and helping teachers to become confident in choosing appropriate and relevant strategies for the particular context – and being flexible enough to adapt them according to what's happening in the classroom.

3. Group work is a method of delivering curriculum aims (for example, understanding a text, getting to know a poem, pooling ideas as a prelude to writing, debating an idea for a presentation). But it is also a curriculum aim for English teaching in its own right. It's more than just a 'take it or leave it' classroom approach. The ability to discuss, respond, listen, collaborate, share ideas, defend a position, play devil's advocate, test out your thinking, hear another view, is a vital twenty-first-century language skill. For children who don't have much of this kind of discussion in their own home, it is all the more important that they are given access to this kind of experience in school. It feeds into everything in the English classroom. What do we expect them to do with texts? Confidently hold different interpretations in their heads and play with them, test them out, have the kind of dialogue with themselves that they might have with others, holding their ideas up for scrutiny and adapting them according to fresh information and fresh thinking. Where can they learn these skills? In group discussion.

4. In the past, a lot of the work on group talk was based on classroom recording, either audio or video. Seminal work by Douglas Barnes and others includes fascinating transcripts of group talk in action, with commentaries analysing what is happening, what is being learned and how one might interpret the potentially confusing signals about what is at stake. EMC for many, many years – less so recently – made small examples of classroom interaction a key part of its courses and teachers were able to discuss what was being learned and why, sharing a piece of visible evidence and considering what might be ways of developing and improving the work they saw. We believe that this kind of work, with teachers, can help refine and extend teachers' confidence and expertise, helping them to make the kind of subtle judgements about when, why, how much, who, and what for, that make all the difference to productiveness or not. Group work requires subtlety, not crude good versus bad, yes versus no decisions. We hope that a project might allow us to do more of this kind of recording, to be shared with teachers and discussed in CPD courses.

We think that the time has come for us to stand up strongly for our principles and practices by publicly announcing where we stand and why. We believe that the work of many highly-regarded teachers and academics, who have dedicated their working lives to close work on language and learning and the social nature of talk and thinking, should not just be cast aside in favour of a range of more or less convincing, new pedagogical theories that seem to us to be based on less rigorous or sustained work. We don't think it is helpful to sway backwards and forwards like a reed in the wind, nor to latch onto the latest craze. We never have. Anyone promising that a single technique or a single theory or a single person offers all the answers, or even that x is good and y is bad, is undoubtedly wrong. We never rushed down the learning styles road or the direct instruction highway, nor did we get stuck in the SOLO cul de sac. We refused to screech to a halt on elements of skills and process, in a headlong dash towards 'knowledge'. We were sceptical about levels and anything that pretended that everything that is important in learning in English could be neatly labelled and quantified. We have always advocated a subtly nuanced approach that says yes and no, and 'it depends' to almost everything and have sought to have the most serious and important conversations not about 'this rather than that' but about how both 'this' and 'that' can be expertly and sensitively used as powerful tools by powerful teachers. We're for knowledge *and* skills, teachers holding the reins and students having a voice, disciplined classrooms but not ones where pupils aren't heard, or are only heard answering in stilted, academic language to the exclusion of their own vital, thinking, exploratory voices. We're for group work, yes. Of course we are! To be otherwise would be simply damaging to pupil learning.

5.2 It's good to talk – changing practice in English

This blog, written in 2016, sets out some of the early thinking generated by the *It's Good to Talk* project and the themes that began to emerge right from the outset. These themes are ones that have recurred through the project, though we have found ourselves addressing some more strongly than others. We have moved a long way since this early discussion of the plans but it is interesting to look back at the thinking we did at the time and the impetus behind it as a way of understanding more about how our thinking and the project then developed.

In our general work in schools, we have seen group work being done a bit less frequently than in the past, and with more uncertainty about its value and less confidence about what makes it successful. This is a cause for concern if one believes that group work is a vitally important vehicle for pupils' learning as well as being important for students to learn how to do well.

We have observed that in discussions about education online and elsewhere the validity of group work as a classroom activity is being questioned. (See the reference to a blog by David Didau in the previous piece on page 94.) The free school in West London, Michaela, states on its teacher recruitment page, 'We would never do group work at Michaela'. Teachers are firmly discouraged from applying if this is an approach that they wish to adopt.[1]

We surveyed the material that exists to support group work, and while we found much of it of real value, we felt that some important questions weren't being asked or answered, particularly in relation to our own subject, English. There is plenty of sound advice about setting up groups, establishing ground rules, giving students roles, structures for group work (such as jigsawing, home and expert groups and so on) but not much on what constitutes success in group work, how teachers should intervene in it, what group work is good for (and, conversely, what it isn't good for), what it does that other classroom approaches can't do, what kinds of tasks work best.

In terms of CPD, there isn't much visible evidence in the form of video clips of students working in groups, to allow teachers to analyse, debate and reflect on the basis of a shared 'text', in the same way that one might moderate a piece of writing for assessment and agree what constitutes success, or discuss how to improve it. Equally, teachers in their own classrooms, find it hard to capture exactly what's going on, to pin it down and examine it more analytically.

So we set up a project, starting with a twilight session at which several teachers put themselves forward to be part of the project group. We set this up to be an open-ended project – with no finish time and no fixed parameters. We wanted to be guided by what we might discover, allowing the project findings to lead us,

---

1. Michaela's explicit statement about not doing any group work seems to have been removed since the writing of this blog. However, it is clear from online debates and statements that Michaela, and other schools like it, continue to advocate whole class teaching with direct instruction and teacher talk foregrounded at the expense of small group talk.

rather than setting out with a fixed agenda to prove a narrow set of hypotheses, for example, tested on the basis of randomised controlled trials. Too often, from our perspective, current educational research is constrained by the limited parameters of what is easy to measure quantitatively and is more about seeking proof of something already envisioned than genuinely investigative. Two teachers, from different schools, volunteered to be part of the first phase of the project. The first phase would involve us going in to observe some group work in KS3 classes, followed by a class from each school coming to EMC to do group work for a whole day and be filmed doing it.

We got started and last term (Spring 2016), two Year 7 classes from these schools, came to EMC. We filmed them working both with their teachers and with us. We emerged with 11 hours of footage that we then edited down to around 45 short video clips, showing group work in action. So far, we have shown a few clips at a workshop at the NATE conference in June – with hugely positive and excited reactions from the people there – and have explored some of them as a staff group, with an equal measure of excitement. Now we are beginning to share our early findings more widely, as well as taking the next steps to broaden our work, and extend our investigations.

So, what has emerged so far? A huge amount – too much to be able to put down on paper here. But I can, perhaps, make a start, by setting out the 10 key themes that we've identified as a result of our observations and work with the students:

1. What kinds of things is group work good for, and conversely, what kinds of things isn't it good for?

2. What's the role of the teacher? In setting it up, in establishing the parameters and the purpose of the task, in pausing/re-directing, in building the framework for future learning.

3. Time allocated and pacing of activities.

4. The role of report-backs and whole class feedback.

5. What's the right level of challenge in group work?

6. What kinds of tasks work best in group work?

7. What if students don't seem to be making good progress all the time?

8. The value of creative work in group work on texts.

9. The collaborative classroom – what insights group work offers into how and what children are learning. What students can tell teachers about their learning?

10. Setting v mixed ability – does this make a difference to group work?

Already our work has been throwing up interesting issues around these 10 themes. They are ones that we want to explore more fully with our project group, extending the range of classes and teachers with whom we test out the ideas.

In the meantime, here are just a few thoughts on the interrelationship between our overarching question, 'Why do group work?', and one of the sub-themes, 'What is the right level of challenge in group work?' It takes us straight back to the David Didau assertion (in his blog of February 2015) that group work isn't the best way of talking in the classroom and therefore nor is it the best way of thinking. And maybe it begins to answer some broader questions. Why do group work? Maybe because it's particularly good for getting students to think hard about difficult things. If group work, as it is often currently set up, demands too little of pupils, because teachers feel impelled to look for signs of instant success – immediate proof of what's been learnt – then perhaps that scope for talking and thinking becomes limited.

In the course of the work we did with one of the Year 7 groups, we set up some activities which were particularly challenging. In one of the activities, for instance, they were presented with two very demanding poems they'd never seen before and were expected to compare them and report back on them. They had to grapple with the poems and their complexities, within a lightly supportive structure, but with no 'direct instruction'. We were hugely impressed by the quality of their response to that activity, as were their teachers. Our observations on the filming day were backed up by student questionnaires (both before and at the end of the day), student interviews to camera, and interviews with the teachers who led some activities themselves and observed their students in others.

One recurrent response from the students was that they particularly liked the level of challenge. Unprompted, the word 'think' came up time and time again in their responses, both in the questionnaires and to camera. They liked having to think hard, to think outside of the box, to talk and find out what they thought, to have to think for themselves rather than being told and so on.

In looking back at the video footage, we were struck by what we saw – students regulating themselves really well, in a group situation and thinking harder by talking to each other. They seemed to learn by bouncing ideas off each other, but also by using their individual talk as a means of thinking through their *own* ideas and taking them further.

In the report back by individuals, one could see the way in which their understanding of the poems and of poetry had benefitted. And it wasn't just a question of 'knowing' more about the two poems for their own sake. One felt that having gone through that process of thinking about those two poems would stand them in very good stead when they had to encounter any poem in the future. Knowing how to think and talk about poetry was what they had been learning.[2] It was time well spent.

---

2. Clips showing some of this early work on poetry in action are available on the EMC website (www.englishandmedia.co.uk). Search 'Barbara Bleiman: What Matters in English Teaching – Video Clips'.

5.3 Group work – had we but world enough and time

There is a constant refrain in discussions about group work that it takes time away from the imparting of knowledge, that it's an expendable luxury, that teacher input does the job more quickly, efficiently and effectively. Group work may be exciting or 'fun' but it doesn't pay its way. In the blog that follows I tackle this issue head on.

One of the things I've been hearing, when I've been presenting the early outcomes of our project on group work, is 'How wonderful! How inspiring! If only we had the time to do this kind of work!' I am, of course, thrilled at the first part of the reaction, where teachers and other education experts clap and cheer when they see the students in our videos engaging in serious, animated and deep discussion of difficult texts. But my heart sinks at the thought that some still see this as an optional 'extra' rather than the very means by which they could be doing all those things they perceive themselves as having to do – preparing students for future examinations, improving students' grades, proving that learning is happening. My contention – contentious perhaps in some spheres these days – is that preparing students for future examinations, improving students' grades and proving that learning is happening is fulfilled much better by doing fantastic group work, and other talk-rich activities, than by eschewing it in favour of simple transmission approaches. That's not to say that transmission is never valuable. It is an essential part of any teacher's repertoire. I'm highly sceptical of any single approach, strategy, theory or directive that claims to be 'the way' to do it. It's always 'yes…and' or 'yes…but' rather than a blunt, crude certainty about one approach working or not. In the right hands, with the right level of subtle thinking about how pupils are learning, all options are open – teacher instruction, modelling and talk, whole-class teaching, individual work, silent writing, silent reading, noisy pair work and high-quality group work. They can all provide the kind of challenge and focus to move students' learning on, developing pupils' knowledge, skills, confidence and pleasure in learning in equal measure.

What can group work do for your students?

Let's take a small example, drawing on a piece of evidence from the EMC group work project *It's Good to Talk*. You are working with a class of Year 7s on poetry. One long term aim is give them the confidence, knowledge and skills to be able to handle unseen poetry at GCSE, as well as writing well about set poems. You also want them to encounter a range of different poems – including perhaps canonical ones. Maybe you have a feeling that pupils don't come across enough challenging texts, that they need to be taught 'content' or 'knowledge', that it's important to introduce them to the kind of literature that they wouldn't necessarily read outside of a classroom. Nothing wrong with that. It's a very important aim but so are other aims that might read a bit differently: introducing pupils to contemporary, living writing and writers; offering diverse texts that speak to them and their identities; allowing them to see the continuities between themselves as writers and the writing of published authors. (A bit of 'yes and…', rather than either/or, is going on here.) A shorter term aim might be that you want your Year 7s to start to write about poetry, beginning to take on some of the terms and ways of thinking about poetry associated with literary study, such as talking about voice, metaphor, rhyme and refrains.

What's the best way of fulfilling these aims? There are many options open to you. One is to have a lesson on metaphor. 'Today we're going to find out about metaphors in a poem. I'm going to give you a definition of a metaphor. I'm going to give you two poems in which there are metaphors to describe a falcon. I'm going to ask you to find those metaphors and tell me about them,' or perhaps, 'I'm going to tell you about what the metaphors are in one poem and ask you to find them in the other one,' or 'I'm going to ask the whole class questions about the metaphors and along the way I'm going to tell you what I think.' At the end of the lesson you say to yourself, 'Good. We've learned about metaphors.' You might feel quite pleased that the concept has been nailed. Next time they encounter a metaphor in a poem, they will be able to spot it. You might even ask them from time to time, 'Where's the metaphor?' just to be sure that they remember.

For your short term aim, this has taken you quite a long way, you think. You can tell anyone coming into your classroom what has been achieved. The children can be tested on what a metaphor is. But what of the longer term, bigger, broader aim, of putting students into a position to be able to encounter any poem and respond to it with confidence, treating it in a way that our subject requires? This involves multiple skills and knowledge of how poetry works. Above all it means being able to test out first thoughts against more measured reflection, being able to observe patterns and identify what is significant, rather than being overwhelmed by every tiny detail. It means feeling comfortable – indeed excited by – ambiguity and complexity. It means understanding how poems work differently from prose, understanding how to read them accordingly, and discovering how multiple and various they are in the techniques they use, from figurative language (including metaphor), to sound patterning, to the look on the page. Does your 'teaching metaphor' lesson take you any way towards this bigger, more ambitious aim for your students?

Working with a class of Year 7s on poetry, we had this more ambitious aim in mind and we wanted to examine whether it could, in any way, be fulfilled by group work. Was group work a luxurious, fun 'extra'? Or could it be the means for doing something demanding, stimulating and significant for the students, in teaching them how poems work, what they have to offer and how to talk (and write) about them in productive and interesting ways? If our reactions, and those of teachers watching our video clips are anything to go by, then the answer is a resounding endorsement of the potential of group work. The students worked in groups. They discussed two demanding poems, one poem per group, supported by a list of statements to debate. These statements put forward some ideas about the poems and how they worked, thematically, stylistically, in relation to voice and other aspects of the poetry. The pupils re-grouped to present their poems to each other and looked for points of similarity and difference. There was no teacher input, apart from to direct the ways in which they talked from time to time, encouraging them to subject their thinking to serious scrutiny, to consider alternative possibilities and prove their thinking to themselves.

What follows is a transcript of a little bit of this group talk. Jacob and Omachi had been working in a group of four on Ted Hughes' poem 'And the Falcon Came'. Devonte and Ryan had been working in a group on Jonathan Steffen's poem 'The Falcon to the Falconer'. At the start of the transcript they had just re-grouped to present their poems to each other and compare them. What follows is a transcript of the first four minutes of talk in the newly formed group.

Jacob: So it's explaining it as a weapon. So, yeah, the falcon is a weapon, it's explaining it as a weapon. What's yours about?

Devonte: I think it's about...you know, the title, I think it's about two people but like about maybe about someone's like captive...maybe about two...a relationship sort of thing. I'm not really sure...because when it says 'unleash me from your hand' our group...I thought... maybe it was something to do with religion.

Jacob: Maybe it's about a bond, as well, with the falcon and the falconer because...

Devonte: Yeah because one of the questions was like, 'Do you think it's about two people?' so I thought it was about two people.

Jacob: Because ours is more vicious, yours is probably more about two people having...

Devonte: ... yeah, a relationship

Jacob: ...yeah, a relationship, whereas mine is very vicious. What did you get for your questions? (*Looking at Devonte's.*)

Devonte: What's yours? (*Reaching to look at Jacob's statements.*)

Jacob: I think they're the same. No, no they're not.

Devonte: 'The voice of the falcon...' [*PAUSE*] What do you think? (*Looking towards Ryan.*)

Ryan: What? About the poem?

Jacob: Yeah, about the poem.

Ryan: I thought it was, like, same as Devonte, like a bond between...I'd describe them as people as well, but like it was a bond between two people and it's technically [inaudible] together, in a way. Like the falcon started as a baby in a way...wait I'm just thinking outside the box...he grew up to trust him and then at the end where it says, 'unleash me from your hand' it's like saying now it's been kept for too long. But then he says, 'I'll be true to you,' so it means he wants to fly away and have a bit of free time but then come back and at the end it says and at the end it says 'All darkness on your hand/I'm hooded, pinned and held by you/O, give me back my wings/That they may bring me back to you' So, he wants to go, and go far away, find his own prey and start hunting and then come back and be true to him...(*inaudible*)

Jacob: What did you think of our poem, Omachi?

Omachi: Ummh. I thought it was, like, describing how the falcon is quite vicious, and quite cynical, and he doesn't have any mercy for others, because of like when it's saying 'the gunmetal feathers' it's saying, like a weapon – it's not exactly a cuddly bear or anything.

Jacob: So it's not...so, what are the similarities then? It's a different poem, yours is more like a relationship between a man and a bird, something like that..

Devonte: Yeah but yours is kind of (inaudible)

Jacob: Mine is kind of... it's quite hard to explain. Is yours anything about like vicious cos ours is just kind of vicious?

Ryan: Our one is like a bit calm... more like the calm sense. Yours is more...

Jacob: Yeah...

Omachi: ...however they are both saying that the falcon likes to go away and get his own things, cos this one says, 'go and get his own prey'. This one is saying how ruthless he is when he is getting his prey.

Jacob: Yeah

Devonte: I think this one's the opposite to that. This is about falconry. One's about wild whereas the other one is tamed.

Ryan: This one's wild, this one's tamed but they both want the same things, in a way.

Jacob: Yeah. They both need food.

Ryan: But this one isn't learning anything because the falconer is giving him the food and he wants to hunt himself.

What one sees across our collection of film clips of this lesson is students who are highly engaged in discussing the poems, for their own sake – not for some external reason, such as to do well in future exams, to get a merit mark, to prove that they know what a metaphor is, or to be able to complete an assessed assignment. They grapple with ideas about voice and perspective – with no teacher prompting apart from that provided by the statements. They talk about metaphor and the question of whether one of the poems is really about falcons or about human beings. The discussion about this is intense and they talk well about the texts.[1] They get to the heart of what is significant about the two poems and some of the key differences between them, in ways that we wouldn't be unhappy to see at GCSE. They report back individually, with sustained contributions that show the quality of their thinking but also demonstrate them continuing to think as they talk, searching for the right words to express complex ideas, weaving fascinatingly between academic language (such as metaphor, voice, whilst, on the other hand)

---

1. Some short clips showing this in action can be seen on the EMC website (www.englishandmedia.co.uk). Search 'Barbara Bleiman: What Matters in English Teaching – Video Clips'.

and a more everyday grasping for meaning. One of the boys who is most engaged, articulate and productive in his own group, reports back with great seriousness and insight into the poetry but at one point says that the falcon is presented as 'weapony'. We all know what he means. It is not a top priority, at this moment, to correct him and replace it with 'militaristic' or another such word. That can come later.

Teachers' and students' reflections

When asked individually what they thought of the group work activities in general, and this one in particular, both in a questionnaire and to camera, there was a consensus that was like a clarion call to all of us to reconsider what we're doing with our KS3 classes. They liked having to 'think' and they liked 'a challenge'. These words came up time and time again – thinking outside of the box, thinking for themselves, the challenge of having to think independently. They were unfazed by the level of difficulty of the poems, they didn't worry about unfamiliar vocabulary – they took that in their stride, without needing explanations in advance – and they quickly began to recognise that good group work didn't involve getting speedy answers to questions but rather involved helping each other, through talk, to understand more fully, in deeper ways, and with more justification, what was going on in the poems. The fact that the poems were challenging made the group work all the more essential. They weren't going to just sort it out for themselves on their own – they needed each other's help. By talking they could hear what other people thought and by saying what they themselves thought, they could clarify their own ideas. They were doing what Neil Mercer so helpfully describes as 'interthinking' – using exploratory talk to think better and find out more.[2]

Their teachers were so impressed with what their pupils did working in groups, with such challenging material, that they went away saying that this was going to make them re-evaluate their curriculum, to make it more demanding. They also identified that challenge and difficulty seemed like an essential element in good group work. If the tasks are too easy, straightforward and manageable without talk, then the benefits of exploratory talk are much more limited.

Where now?

So where does all of this take us? It makes us want to reassert the importance of doing good group work. It makes us clearer that group work can help fulfil substantial long term aims, enabling students to learn how to think rigorously and encounter challenging texts. It makes us aware that the tasks and the level of demand need to be finely judged. It doesn't negate the powerful and subtle role of the teacher in shaping the experience and drawing out what has been learned. It doesn't in any way silence the teacher's voice or take away their agency or authority. If anything the reverse – they need to be alert to what's happening and responsive in thinking about how best to push pupils' thinking on.

---

2. At an EMC twilight session in 2014, Neil Mercer demonstrated this beautifully with a group of teachers, asking us to talk about an aspect of physics that none of us knew know much about but where pooling our thinking allowed us to get a lot further than each of us individually might have ever imagined.

It doesn't make us think that group work is the only method, for every circumstance. A teacher might talk to the class about a poem, sharing their reading, with no student interruptions – this might teach the students a great deal. Another great lesson might involve students' asking and answering their own questions, or writing in silence about a poem. Another might involve creating a dramatised reading. Group work isn't everything, but it is vital. 'Yes and… yes but…' And we shouldn't worry about not having enough time to do it, because what it fulfils in the longer term matters so much more than some of those smaller, short-term aims with which we crowd out our curriculum.

5.4 Creating as well as thinking in group work

Other blogs in the series on group work concentrate on the value of group work for grappling with difficult texts – on talking to help you think. However, this isn't the only aspect of collaborative work that we were testing out in our project. In our initial work with two Year 7 classes, we were equally interested in exploring how pupils work together to create something. Here we explored what happens when pupils try to write a poem together.

Creativity means different things to different people – one could justifiably argue that everything, even the most analytical and discursive work is highly creative – but in this instance we were focused on the narrower idea of creativity as 'creating something' together. (Later in this blog, you'll see how we witnessed the two coming together in the work that the pupils did.) In our trials, we did two activities with two different classes, in each case creating collaborative poems.

The first class, a higher attainment set, having worked on poetry all morning, went on, in the afternoon, to produce poems of their own about falcons.[1] The second class, a lower attainment set from a different school, read a short story, 'The Paradise Carpet', by Jamila Gavin, from EMC's publication, *Literary Shorts*. Instead of responding to the story by discussing it, or writing about it analytically, they produced a poem based on it, using words and phrases from the story. In both instances, the students were given the opportunity to 'find' the material for a poem from the words of published writers. This gave them a pool of rich language to draw on. They worked together to select, organise, structure and make poetic choices and choices of meaning, including introducing those elements of patterning and repetition that we strongly associate with poetic writing. In both lessons, the work culminated in a reading aloud of each group's poems, which provided a strong focal point and incentive to work with intensity and purpose towards a public outcome.

Falcon poems

The students in the higher-attaining group worked in threes. Each member of the group was given either a 150-200 word non-fiction extract from Helen Macdonald's *H is for Hawk* or 'Peregrine Falcon', a poem by Gillian Clarke. Each student selected five or six words or short phrases that they particularly liked and cut them out. The group pooled their selections and then worked together to choose from the words and phrases to create a poem. They were told that they should bear in mind what they'd specially liked about the poems they'd encountered in the morning and include some of those favourite techniques in their own poems. For instance, they might want to repeat a phrase, a line or a single word. They might want to set up rhymes or echoes between words. When they came to read out their poems, they were asked to make sure that every member of the group was in some way involved and that, at least once, all their voices should come together in unison.

---

1. The earlier discussions of the morning are described in the previous piece, on page 102.

A few interesting things emerged, that offer us food for thought:

1. All the students were highly engaged, including one boy, M, who can be seen on film in other sessions looking rather detached and bored. He was the only student in the class who, at one point in the day, had to be taken to one side by his teacher to ask him to behave properly. Yet, in this activity, he was totally involved, contributed greatly to his group poem, and confidently expressed his views and preferences working alongside two students who had been much more focused throughout.

2. Many students, in their interviews to camera and their questionnaires at the end of the day, identified this activity as their favourite one. Here is a flavour of the reasons why:

   > Because I got to work in a group and it was so much fun.

   > Because me and my partner both got to put in our own ideas and combined them to make a great poem.

   > Because it was challenging and it got our minds working and it was also very fun because you got to hear other people's ideas.

   > Because it was lots of fun working with my friends and using different techniques to make the poem as good as possible.

   > Because you had to work as a group to write *and* perform a poem, so everyone shared their ideas.

   > Because my group had lots of ideas so it was really good.

   > Because we got to be really creative with our ideas and we made a brilliant poem.

   > Because I thought it was really creative and that there were some really powerful phrases in a lot of them.

   It was interesting to see the pleasure and pride in the work – not for any external reasons such as to get a good grade or to achieve a target, or fulfil a specific objective, but for the intrinsic value of the activity itself. Writing a poem you can be proud of, using techniques you've already been thinking about, appears to be reward enough. Fun in the classroom gets a bad press sometimes these days, but it's interesting to see how the students identified the fun with other elements of learning – 'a brilliant poem', 'powerful phrases' – that we would all be pleased to see our students thinking about; the two go hand in hand.

3. The poems themselves revealed the students' developing understanding of how poetry works – building on the work they did exploring poetry through discussion earlier in the day. The vocabulary was drawn from the work of published writers, but they confidently made it their own, trying out the sound of words that they wouldn't normally use in their own mouths. Here is the poem written by M's group:

a flying rain cloud
a complicated grey cloud
it lands, mobbed by crows, disguising itself
its prey there before him, a grey pigeon
a couple of flaps, fast like a knife-cut
there was new blood in the killing ground
blood still warm.

And just to give a flavour of how different the poems were, despite the common pool of words, here is another:

I don't remember looking down or away
From the beast within him.

I saw him whoosh past me.
And in that tiny black gap,
I saw a pigeon burst like a city but I smelt ice in my nose.
I saw a bright light in the corner of my eye.

A crow barrelled down
like a knife cut.
The crow was not stupid.
I took one step towards him and he flew away.

I don't remember looking down or away
From the beast within him.

In both cases, it's worth asking the question, 'What do these students understand about poetry?' It seems clear to me that they understand that:

- Poetry often includes repetition, including parallelism (grammatical repetition).

- Poetry does not have to rhyme.

- Poetry uses language in different ways from prose.

- Echoes and patterns are an essential, and pleasurable, aspect of poetry.

- Lineation is part of the meaning and choices of lineation allow you to emphasise certain things.

- Spaces between lines are part of the meaning and these are chosen deliberately rather than being accidental or random.

- There needs to be a satisfying ending – brought about either by repetition or by a return to the opening, or by focusing on something especially powerful, or a mixture of these.

- Poems are there to be read aloud.

One might justifiably say that these students could have come to this activity with some of this knowledge already in their heads – though interestingly, in the very first activity of the day, working on extracts from a range of different poems, their immediate focus was much more on 'What's it about?' than on 'How does it work as poetry?' However, it seemed to us to be clear that writing poems themselves, and putting themselves in the role of poets, brought this element of their understanding to the fore.

If we want students to be attuned to the way poetry works as they progress through KS3 and into KS4, so that they can write confidently about line length, patterning, lineation, repetition and other key elements of language, structure and form, then what better way than to allow them to play with these elements, beginning in KS3 and carrying on into their studies at GCSE and beyond?

'Paradise Carpet'

The other group of students, working on a short story by Jamila Gavin, also wrote poems but the aim of the activity was very different – not so much to discover how poems work but more to use the writing of poems as a way to explore a narrative text independently. This is the kind of thing that we might also encourage at A Level – holding off from quick analytical or formal responses to allow for a more exploratory, almost oblique first response, that encourages something authentic as a first stage. Transforming a text takes the pressure off and avoids the leap to instant judgements, with a focus on 'What's it like?' and 'What's interesting about it for you?' rather than 'What's it about?'

Like the first class, they were asked to write poems for performance, in groups. The story was read aloud first. The students then went straight into groups to create their poems. One group was given a long list of words and phrases from the short story to select from. Another selected their own 'favourite' words and phrases. A third was just given a title, 'The Wealthy Man'. A fourth was told that each line of their poem should start with the name of the main character, a boy called Ishwar. For example, 'Ishwar knew…Ishwar longed for… Ishwar heard… Ishwar thought…' A fifth had to pick words and phrases from the dialogue only. The different prompts allowed us to try out a range of different ways into the task.

It was interesting to observe how much the work took the students back into the short story. We witnessed them delving back in and, almost with a sideways glance, discovering more about it as they constructed their poems. One group became fascinated by the ending, trying to grapple with the puzzling issue of what exactly had happened to Ishwar and the underlying question of whether his life had been so bleak and depressing that he had escaped into the carpet – just the kind of reflection we would have wanted. Another group excitedly came up with a refrain that summed up the trajectory of the story – 'One knot blue, two knots yellow, three knots red, four knots dead', the words 'four knots dead' being their own invention.

One of the groups wrote this poem. (The different text formats represent each of the three different voices in the performance.)

One knot blue, two knots yellow, three knots red, four knots green.
The paradise garden shimmered on the loom.
When I look behind me I see a gold-spotted deer leaping through undergrowth.
One knot blue two knots green, three knots red, four knots green.
Thread of every colour in the rainbow.
The glowing colours of hummingbirds and nightingales.
A dozen shades of blossom of red, pink, purple and violet.
One knot blue, two knots yellow three knots red, four knots green.
A paradise garden of strutting peacocks with sweeping tails
twisting, coiling branches
exotic birds swooped and trilled and pecked.
One knot blue, two knots yellow, three knots red, four knots green.
The paradise carpet shimmered on the loom.

This was produced without any discussion of the story as a class, yet by writing the poem the students found a way of conveying some of the rich descriptive qualities of the original. They went beyond extracting the most basic elements of the storyline; the phrases they selected and repeated stand out as being particularly magical, exotic and vibrant, showing the students' pleasure in the sounds of the words and the images created. The choice of refrain is also a clever one, constantly returning to the endless work of the boy in making the carpet.

What this work reinforces is that creativity and analytical thinking in group work are both valuable. Both are also fun. And, importantly, they are not neatly, or easily separable into rigid binaries. Analysis is creative; creativity involves analytical thinking. They work together hand in glove, to support students' growing understanding and knowledge of how texts work. Working in groups on a creative task, with the incentive (and pressure) of a performance, can be a powerful way of developing understandings about texts and how they work, and a stimulus for students to write themselves.[2]

2. This blog relates to the piece on page 139 on creative/critical writing and the relationship between them, as well as the piece on page 142 on the teaching of writing about poetry.

5.5 Group work or teacher transmission of knowledge – a false dichotomy?

Group work is often presented as being in opposition to teacher talk, as if the two are diametrically opposed and entirely distinct from each other. In polarised debates, group work is characterised (or caricatured) as a great big, loose, baggy activity lasting for an extended period of time, in which the teacher gives little direction, no input and is merely a passive observer of students' self-directed activity. In this blog, written in 2017, I seek to dispel some of these myths, drawing on the work of the EMC project to show how in good group work the teacher is playing a very active, 'talking' role, with plenty of input of his or her own knowledge. The interplay between teacher questioning and input, group talk and individual pupils' contributions to whole class discussion is of vital importance.

There's been a lot of debate recently about the relative value of group work, pupil talk and teacher transmission of knowledge. On January 24th 2017 Government minister Nick Gibb made a speech entitled 'The Evidence in Favour of Teacher-Led Instruction'. It's worth following the train of his argument, at least in the exposition of his main ideas. First he says that one must have knowledge and, of course, he says, one must be able to apply it. Next he goes on to say that 'child-centred' pedagogies 'focus on eliciting and developing ethereal and often poorly-defined skills in pupils' and that teacher focus is 'turned away from ensuring all pupils are taught the core of academic knowledge that they need, and instead teachers attempt to inculcate creativity and problem-solving as if these skills transcend domains of knowledge.' The two major points in his argument are presented by him as a logical development one from the other. But what if – as is the case for many of us – we believe, like him, that 'one must have knowledge' but we disagree with his characterisation of 'child-centred pedagogies' as not being interested in knowledge? What if we also disagree with his view that transmission, pure and simple, and only transmission, is the way to develop important knowledge in our pupils?

I've been thinking about this a great deal because of the work we've been doing at EMC on group work in our project *It's Good to Talk* where I've been going into classrooms and seeing English in action. Some of the time I've been setting up activities as part of the research; at other times, I've watched classes doing the tasks that the teachers have generated for them.

Most recently, I've been fortunate enough to be invited to work with Richard Long and his department at St Michael's in High Wycombe, filming four Year 7 mixed-attainment classes working on poetry, with an emphasis on small group activity. You may note already the care with which I describe this – 'an emphasis on small group activity'. The way that group work is often characterised by those who don't see its value is as only group activity. In this caricatured version of it, teachers set up groups, are only interested in nebulous ideas like 'working together' or 'creativity', privilege above all else students' interactions for their own sake and 'skills' such as 'collaboration, co-operation' and so on. The caricature has the teacher almost absent – unwilling to offer information, ideas, knowledge, wisdom or anything else, because 'it's only what the children think that counts'. The caricature has no shaping, no transmission of information or knowledge, no drawing out of key ideas, no pushing students to think more deeply, no questioning of their ideas or building on them with the offer of information and ideas that will take them further.

It would be interesting to know whether those who are so critical of group work are fully aware of the vital role that the teacher must play to make it really effective. Equally, it would be interesting to find out whether they realise that, in really good group work lessons, the time spent in groups is likely to be only a part of the whole lesson. Even in the phase of the lesson that involves group work, it is likely, when it is working at its very best, that the teacher will be constantly weaving between whole class intervention and group talk. This is what I saw in the course of the lessons at St Michael's.

Let me just give you one or two of the most memorable examples. I constructed a lesson plan (and provided materials) for the Year 7 students. They were to read a small selection of five to seven poems, selected by me, and choose one individually to share with their group. They were asked to read their poem to each other, explaining why they chose it, and then decide, as a group, on one that they all liked enough to present to the whole class. The aims of the lesson were broad, big picture ones in terms of knowledge – to give students an understanding of how poetry works differently from prose, what pleasures it offers and how one might enjoy complexity and ambiguity, persisting with puzzling elements rather than being intimidated by them. The objectives were not little ones like 'know what a metaphor is' or 'identify sound effects' but rather much bigger, more significant ones that I believe will stand students in good stead in all their future encounters with poems. In each of the Year 7 lessons on poetry, I asked the teachers to start the lesson by presenting a poem that they particularly liked and talk to the class about it. They were asked to say what they liked about it, what they thought was special about it, any aspects that were complex or puzzling and how they felt about that, with strong guidance that they should indicate to the students that difficulty was something they didn't fear or shy away from but was a source of great interest and pleasure. (Adult critics and poets, writing for adults on how to read poetry, emphasise all of these things.[1]) The idea was for the teachers to model their 'knowledge' about a single poem and the way in which poems can and should be read. Each of the teachers did this, and the children sat rapt, listening to their 'transmission' of knowledge about poetry. It was so much more than 'transmission' though. It was an entry into how to 'do' the subject, how to be a serious student of literature but it was also personal, and at times, inspiring. Two teachers chose a Shakespeare sonnet, another a contemporary poem by Andrew Waterhouse, a fourth Yeats' 'Lake Isle of Innisfree'. This latter was a tour de force – a stunning example of a teacher conveying her passionate commitment to a poem, its complex

---

1. See the chapter on poetry teaching on page 148, for more on this.

ideas and the way it works. She was the expert guide for students starting out on the same road towards an understanding of the pleasures and complexities of poetry.[2] In their evaluations, several of the pupils commented on how much they'd enjoyed this, for instance: 'Poems have changed for me because I was not interested in poetry. Now I am because we wrote about lots of them and sir told me about his favourite poem, 'Sonnet 130', which I really enjoyed.'

After the teacher presentations, the students went into groups. The students chose their own poems and it was notable that they didn't always opt for the easiest ones but rather ones that intrigued or puzzled them. Poems like William Blake's 'A Poison Tree', Yehuda Amichai's 'The Diameter of the Bomb' and Emily Dickinson's 'I'm Nobody – Who are You?' were chosen in preference to more straightforward poems of the kind one might expect 11 and 12 year olds to choose. Though the conversations were sometimes hesitant and fumbling, students could be seen grappling for meaning and enjoying the struggle. The student evaluations were extremely positive about the way group work allowed them to make their own choices and work together on difficult texts. One said, 'Now I find challenging poems more interesting than others.'

In one lesson, following on from this open-ended activity in an earlier lesson, Richard Long introduced a single poem 'Wind' by Ted Hughes, using a 'collapsed poem' as the starting-point.[3] Groups talked about the collapsed poem and were then given the whole poem to read, in the light of their speculative thinking about the collapsed version. The poem is one that many of us might consider to be very challenging for Year 7. I chose the poem. When we talked about this before the lesson, I suggested that I was less interested in the pupils 'doing justice' to the poem itself and more in them learning about how to approach difficult poems with interest, openness and a willingness to work through difficulty towards interpretation.

In the lesson itself, lots of issues were raised about the specific use of the collapsed poem and whether it provided enough support for the students and one could talk at length about this. However my focus here is on the question of teachers imparting knowledge as groups work on their own. What was fascinating to observe, and then to reflect on again when watching the film footage[4], was the way in which Richard moved in and out between whole class instruction, questioning and pulling things together, and the group work itself (in which he played a strong role, intervening in individual groups, asking students questions, pausing to share ideas with the intention of highlighting productive ideas and prodding struggling groups in the right direction). He would agree with me, I'm sure, that the extent of that intervention, the timing of it and the nature of it was of critical importance, and we would also agree on the fact that sometimes it's tricky to know

---

2. The video of this is available on EMC's website. Search 'What Matters in English Teaching – Video Clips'

3. A collapsed text is one that is presented as an alphabetical list. It allows students to speculate about the words and what they suggest about the poem before reading it. When they see the words in context, they have already thought about patterns that they can then begin to make sense of in the text itself.

4. The clip of this is available on EMC website (www.englishandmedia.co.uk). Search 'What Matters in English Teaching – Video Clips'

when to challenge an interpretation that is plainly wrong, without undermining students' confidence. There were times when groups' ideas went a little astray. Teachers need to challenge, prod, and come clean and be honest about times when interpretations are unconvincing. But when and how? Might my suggested lesson plan have offered more information to the whole class earlier on? Or part way through? These are all aspects of the management of group work that the project is considering, by observation, reflection and shared thinking.

What is absolutely clear is that in all the lessons I saw students were not being left to their own devices, without the teacher contributing knowledge and expertise. Nor was the focus of the teachers on what Nick Gibb describes pejoratively as 'eliciting and developing ethereal and often poorly-defined skills in pupils'. The focus in the lessons was on knowledge about poetry. Students were being expected to think about poems in the way that adult readers of poetry do, in exactly the way that they'll need to think about poetry to do well in GCSE unseens, for English Literature A Level and beyond. In other words, they were imbibing serious, significant knowledge related to the subject. The idea that group work and teachers imparting knowledge are entirely distinct from each other is hugely simplistic. In the best classrooms teachers weave nimbly between the two, gaining the benefits of both by offering their own understanding and ideas, and allowing students to develop their own.

References for Chapter 5

Barnes, D., J. Britton and H. Rosen. 1974. *Language, the Learner and the School*. Harmondsworth: Penguin.

Bullock, A. 1975. *A Language for Life*. London: HMSO.

Coultas, V. 2006. *Constructive Talk in Challenging Classrooms: Strategies for Behaviour Management and Talk-based Tasks*. Abingdon: Routledge.

Didau, D. 2015. 'Why the hell should students work in groups?'. Learning Spy blog.

Gibb, N. 2017. 'The Evidence in Favour of Teacher Led Instruction'. www.nickgibb.org.uk/news/evidence-favour-teacher-led-instruction

Hattie, J. 2011. *Visible Learning for Teachers*. Abingdon: Routledge.

Language in the National Curriculum Resources (LINC). 1991. Available, Nottingham University Online Store.

Littleton, K. & N. Mercer. 2013. *Interthinking – Putting Talk to Work*. Abingdon: Routledge.

Myhill, D. 2006. 'Talk, talk, talk: teaching and learning in whole class discourse'. In *Research Papers in Education*, 21 (1).

Reid, J., Forrestal, P. and Cook, J. 1989. *Small Group Learning in the Classroom*. Enlgish and Media Centre: London.

Vygotsky, L. 1986 [1934]. *Thought and Language*. Cambridge MA: MIT Press.

6. Teaching Writing

6.1 The transition from artlessness to art

This overview piece, newly written for the book, brings together ideas and insights about the teaching of writing from the past, with more recent thinking and developments. It provides some of the history of how we've got to where we are, through the National Literacy Strategy years and beyond.

It starts with a focus on something that has become an overriding concern for me, and for many English teachers – the way that an exaggerated emphasis on form and formulae has diverted our attention away from writing being the expression of students' ideas, meanings and purposes. Though this is most clearly the case in critical writing, with PEE paragraphs being the most obvious example, formulae for writing have also found their way into non-fiction writing and other forms of creative writing, where checking off the inclusion of certain features or adopting set structures has become as important as having a 'voice' or something interesting and authentic to say.

The history of education in the late twentieth and early twenty-first centuries provides us with plenty of clues as to why all of this has happened. I explore these, and in doing so, seek to show that current problems in the way we teach writing arise out of a set of policy initiatives, government interventions – and even a few promising new ideas that became distorted in their translation from theory to practice. English teachers now, as in the past, have sought to do the best by their students but the parameters within which they have been working have changed, and these have brought a new set of problems.

The later part of the piece focuses on how, despite the pressures on English as a subject, we can help students to develop as writers across the full range of writing purposes, by teaching them the 'craft' of writing as a means of 'expressing themselves', whether that be in storytelling, comment, poetry, autobiographical writing or literary critical essays. Writing is a way of putting onto paper thoughts, feelings, lines of argument, personal ways of thinking and being. Teaching students to write, and write well, should allow them to do that. It involves developing ideas as well as skill, art as well as competence, freedom as well as structure.

A Language for Life (The Bullock Report, 1975) talks of 'spontaneity [...] surviving the transition from artlessness to art' and of teachers who aim 'to extend the pupil's power as a writer' needing 'to work first upon his intentions and then upon the techniques approriate to them'. The role of the teacher is to support young writers to find 'new techniques appropriate' to their 'novel intentions'. How wise this seems and how relevant to today's teaching, classrooms and students. For what seems to me to have happened over the past decade or more is that we have lost sight of these fundamental ideas, that students own thinking and intentions should be at the heart of learning to write and that technique should be at the service of their purposes, not in the driving seat, controlling the whole operation.

From KS2 up, we seem to have forgotten what learning to write is all about. Primary school pupils have been told to use 'wow words' in their creative writing or are required to include fronted adverbials or 'interesting' adjectives. Secondary students have been expected to use 'ambitious' vocabulary or vary their sentence structures. In critical writing they have been asked to provide topic sentences or write to an increasingly rigid formula, ranging from the basic PEE to PEETAL or even, on one blog, the extraordinary, byzantine PETAETAETAAAAL.[1] In non-fiction work, the acronym AFOREST[2] has been used for persuasive and argument writing while for descriptive writing the 'Drop, Shift, Zoom in, Zoom out' technique has been used. Intentions seem to come second – or don't come anywhere at all. So long as students have followed the formal procedure, teachers have been willing to overlook the fact that the P, the point that should be the driving force of a piece of writing, has no significance or even validity, that it rests on shaky E (evidence) and has been E'd (explained) to death – micro-analysed to a point of absurdity, with individual words defined and explored for every possible connotation, regardless of relevance, and to the point where all meaning is lost. Students' heads have been crammed full of acronyms and the need to follow set procedures, leaving little space to have genuine thoughts about texts and ideas. (If cognitive overload ever had validity as an educational idea, surely it is here!)

Exam reports, at GCSE and at A Level have, for decades, been making strong points about the counter-productiveness of approaches which emphasise form and formula over fresh thought, clear intentions and genuine 'art'. Here are just a few recent examples from AQA GCSE Examiners' Reports:

> Students who answered the question generally did better than those who were confined by formulaic, AO-driven responses. (English Literature Paper 2 June 2017)

> Some students continue to produce formulaic responses with a contrived use of senses: I can see/I can hear/I can smell. Others continue to include over-ambitious vocabulary that is misused and obscures meaning. Writing skills obviously need to be taught, but there is also an argument for not over-preparing students with formulaic methods, especially for creative writing. There is much to be said for an honest response where the student's voice can be heard, rather than an artificial, contrived construction. (English Language Paper 1 June 2018)

> This increasing confidence in addressing the demands of the paper suggests teachers have prepared students well for this assessment, and students are well-versed in each of the key skills. However, the best answers continue to be those which spring from a spontaneous and individual response to the stimulus material, rather than those which are the result of overly mechanistic, prescriptive or repetitive approaches. (English Language Paper 2 June 2019)

What's been going wrong?

So why have so many teachers been swayed into believing that such approaches are valuable enough to put them at the very heart of their teaching of writing? One answer undoubtedly lies in the tremendous pressure on teachers because of

---

1. This was an approach outlined by a teacher in a blog in March 2016.

2. AFOREST: Alliteration; Facts; Opinions; Rhetorical Questions; Emotive Language; Statistics; Triples

stringent accountability measures. Senior management teams are looking for silver bullets, quick answers. They don't necessarily understand the differences between subjects. English has always been notoriously difficult to pin down. What makes good writing simply doesn't fit a rigid, set pattern, in the way that perhaps the write-up of a science experiment or an answer to a Maths problem, or an explanatory paragraph on a geography feature might. Creative writing cannot be reduced to a formula but a literature essay also has multiple possible starting-points, all equally acceptable, whether it's tonal, thematic, structural, concerned with voice or emotional power. Ideas can be expressed starting with a great quotation and building out from that into a significant point, rather than vice versa. Evidence is selected by each individual and they will invariably choose slightly different things. Ten different students might make quite different points, while still all writing a very good essay. And a really great student might say something, even in an exam essay, that the teacher or examiner has never thought of before themselves. In the past, English teachers and Subject Leaders, who had more control over what they did, could – and did – argue vociferously for the uniqueness of the subject, in the face of whole school directives to apply common processes that simply didn't fit English.[3] But in the current climate, with experienced teachers leaving the profession and many non-specialists teaching the subject, this confident, determined advocacy for the subject has diminished.

One has to go back in time to find another major reason for some of the embedding of these practices in the teaching of critical writing and their transference into creative writing as well. In the 1970s, 80s and early 90s, the dominant forms of writing in secondary English were writing creatively (mainly stories and writing about oneself) and writing about literature. In the early 1990s, there was a growing sense that English should more systematically incorporate non-literary, non-fiction genres – the kind of texts that students would go on to encounter in their everyday lives, and would be required to write as part of being seen as 'functionally literate', in adult and working life. It was not enough to base English entirely on literature – it also had to include reports, articles, letters, health and safety notices and leaflets. Some of these forms had been taught previously, usually in the context of media work, for instance the study of newspapers, but as part of broader understandings, not necessarily as genres in their own right. In classroom projects such as EMC's *School Under Siege* (1979) and *The Island* (1985) students did varied kinds of non-fiction writing in the context of a simulation, but the emphasis was on the imaginative context more than on teaching the detail of different non-fiction genres.

A growing pressure to see English as being about 'literacy for life' coincided with the development of a new strand of thought among a group of progressive Australian 'genre theorists', who focused their attention on the features of different non-fiction genres, arguing that many students had much less experience of these

---

3. Judith A. Langer in *Envisioning Literature* says of the US context, 'Too often graduate teachers have little understanding of what the process of literary understanding entails, or of what literature education has to offer to the developing mind. Pre-service teachers are taught about mathematical reasoning and scientific thinking, for example, but not about literary reasoning.'

than of narrative genres. They would sit on the primary school carpet from an early age listening to stories, immersing themselves in the features of storytelling but had scant familiarity with non-fiction genres (reportage, interviews, features, editorials, promotional material and so on). The Australian genre theorists argued that all children needed to be taught explicitly the conventions of current non-fiction forms and genres, to give them access to powerful knowledge and skills. In the late 1990s, David Wray and Maureen Lewis wrote several books, taking the work of Australian genre theorists and translating it into some highly practical approaches for classrooms, including *Writing Across the Curriculum – Frames to Support Learning* and *Writing Frames: Scaffolding Children's Non-fiction Writing in a Range of Genres*. It was at this point that two things happened. First was the emergence of the idea of the 'writing frame', never intended as a rigid structure but rather as a light support that should only be used where needed and then removed. That 'scaffold' intended to be taken down when the building was stable became, instead, a permanent, unsightly structure. Here's how David Wray describes this process in the online blurb introducing his book, *Developing Factual Writing: An Approach through Scaffolding* (2001). It is interesting for its clear signalling of the fact that writing frames should only be a temporary support for some students (and should only be used as the 'skeleton' for writing, to be fleshed out).

> Most teachers would agree that children should undertake a wide range of types of non-fiction writing, but there are many questions about how this aim should be achieved and about how teachers can help children learn about the various structural demands of particular writing forms. 'Writing frames' are one strategy which can help children use the generic structures of recounts, reports, instructions, explanations, persuasion, and discussion until they become familiar enough with these written structures to have assimilated them into their independent writing repertoire. A writing frame consists of a skeleton outline to scaffold children's non-fiction writing. The writing frames concentrate on the six types of non-fiction genres identified by the Australian genre theorists, Christie (1989), Martin and Rothery (1986), and Rothery and Callaghan (1989). Children experience problems in practising non-fiction writing. Writing frames are helpful to children of all ages and particularly useful with children of average writing ability and with those who find writing difficult. Use of a writing frame should always begin with discussion and teacher modeling, and not all children in a class will need to use a writing frame.

It was during this period that the systematic categorisation and teaching of 'text types' came into being – writing to argue, persuade, inform or describe, each with its own characteristic structures and grammatical and rhetorical features. Here was the start of a system-wide focus on the 'techniques' of persuasion, the structure of argument and so on. Listing in threes, rhetorical questions, alliterative phrases in all persuasive texts took root in classrooms. When Wray and Lewis's book came out, EMC welcomed it, as it had done the work of the genre theorists. It promised much. However, as with so many new ideas, as soon as it became fixed in an assessment system and taught as a set of rules and formulae rather than as a useful set of ideas to explore and think about, it became a rod for teachers' (and students') backs. The non-fiction 'triplets' – 'argue, persuade, advise', 'analyse, review, comment' and 'inform, explain, describe' – became the structure for GCSE questions, with mark schemes that required such features as 'listing in threes' and the whole idea of non-fiction genres turned into a huge edifice of falsely rigid features to shape and control student writing. This was the first moment when students started to be told that they must 'include' certain elements in their writing as proof of knowledge of the genre. Persuade was different from argue or inform, despite the fact that in the real world, no non-fiction writer would set out to do one of these things in isolation but would almost certainly have many overlapping purposes and techniques to fit his or her intentions. Their introduction was concurrent with the National Literacy Strategy, which cemented their status.

When the triplets were finally abolished, no-one was sorry to see the back of them. However the habit of teaching small features, detached from the student's own ideas and intentions, has sadly remained, and been incorporated into the various more recent iterations of formative assessment. It has been hard to row back from this atomistic approach to the teaching of writing, where students are rewarded for demonstrating particular features rather than for their broader understandings and ability to structure coherent lines of argument and thought to fulfil their own purposes. (See Chapter 10, page 160, on assessment.)

Where do we go from here?

How can teachers wrest back a sense of confidence and authority about how to teach students to write, and to write well, that strips away some of the unhelpful accretions of the 1990s and 2000s? What follows are a few ideas and initiatives that suggest a way forward, and some more fruitful and supportive ways of thinking about writing that have emerged over the time that I have been involved in education.

Global moves take precedence

One helpful way of looking at student writing is to recognise the difference between what Lapp, Fisher and Wolsey call 'global moves' and 'local operations'. (This has already been discussed in Chapter 2.3 on page 31, in the context of the shrinking of English as a subject.) The authors of this study conducted a fascinating piece of research, 'Students' and Teachers' Perceptions: An Inquiry Into Academic Writing' published in 2012 in the *Journal of Adolescent and Adult Literacy*. They found that teachers were teaching small scale manoeuvres in writing (such as signposting, using quotations correctly and so on), while actually holding much more substantial subject-disciplinary ideas about success in writing[4]. Students who fulfilled these 'local operations' were often confused as to why they weren't getting

---

4. Helen Lines, working at the University of Exeter, has been doing an ESRC-funded longitudinal study of students' uses of linguistic terminology in their writing, including interviews with the same students over time (2013-16). Her interim findings indicate the problems in a very narrow, localised focus in the teaching of writing in the UK too. She quotes a very able Year 9 whose writing she has been tracking: 'I just used to love reading and I used to pick up vocabulary just like unintentionally and use it. Now the focus is really on getting a high grade…you almost have to have a checklist when you're writing so you have to make sure you've got all the techniques you need to have in order to get a high level…semi-colons are drilled into us' (Rose, Y9). http://socialsciences.exeter.ac.uk/education/research/centres/centreforresearchinwriting/

good marks when they'd been doing just what their teachers told them to do.

The researchers argued that the teachers' own understandings about good critical writing were significantly different from the advice they were giving. They had much more complex ideas, involving ways of thinking about texts and operating within the terms of the subject discipline. Too much attention to 'local operations' was actually getting in the way of developing good writing. So what might global moves look like? The list of points showing the kind of thing one might focus on as global moves or local operations, gives some idea of the difference between them. Let's assume that the written task is a literature essay, based on an unseen poem.

Global moves

1. Has a good sense of what the poem is about, the most important things at stake – an overview of its major idea or mood.

2. Has a strong sense of some of the most significant qualities of the poem.

3. Traces how the ideas/mood/feelings are developed through the poem, bringing in detail at the service of these major patterns.

4. Notes and can explain major shifts and changes in thought or mood.

5. Provides a satisfyingly coherent interpretation, taking in possible ambiguities along the way, but ending up with a convincing personal view of what the poem is doing and how.

6. Is fully aware that this is a poem, rather than a text in any other genre, and treats it as poetry in analysing how it works.

7. Has a personal, authentic voice, showing engagement with the ideas and feelings – pleasure, uncertainty and so on.

8. Recognises what's special about this poem in relation to poetry more generally, and even perhaps to other poems read previously on a similar topic, revealing intertextual understandings.

9. Writes about the poem in such a way that someone who's not encountered it before would understand a lot about its most salient features.

10. Is written in a direct, simple and comprehensible style, which allows the reader to follow the line of argument.

Local operations

1. Makes a point and backs it up with quotation.

2. Has a topic sentence to introduce each paragraph.

3. Writes in paragraphs.

4. Uses quotations accurately in quotation marks and set out correctly on the page.

5. Includes a paragraph about structure.

6. Includes a paragraph about the writer's use of language.

7. Explodes quotations – makes sure that every bit of evidence is unpicked to show what it reveals.

8. Uses literary terminology such as alliteration, onomatopoeia, assonance, caesura, zeugma to demonstrate literary knowledge.

9. Has an introduction and conclusion.

10. Uses signposting words like 'furthermore', 'hence', 'in addition', 'thus'.

This is not to say that the detail of how students write is unimportant. It's just that it has become the be all and end all. Intentions and ideas have been swamped by small details and the expectation of fulfilling 'formal' requirements rather than expressing authentic ideas. The metaphor of 'global moves' seems like a good one to use as a way of judging whether we are getting lost in the detail or giving students a real sense of what academic writing is all about.

Teachers as writers

Another way for teachers to teach writing better is to write themselves. There has been a growing movement both in the USA and the UK to focus on teachers as writers. The idea is that if you experience the process of writing yourself, both critically and creatively, that will give you insights that will help shape your teaching. There is a well-established National Writing Project in the USA that funds and develops this work. In the UK, Simon Wrigley and Jen Smith, under the aegis of NATE, have been running teacher/writer groups for many years, where teachers write for themselves and then share the implications for their teaching. Their book *Introducing Teachers' Writing Groups* (2015) documents this work. EMC has also, for many years, incorporated elements of teachers writing on CPD days, to give them experiences to draw on in their teaching. Most recently Arvon and the University of Exeter ran a fully evaluated two-year study of how teachers writing for themselves can feed into their work with students, funded by the Arts Council.[5]

---

5. The full report, published in 2017, is available at teachersaswriters.org

Many issues are raised by teachers writing for themselves, including the following:

- The role of planning: teachers asked to write can sometimes surprise themselves by how little they use the planning structures they impose on their students.

- It is often an eye-opener to teachers to discover how much their ideas develop through the writing itself, rather than being there, fully formed at the start. This is a real encouragement for allowing students to do more developmental, exploratory writing, as a way of sorting out their thinking.

- The role of drafting and re-drafting has shrunk, since much of student assessment is now in the form of short, end-of-course exams. When teachers write themselves, they become aware of how much more can be done to a first draft to sharpen it up and develop it.

- Teachers often comment in equal measure on how pleasurable and how difficult writing can be. These two feelings are absolutely at the heart of the process. Pleasure doesn't always come without pain – hard work, grappling with difficult ideas, struggling to get the right structure and find the right words, frustration at blocks and difficulties. That's the case for all writers, whether young learners or adults. It's very helpful for teachers to acknowledge that and allow their students to see it as an inevitable part of the process of formulating ideas on paper.

Freedom and choice versus control and limits

Constraints can be helpful. At EMC, we've done lots of little writing exercises in CPD courses and publications where being required to do something very narrow and precise frees you up to think imaginatively. Some of the decisions are made for you and this seems to release students' creative potential. Mark Haddon did a lovely exercise on a course in 2012 at EMC with teachers using postcards and limitations – write about the postcard only using the 2nd person, or only using the vowel 'e', or only in the present tense, or without using any adjectives or adverbs. The results are often fantastic. Equally, in EMC's OCR Language and Literature A Level, there is a narrative writing task in the exam which gives the bare bones of a storyline and asks students to tell the opening as a fully formed narrative. The removal of the requirement to 'invent' the plot frees students to be inventive and individual in their ways of telling.

On the other hand, students often lead very constrained educational lives. It's rare for them to have the freedom to make choices, because their programmes of study have become increasingly rigidly mapped out, setting them on a pre-planned path towards GCSE exams, even sometimes from Year 7 (though this seems to be increasingly acknowledged as inappropriate and is being addressed by Ofsted in its 2019 Education Inspection Framework). Choice, whether of genre, or style, or in the title or topic, offers a chance to make something your own and do something individual and unique. Students can rise to this challenge. This was demonstrated during the National Writing Day activities offered by EMC under the banner 'Let

Them Loose', in 2017 and 2018 and 'Just Write' in 2019.[6] It seemed to strike a chord with teachers and with students. They were given a number of prompts, in the form of visual images and fragments from poems as the spark for their ideas but beyond that they were given the freedom to write in whatever ways they wanted. The results were stunning – students writing personal accounts of their lives, poems in all kinds of shapes and sizes, words and images matched in shape poems, cartoons and texts sprinkled with drawings, stories in every imaginable genre, speeches and pleas from the heart. Many teachers commented with surprise at the energy, imagination and individuality of the writing. This isn't something that should only happen on one day a year. English lessons are there for us to offer more freedom and choice in the curriculum as a whole. EMC has taken this forward with the publication of *Just Write*, a writing book for students, designed for them to pick and choose, for use as homework or for free writing in class. Judging by the numbers of schools buying it, it seems that there is a real appetite for giving students more opportunities to simply exercise their writing muscle and discover for themselves what they're capable of. Doing more of it, doing it without constraints, doing it outside of assessment, without risk is something that all adult writers will identify as the way to develop as a writer.

The creative and the critical

EMC has always recognised the relationship between reading and writing as a key part of the development of good writers. Professional writers queue up to argue that their own writing has been influenced by their reading – that you cannot write well without being a reader. Francine Prose's book *Reading Like a Writer: A Guide for People Who Love Books and for Those Who Want to Write Them* (2006) is a powerful testament to that, showing how a writer reads differently (and better). There is also a lot written in the field of academic English about the way in which creative experiments and writing around texts are themselves a critical act, and can enhance one's understanding of texts. Writers such as Ben Knights, Chris Thurgar-Dawson and Rob Pope, and more recently Catherine Maxwell at Queen Mary University of London, Thomas Karshan at UEA and the poet/critic Sarah Howe, have shown how a blurring of the boundaries can be a fruitful way of developing the act and art of critical writing.

In my period as Head of English at an inner city sixth form college in the 1980s my student coursework always included creative writing based on a text. The folders sit on my desk at EMC as a reminder of what was possible then and include my student Abena's superb additional chapter for *Jane Eyre*, with a commentary that shows the depth of her understanding of Brontë's use of narrative voice, symbolism and her prose style. In the era of the AEB 660, a 50% coursework A Level, she achieved a top grade for this work.

At EMC, for as long as I can remember, we have been arguing for creative exercises and activities in work on texts, building them both into our classroom resources and our CPD courses. Teachers on one-day courses can often expect to write in

---

6. For more on this see page 136 on 'Freedom versus constraint'.

the style of a text, or make a 'micro-intervention' to see what difference it makes if you change an aspect of the telling, or write a poem themselves built out of short quotations they have chosen from a novel. In our *emagazine* competition (in partnership with the Forward Arts Foundation) the creative/critical task of writing a poem inspired by one of the poems shortlisted for the Forward Prize for Poetry has resulted not only in wonderful winning poems but also in exceptional critical writing in the commentaries.

Collaborative practices in writing

Debra Myhill's work emphasises the importance of exploratory talk to improve writing. For instance, *Using Talk to Support Writing* (2010), demonstrates clearly the value of discussing writing, at the start of the process, during writing and in the sharing of completed writing. In EMC's own work, the planning of writing collaboratively has always featured strongly. A few examples include:

- The use of 'post-it note planning', where students work together to generate ideas for a formal essay, put the points on post-it notes and then select, reject and organise the points they think will make a good essay. They can send envoys out to other groups to extend their group's thinking, have additional ideas offered along the way by the teacher, and ultimately use all the thinking that has gone on, not only to write the essay but also to have thought at a metalevel about what makes a good essay. Students can then go on and write the essay individually, drawing on the planning. The process allows ideas to be questioned, sharpened, or rejected, to interrogate their validity, significance and relevance to the topic under consideration.

- Workshop approaches such as drafting, re-drafting and proof-reading in pairs or threes, to provide support for writing at the point of production.

- Modelled writing, where the teacher collaborates with the class to write something together, revealing the thinking processes involved and making judgements about what works, what could be improved and so on.

- Writing together for a common purpose, for instance to prepare a presentation, speech, scripted play, joint statement, letter, or other written communication. EMC's unit, mimicking the 'The Apprentice', for its *Language Works* publication, involved students in collaborating over writing to agree promotional material.

Exploratory writing and thinking

Queen Mary University of London's 'Thinking Writing' website is an interesting initiative by a university to help students write better. At its heart is the idea that writing is not just a way of getting pre-existing ideas down on paper but is a way of developing one's thinking. Here's a short extract from the introductory section:

In 'Thinking Writing', we take writing to be not only a means for showing one's thinking in a discipline but also a tool for developing that disciplinary thinking. In fact, we consider writing to be part and parcel of participating in, and contributing to a discipline. [Writing is] an important means by which disciplines themselves create and communicate thinking and knowledge. It is more than just a tool for showing you can apply knowledge or what you have learnt. [...] So thinking, writing, being, knowing, communicating are all tied up together; inextricable from one another, part of practice.

This chimes strongly with EMC's thinking and my own. When Lucy Webster and I have worked with underperforming students, asked in by teachers to help them improve their writing, it has always been the case that the technical aspects of their writing are a less significant problem than their uncertainty about what they should be saying. Having good ideas, being in charge of the material, and having confidence in exploring them, is a bigger problem than paragraphing, punctuation or academic signposting. Exploratory writing, in which students are freed up to think and develop their ideas seems a vital part of this process.

Most recently, EMC's project *It's Good to Talk*, working on a novel with four Year 9 classes and comparing the outcomes with four others, has demonstrated how a very different kind of approach – putting ideas and intentions first, allowing much more exploratory writing and handing over more control to students themselves – can produce very high-quality writing, as well as rich thinking about texts. Both with Year 7s writing (and blogging) about poetry, and with Year 9s writing about a class novel, we have evidence of the kind of thinking that can be developed at KS3, in coherent and authentically personal writing.[7] The response to this project suggests a real appetite among teachers for moving beyond a narrow focus on atomised teaching of formulae and writing solely for exam purposes. The relationship between talk and writing and the opportunities to write in exploratory ways have been central to this work.

One strong aspect of this is authenticity – not what you think will impress an examiner but what you genuinely notice, think, feel, find interesting about a text. Another is the authentic use of vocabulary suited to purpose. There is plenty on vocabulary elsewhere in this book so suffice it to say that a genuine, rich exploration of texts in classwork and group work can lead students to use subject-specific vocabulary in ways that are solidly rooted in an experience of hearing it well used as part and parcel of the everyday business of doing the subject, rather than as window-dressing to catch the attention and impress. The students in the Year 9 project used words like 'symbol', 'narrative arc', 'characteristic style', 'point of view', 'child's eye perspective' entirely appropriately and correctly, rather than cramming in unfamiliar words in discordant and inappropriate ways.

A repertoire of approaches to the teaching of writing

I once had a phone call from an English consultant working with a large number of trainee teachers asking me for advice about the teaching of writing. It was in the early days of her work and she was hoping that, over the phone, I could tell her 'the way' we encouraged early careers teachers to teach writing. She was looking for

---

7. A write-up of the *It's Good to Talk* – 'Teaching a Novel at KS3' is available on EMC's website and includes examples of such writing.

just one single, fool-proof approach. I was flummoxed. There wasn't a single way, either of writing or of teaching writing that I could possibly hope to offer. There couldn't be. There are so many different kinds of writing and so many different approaches that identifying just one as 'the' approach was impossible. Our role as teachers is, at least in part, to select the most useful and appropriate strategy for the kind of writing, the students we're teaching, the stage they've reached, the purposes and context (for exam, for developing ideas, for self-expression, for a public audience), for the short-term goal or the longer term outcome. In a truly responsive classroom, the teacher is making judgements about what might work best, drawing on a rich repertoire of different strategies – not just to ring the changes but to adopt the best approach for the task at hand.

This repertoire is vast and is being added to daily, by excellent teachers finding new ways of working on students' writing. Here is a list of twenty things I might incorporate into my teaching – a repertoire of ideas that an experienced teacher might draw on in different circumstances, to help students become more confident, assured writers of a variety of kinds of texts. It draws on some of the overarching ideas explored above.[8]

1. Write creatively to think critically.

2. Plan collaboratively, with students in groups, or with you (for example, post-it note planning).

3. Read widely in the genres students are writing in. Bring in examples of excellent writing, not just in fiction but in other kinds of writing. Encourage students to read widely themselves.

4. Offer students statements, all of which could be true of a text, or valid in an argument, expressed in a good, lucid style appropriate to the kind of writing being done. Get the students to select and argue for ones they would use in a piece of writing.

5. Sometimes offer a choice of titles or tasks.

6. Sometimes offer tight constraints, almost like a 'game'.

7. Focus on the validity of ideas, not just the formal aspects of the writing.

8. Write alongside students.

9. Share the processes you're going through in writing (live writing/thinking aloud).

10. Offer plenty of opportunities for exploratory, developmental writing – not for a public audience or for assessment, so low risk.

11. Set up a class blog, where students write to each other, sharing their thinking about topics or texts under discussion. Make this a homework task, so that all students participate.

---

8. Some of these feature in EMC's publications *Spotlight on Literacy* and *English Allsorts* which both offer many different strategies for teaching writing.

12. Make room for drafting and re-drafting of work, even if this isn't required or possible in examination writing.

13. Encourage students to read their own work aloud, to hear how it sounds and notice places where it doesn't read well, sounds confused and could be improved.

14. Get students to identify their own criteria for success, according to what they're aiming for and the particular context for their writing.

15. Provide opportunities for students to read/hear each other's writing.

16. Provide opportunities for real audiences for student writing (to offer them the experience of writing for an actual reader).

17. Provide publishing opportunities – booklets, class magazines, school magazines and so on – to share and celebrate great writing.

18. Bring writers into school, to work with students on their writing and share their experience and expertise.

19. Help students to write clearly by getting them to express their arguments and ideas orally first: 'What I want to say is this…'

20. Ask students themselves what's proving most helpful, what advice/ techniques, activities are making the most difference to their writing, what else might make a difference.

6.2 Exploratory talk and writing – pupil progress at KS3

This blog focuses on writing emerging from exploratory group talk. It is based on a return visit to St Michael's School, where teachers worked on poetry with their Year 7s as part of the *It's Good to Talk* project in 2016 (see Chapter 5.5 on page 113). We looked at the writing students had done as a result of their discussions, and considered the most fruitful ways both to respond to it and to assess it. It has broader implications for assessment that are picked up again in Chapter 10.

I recently went back to St Michael's to talk to the teachers about their perceptions of the work we had done in the group work project – two lessons on poetry that I had set up followed by their own sequence of lessons on a wider range of poems. I had my own list of issues and questions to raise but was also very open to listening to what had been of most interest to them. The conversation ranged across all the big 'themes' that the project has been trying to address: everything from size and composition of groups, to level of challenge, to the role of the teacher in imparting knowledge and directing the groups, to the offer of choice to students and the difference this made to their pleasure in the work.

One of the most interesting areas of discussion – and a major concern for them – was the writing that the students did as a result of this unit with its strong focus on group work – and how this fitted into the school's own requirement for regular formal assessments of students' work, tied to a set of descriptors of pupil progress that is linked to GCSE. I'm sure that this is a live issue for many English departments, who are expected to measure student progress at regular intervals in relation to future attainment in external exams.

Richard Long, the Head of Department, had been getting his students to do lots of blogging in the course of the group work activities. This was informal writing but it seemed to me that its informality didn't mean that it wasn't – at its very best – analytical, reflective and highly academic in its own way. Take this example of (uncorrected) student work:

Hi sir, it's Shannon here.

This is my opinion for 'Women Work'.

The poem is from Maya Angelou and she is American and I like it because she expresses all of the jobs that a woman has to do and near to the end when it says 'let me rest tonight' implies that she wants a rest from all the jobs that needs to be done and when it about all the jobs, it can create an impression of breathlessness when the reader reads it. The last parts of the poem give of a calm mood because it gives you an image of her feeling more calm and relaxed than when she was doing all the chores.

Hope you like my opinion on the poem that I have chose.

P.S Maya Angelou has had seven published autobiographies, three book essays and seven books of poetry. I also thought of a way to describe poetry, poetry is like a cake there are three layers of detail and the last layer is the topic. If you make your poetry really 'tasty', then the reader will feel engaged into poetry that will want to read more.

What might one notice about this writing? The genuine audience of her teacher and peers? The informality of her address to him and them? The clear signalling that what she's going to offer is an honest opinion of her own? A sense that she has gone off to find out more about this poet and then suddenly, the joy and surprise of her throwing in something about what she understands poetry to be, that itself uses the figurative, metaphorical language of poetry. She's saying something that even many A Level students find hard to grasp, that 'topic' or 'content' is just one part of poetry – if you try to reduce it to a single layer, you diminish it. Here's Shannon really thinking for herself about the nature of poetry. Her understanding about poetry – aged 11 – is very impressive. But where's the learning objective, or progress descriptor that could capture this? It's so much simpler to ask whether she can infer or deduce, whether she can understand what a metaphor is, or identify assonance or a determiner and say yes or no, than to pin down this bigger, more conceptually complex understanding about how poetry differs from other forms. I find myself thinking, please don't knock this kind of knowledge out of her by the time she reaches GCSE and A Level. Of course, some might also mention the spelling mistakes and her predominant use of a sentence structure that proceeds largely through co-ordination rather than subordination. I would be concerned about this if she were not addressing these issues in other, more formal contexts as she develops, but here, in this blog, the focus is different. It's exploratory writing and the hard task for an 11-year old of thinking through difficult ideas. For me, the question of technical accuracy and writing style can be addressed in other ways, at other times.

Below is another rather more formal blog entry by Beatrix. We discussed this piece when I met the department and agreed that it was exceptionally good at getting to the heart of what's important in this poem. This is something that, as co-editor of *emagazine*, I'm sometimes depressed to find missing in student submissions and in many entries for our poetry and close reading competitions. Far too many GCSE and A Level students seem to have lost the ability to make a concise and sharply focused statement about the whole text, in favour of more diffuse and ill-judged micro-analysis that misses the obvious. What's great about Beatrix's writing is its big picture thinking – its ability to grasp some of the key ideas behind the poem, and explore them with some subtlety. In fact, the only places where it seems to falter are where she suddenly seems to feel obliged to 'prove' her knowledge of technical literary terms and her mastery of academic language. Her sentence about the poet using 'the determiner 'my' to indicate that the floor and window was hers' and her awkward use of the term 'enjambment' are the least convincing elements in her account of the poem. It is interesting that they come at the end, almost as if she has felt obliged to add them in, rather than seeing them as being central to her thinking.

In the poem, 'Children in Wartime', Thrilling uses sibilance to give a calm mood however, it is set in a dark, 'moated' place. The poem is in a child's perspective during wartime. The narrator seems confused especially when she says, 'people said it was a storm, but flak had not the right sound for rain' this implies that the child doesn't believe the people. The 'people' sound like adults who were trying to persuade and comfort the children and trick them into thinking that there are not in danger. Although, the children are doubting it.

Thrilling uses onomatopoeia to describe the damage the thunder could not do – 'thunder left such huge craters of silence'. Those craters could be craters from a bomb however, even though the explosion of the bomb was loud what it left behind was silence. Yet the children were told it was just a, 'giant playing bowls'

The narrator's window gives a dreamy mood as it is, 'spun with stars,' this is another use of sibilance. During wartime the window fell and the reflection of the sky ,'lay broken' on her floor. This could be the reflection of the sky on the broken glass because the window represented her hopes and dreams, the broken glass is a symbol of the child's broken dreams and hopes. The poet uses the determiner, 'my' to indicate that the floor and window was hers.

The poem is enjambment and at a quick pace. This gives the poem a fast, pressured mood. The whole poem is in one stanza to show that there is no pause.

Beatrix

Even in the briefest of writing that took place during the group activity itself – the note-taking in the very first group work lesson, there was evidence that students were – individually – pulling out some key idea about the poems they'd chosen and in the discussions, were able to 'think big' in these ways. They weren't getting bogged down too quickly in the detail. The reading of several poems in the lesson, and the quick reading and discussion that ensued, may have meant that they didn't always 'get' everything about the poems but this kind of reading was giving them the experience of reading fast, having a quick 'gut reaction', making overall judgements and thinking about what leapt out for them in terms of what they liked. The 11-year old student who read 'This poem is dangerous' and questioned whether it was really a poem or 'more like a public health advert' was fearless in getting to the heart of what makes that poem special, odd and different and even more stunningly perceptive in saying that perhaps the poet was right because poems really do get to your emotions! What might that student have written if they'd been given a formula for sentence openers, or told to make sure that they do PEE, or told that they must write about sound, imagery, form or anything else? Would this kind of perceptive, broader understanding emerge? That's a question for us all to think about.

This particular unit was positioned in the Year 7 curriculum just before one of the school's periodic, formal assessment points, which raised very interesting – and not always straightforward – issues. The teachers felt some degree of uncertainty about whether the formal assessment they'd devised – an essay on an unseen poem – would show the kind of progress they hoped for. In some cases, it really did.

The work of some students showed real confidence and maturity. Oliver's writing (below) also shows some clear footprints from the group work we did – the kind of open exploration we'd encouraged. He seems to have the confidence to explore ambiguity and wrestle with difficult ideas. He's unafraid to express a degree of uncertainty and then try to resolve it. His use of quotation is not cold 'after the fact' evidence but part of an ongoing tussle with the meaning of the text:

> At the beginning of stanza 4 Pastan confuses me when she says, 'while you grew smaller, more breakable,' but I read it over and over and noticed that she meant more breakable as in more delicate to the outside world and less protected from dangers. In stanza 4 Pastan also goes on saying 'pumping, pumping for your life, screaming with laughter.' This makes me think that the daughter has some doubts and doesn't want to leave her mother.

> In stanza 5 it is clear the girl is leaving when speaker says 'the hair flapping behind you like a hankerchief waving goodbye.' I know she is sad as hankerchiefs are somthing you could use to get rid of tears. This is a simile as her hair isn't literally a hankercheif but is like a hankercheif. This end stanza also makes me think the daughter has left without saying goodbye. At this point the speaker sounds emty and feels like they have nothing left without the memorys that were shared with her daughter.[1]

Some students' formal assessments raised more problems. One student, James, had really taken to heart our message in the group work that it was fine to be uncertain about meanings in poetry. He wrote his whole formal assessment with a repeated refrain of how confused he was about the poem he chose to write about. My initial reaction was to feel quite worried, along with the teacher, about the clear weaknesses in his writing. He'd really not done very well at all in his assessment. But when I came to look at the writing in more detail and reflect on it, I became aware of just how much this piece of assessed writing had to tell us about what the student knew, or didn't know. It was a brilliant insight into what needed to be done to move him on – to help him make progress in future. In particular, what emerged was his difficulty in reading beyond the literal, recognising fully that poems often work in metaphorical ways. Just because a poem is about a girl riding a bicycle, it doesn't mean that it can't also really be about something else. The boy's assessment piece gives a clear, transparent window onto his thinking and misunderstandings. And isn't this what progress tests should be about? Rather than fretting about whether he has met a target for 'achievement' at this given moment, in this one test, and therefore what he might achieve at GCSE, shouldn't we be using the test as a valuable tool to find out more, to allow us to respond in ways that ensure that progress is genuinely made? He has four and a half more years left to make the progress we're looking for and this helps us achieve that.

There were other questions around the issue of assessment. If blog style writing wasn't acceptable (despite the fact it demonstrated so much about what the pupils

---

1. You can read the whole of Oliver's piece of writing in the online version of this blog on the EMC website (www.englishandmedia.co.uk/blog). The work of another student, Naomi-Lee, is quoted on page 205 of this book.

had learned) then what else would be? I put to the department that perhaps the mismatch between the formal assessment and the work on the unit was worth unpicking. First, was it necessary (and helpful) in Year 7 for the formal assessment to have such a direct relationship to a GCSE task many years down the line – an unseen critical commentary? Might it not be better to make the assessment match the learning more closely, for instance to give students two or three poems and ask them 'Which of these poems would you advise your teacher to work on with next year's Year 7s and why?' This assessment would have involved formal writing, a close focus on a single poem (in relation to others) but might have been more closely allied to the work the students had been doing in the unit and the 'big picture' understandings they were developing about poetry. I wonder what James might have done with a task of this kind?

Second, I would come back to the question of whether or not there are some vitally important elements of textual study that need to be taught (and if possible assessed) that are missed if you're assessing progress in relation to narrowly defined progress descriptors. The progress descriptors that the department have used since the scrapping of NC levels have been taken from a set of descriptors designed by an external body for the new GCSE grades 1-9. 'Having an overview of a whole text' or 'confidently making choices and justifying them' or 'understanding the multiple meanings and complexity of poetry as a form' or 'being able to sustain an interpretation and develop it, or 'being able to talk about one poem in relation to others' didn't appear in these. However these broader skills and understandings do make the difference between high grade responses and lower ones at KS4 and beyond. There's a danger that in only assessing what can apparently be easily assessed, the bigger picture elements are perhaps not given sufficient value and attention. Going back to Oliver's piece, or that of Shannon and Beatrix (or Naomi-Lee, another student who wrote powerfully about poetry after these lessons), it is these bigger ideas that mark them out as being so exceptional. They don't actually use masses of subject terminology. But does that matter? Great writing at KS4, KS5 and even in university English is highly judicious in its use of terms, only using them when appropriate rather than for the sake of show. If the mark scheme on the assessment says 'Uses subject terminology effectively' and the teacher marking says as justification for a high mark, 'Lots of subject terminology mentioned', then that's the message students will be getting. Yet, as Beatrix's blog and Oliver and Naomi-Lee's assessment show, it's not subject terminology that makes the writing so good but the genuinely reflective ideas about what's 'going on' in the poem. Making your focus 'using subject terminology' might actually make your writing worse rather than better.

These are some thoughts emerging from the writing that came out of these lessons. They pose many questions, not least of all because of the pressure on English teachers to work within national and whole school assessment structures that don't always seem to be either well-timed or fully integrated into learning[2]. There is more on this in Chapter 10 on page 160. But these reflections also seem to

2. For more on this, see Chapter 10, page 160.

answer a few questions, particularly in highlighting the ways in which exploratory talk and writing can offer something genuinely helpful and developmental, encouraging exactly the kind of thoughtful, genuine responses to texts that we're ultimately hoping for. Our work also suggests that we may be getting KS3 progress assessment a bit wrong, if we tie it too closely to GCSE requirements and only see it as a measure of progress, a bit of data to worry about or reassure us about a pupil's position at a given moment, rather than viewing it as a window into what students are thinking and learning and what they (and we) need to do next.

6.3 Freedom versus constraint – EMC's 'Let Them Loose!'

In 2017, EMC launched a new initiative for National Writing Day, called 'Let Them Loose'. Its rationale was to give students the freedom to write in unconstrained ways, for pleasure and without the pressure of assessment. It had a fantastic take-up from schools. We collected a large sample of the writing that emerged and did an analysis of the work produced and shared on the day. Writing expert and educationalist, Simon Wrigley and playwright Sarah Hehir joined us to read the huge volume of writing that was sent to us and shared on Twitter. We gained important insights as a result. We have continued to offer this on National Writing Day each year. This blog, written soon after 2018's 'Let Them Loose!' draws on our experiences of it so far. I share what it seems to tells us about what, how and why young people write when given a degree of choice, as well as how we can help them to develop as writers.

> Students had a fab time writing whatever they wanted!
>
> Loved taking part in #EMCLetThemLoose2018!
>
> These pieces of work are fantastic!
>
> What an amazing batch of work!
>
> We've all enjoyed the freedom of telling our own stories.

Many schools tweeted on National Writing Day using #EMCLetThemLoose2018. Many other schools almost certainly took part, either without tweeting, or using the National Writing Day 'I feel free when…' prompt, or doing EMC's activities, alongside a range of other initiatives, such as working with a poet or children's author for the day. The event went far and wide. The British School in Panama tweeted about their involvement, and amazingly, the fresh out of the egg, newly-hatched writers of Banks Lane Infants shared some of their writing! One lucky class were let loose in Shakespeare's own classroom in Stratford-upon-Avon.

Like last year, we watched the unfolding stories of the day, the tweets of student writing, the photographs that were shared, the accounts of what had happened, with a sense of wonderment and joy, that was clearly matched by that of the teachers who decided to offer it to their classes. The students took to it like ducks to water. There seemed to be little need to persuade them to write and the chance to pick a prompt that they were drawn to, or an image that interested them, or just to determine for themselves what they wanted to write about, was a spark for the most incredible range of writing. There was everything from science fiction, to life writing, poems, songs and raps, to graphic novels, film reviews, rants, playscripts, short stories, descriptions, and powerful, urgent comment pieces on issues that students wanted to speak out about. There were some bits of writing that defied categorisation. Some students wrote in home languages, some also wrote translations to go with this, sharing with classmates their writing in another language, possibly for the first time.

The writing happened in lots of different places and in different formats – in playgrounds, on the grass, at desks, on the classroom floor, on paper, word processed, on sugar paper, posted up on fences in the playground. The ICT department at one school was roped in and students wrote in html. In the same school, all the teachers wrote an emailed line or two of poetry that formed a whole staff poem. One member of staff in a third school was given a visual prompt for writing by a student and took up the challenge with gusto, writing alongside his students and sharing his work in the same document.

Reading the pieces gave us a fantastic insight into this cohort of students – what matters to them, what literary, cultural and linguistic styles they are drawn to and want to test out for themselves, what textual influences they are making use of and what they want to use writing to do, if given the freedom to do it in ways they choose. Some actually used the act of writing to question whether they were themselves writers and what it meant to be a writer, in one case being replied to by a published author assuring him that he was, indeed, a writer. Others revealed private hurts and wounds, using their writing as a way of exploring that grief and sharing it with classmates, sometimes for the first time. Others revelled in the chance to be silly, witty, satirical, clever, working both outside of genres or within genres that they were clearly well versed in – science fiction, fantasy, Gothic horror. One thing they were not doing was writing for assessment, with a possible examiner in mind. They were not trying to impress someone else or feeling under pressure to perform. That was very obvious from much of the writing. The students were pleasing themselves, writing for themselves or for each other. In amongst it all, there was some brilliant writing which had very little 'peacocking' of linguistic ability and no ticking off of required elements – no forced fronted adverbials, no showy vocabulary, just a strong, authentic voice. Noticeable was the number of students whose language was genuinely fresh and original, for instance the description of Grenfell Tower that never mentions it by name but describes 'it' as 'a burnt match box in the sky'. A particular favourite of mine – and of others on Twitter – was the piece by Jack, from Hellesdon High, who brilliantly sustained a metaphor of getting a car started to describe getting going on his own writing, with lovely little visual images of spark plugs, gear boxes, wrenches, warning lights, timing belts and more, peppering the lines (Figure 1). (Eat your heart out Brian Bilston[1]!)

Equally, there were some wonderful pieces that took as their starting-point a snippet of poetry offered in the EMC prompts. 'Let us go then you and I' was beautifully handled as a repeated refrain by a student at Cardinal Pole School and the Driffield student who chose the snippet 'Think of a sheep/knitting a sweater' used it to create a superb, witty fantasy story of goblins and centaurs, full of laugh out loud lines.

---

1. Brian Bilston writes clever, topical poems online, sending them out over the internet on Twitter. *You Took the Last Bus Home* (Nov 2017) is a collection of some of these.

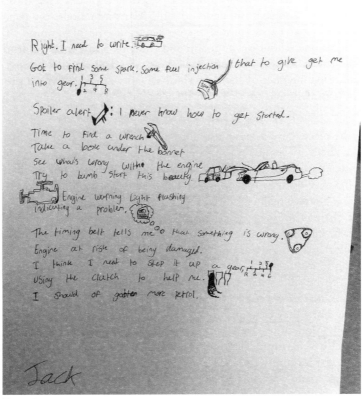

Right. I need to write.

Got to find some spark, some fuel injection that to give get me into gear.

Spoiler alert: I never know how to get started.

Time to find a wrench
Take a look under the bonnet
See what's wrong with the engine
Try to bump start this beauty.

Engine warning light flashing
indicating a problem.

The timing belt tells me that something is wrong.
Engine at risk of being damaged.
I think I need to step it up a gear,
using the clutch to help me.
I should of gotten more petrol.

Jack

Figure 1

The writing was obviously great for the students but also very revealing to us (and no doubt the teachers too), in what it could tell us about them. When left to their own devices would they plump for easy options, safe bets, undemanding angles, the least challenging tasks? Would they write as little as possible? Would they be stumped and have nothing to say. No. Definitely not. They wrote loads, thought hard, rose to the challenge. It's a salutary reminder that children aren't just empty vessels to be filled. They don't have blank cultural or intellectual lives. They aren't to be viewed through a lens that sees them in terms of deficits. There were many instances of children revealing hidden depths, like the girl who let it be known to her teacher that she had 72 poems that she had written in the 'Notes' of her mobile phone. 'Let Them Loose!' was the first time that she had opened up to her teacher about these.[2]

References for Chapter 6

References for Chapters 6 and 7 combined can be found on page 146.

---

2. Since writing this blog, EMC has continued to offer free writing activities on National Writing Day and has built on the momentum by publishing a student workbook called *Just Write*. Some schools are now using this as the basis for regular free writing, both in class and for homework.

7. The Creative and the Critical

The two pieces that follow could have fitted equally well into the chapters on writing or on teaching poetry, the novel or other aspects of literary study. I've talked about reading as a writer and writing as a reader in some other chapters[1] but here I bring it into the spotlight, because of its significance for me and other colleagues at EMC. The interrelationship between reading and writing seems to me to be of huge importance in the teaching of both. Students trying to write well need to read a great deal. They pick up understandings at every level – from sentence structures and vocabulary to awareness of style and rhetoric, generic understandings, awareness of conventions, traditions, audiences and purposes – that they can then draw on as they develop as writers. Equally, writing can offer students insight into, and understanding of, the myriad decisions and choices made by writers of texts they are reading. Adapting a text, or writing in the style of a writer, or doing your own piece of writing on the same topic, is a valuable critical activity in its own right. This is acknowledged and understood by writers and critics but also in the universities where creative criticality is increasingly regarded as a valuable part of the discipline and where academics have been reminding us of it as a very long tradition, stretching back to the educational practices of rhetoricians of the sixteenth century.

7.1 Reading as a writer, writing as a reader

Every creative act begins as imitation and ends as invention

Octavio Paz

At the NATE conference in 2015, EMC ran a couple of workshops. The one I led with Lucy Webster, was about 'Reading as a Writer, Writing as a Reader', an idea that is very dear to our hearts. That simple pair of phrases has been used by writers and others in recent years to describe the process by which reading widely and deeply informs your writing, while trying to write yourself informs and enriches your response and ability to be analytical about texts. Two sides of a very precious coin.

In the workshop I mentioned a couple of writers who very neatly make the point about the impact of reading on writing. Stephen King is famously quoted as saying:

If you want to be a writer, you must do two things above all others: read a lot and write a lot.

and

If you don't have the time to read, you don't have the time (or the tools) to write.

And in a more developed way, the wonderfully aptly named writer Francine Prose says in her book *Reading Like a Writer*:

In the ongoing process of becoming a writer, I read and re-read the authors

---

1. See, in particular, 'Creating as well as thinking in group work' on page 108.

I most loved. I read for pleasure, first, but also more analytically, conscious of style, of diction, of how sentences were formed and information was being conveyed, how the writer was structuring a plot, creating characters, employing detail and dialogue. And as I wrote, I discovered that writing, like reading, was done one word at a time, one punctuation mark at a time. It required what a friend calls 'putting every word on trial for its life'.

A favourite poet of mine, Derek Walcott, describes his own process of learning to write poetry as being like an apprenticeship, where you learn the tools of the trade by apprenticing yourself to the writers you admire, following their techniques and trying them out for yourself till you gradually find your own voice. He talks of starting off by imitating the exact forms of poems he admired, superimposing his own ideas on those structures.[2]

These are published writers speaking and, obviously, in schools we're dealing with children, not all of whom will become novelists or poets! However, the basic idea that reading and writing are not separate things still holds true, at whatever age or stage. At a very basic level, if you were asked to write a sentence, without ever having read a sentence, how would you know what's expected? Or a haiku, without having read many haikus? If your teacher tells you to write the opening of a crime story but you've never read one, or even only one, how do you know what the conventions are and what choices are available to you? If you've just read Agatha Christie and nothing else, you may have a rather limited sense of what's possible. Likewise, if you're a KS3 or KS4 student and you've only ever read one first person narrative and that happens to be *The Curious Incident of the Dog in the Night-time*, would you realise that, in your own autobiographical piece, or short story, you could use a retrospective adult voice, as in *Jane Eyre*, or *To Kill a Mockingbird*, or an angsty, funny, teenage voice, as in *Catcher in the Rye*? Offering a few openings of different kinds would extend your reading experience to show you what else you could do as a writer.

Flip the reading/writing coin and perhaps if you had a go at imitating the writing in your set text, or writing back to or around it, you might discover more about it. Here's a bit of writing around the opening of *Great Expectations*, for instance, a really quick, playful little experiment:

> *My father's name being Bleiman and my first name being Barbara, the pleasant alliterative ring of the two words did little to assuage my feeling that the name was both bland and undistinguished,'*

followed by

> *Ours was a different country, a world away, thousands of miles from the London where we finally planted our shaky, immigrant feet. My first, intensely vivid memory seems to have been gained at a moment when I lay in my bed, in a house in Cape Town, watching the shadows of the fig tree swaying gloomily on my bedroom wall.*

2. In an interview with Edward Hirsh in 1977 Walcott said: 'You know that you just ravage and cannibalise everything as a young poet: you have a very voracious appetite for literature. The whole course of imitations and adaptations is simply a method of apprenticeship.'

As I do this, I discover more about that formal, retrospective voice of Pip, the immediate scene-setting, the sense of a confessional relationship with the reader, in which the reader is being let in on the deepest thoughts and feelings of the narrator about his childhood and the sense of emotional uncertainty he has, of piecing together knowledge about himself and his origins.

One key element of both reading as a writer and writing as a reader is the idea that small experiments, tests, trying things out, having a go, being playful, taking little unrisky risks, is extremely valuable, regardless of the 'success' of the end product. The end product of these little experiments is not to produce a great piece of writing (though it's amazing how work like this can spawn great stuff, as was evidenced by the work read aloud by the teachers at the NATE conference). But that's not the main point. Something that doesn't work may still teach you a lot about the text you're reading or the process of writing. My 'mock' Dickens above, is no great piece of writing! In any other context than this blog, I'd be embarrassed to share it with others. But it did teach me something about the text. I 'put every word on trial for its life' as I was writing, in the sense of weighing each word for its Dickensian appropriateness. It felt like time well spent.

And this is one aspect of this kind of work that perhaps has lessons for us in all the work we do with pupils, that 'success' isn't always about measuring how good a piece of work is. There are times and places where end-products are very important – terminal exams, finished pieces for non-exam assessment, university dissertations, job applications, writing within one's job after leaving school, publishing a novel or collection of poetry or short stories. However, in the work of the classroom, there must be time to try out, experiment and learn, where the question of whether the final product is brilliant or not is not especially relevant. Pupils need to know that. If pupils have a go at writing three different first person openings to get a feel for how they work and how different they are, none may be a brilliant opening. But they may have discovered a lot more about the choices open to them and to other writers, including the one they are studying. And if that was the point of the activity, then that's fine. The learning is what counts.

7.2 Learning how to write critically by writing creatively

In eighteen years of editing *emagazine*, alongside my colleague Lucy Webster, we have run several competitions for students. These have given us unique access to writing by sixth formers from across the UK (and beyond), from schools of every type, studying for all specifications of A Level, as well as IB and Pre-U. This has been a privilege but also it has given us an unparalleled window into the state of writing across the nation at this level. Other blogs focus on what's happening to the use of terminology, or the ability of students to engage in the practices of close reading. This one draws on our experience of setting the challenge either to write critically or, alternatively, to write creatively and then apply critical insights both into one's own response and the original text. The blog explores the idea that creative writing can be a powerful critical tool and means of responding to literary texts and can lead to an equally good, if not better, critical response.

Lessons from the *emagazine*/Forward Student Critics' Competition

It seems like a paradox. Critical writing is analytical, reflective, structured in terms of argument and evidence, planned, rule-bound, thought-through, high stakes, the main business of examinations. Creative writing is spontaneous, often semiconscious or even at times unconscious, free of rules, personal, idiosyncratic, subject to the writer's flair or talent, worked on over time, sometimes not shared with anyone else, often not highly prized (except if you're entering for the Booker or the Forward Prize, or appear on the shelves of Waterstones), rarely examined as part of a literature course.

Of course, this characterisation is full of false dichotomies and stereotypes. For instance, if you stop to think, even for a moment, you realise that creative writing follows lots of rules – the conventions of genre, the expectations of audience – while critical writing of the best sort (hopefully much of what we publish in *emagazine*) has a strong, personal voice, breaks rules in order to bring ideas to life and is highly creative. But nevertheless, they are often perceived as distinct aspects of English as a subject, and are taught in isolation from each other.

There is a long history, however, strongly supported by EMC over the years, of bringing the two together, in recognition of the fact that not only are the boundaries blurred but also the two complement each other. Our broader CPD courses and publications on texts and critical analysis are always full of creative activities on literary texts. One aspect of our premise is that teaching about texts helps you to write – an idea at the heart of all Creative Writing courses at university level, and confirmed by countless writers.

But the reverse is also true. Writing yourself helps you to understand better what other writers do. This might be discovering more about how a choice of narrative voice or point of view works, or learning more about a literary idea like symbolism, or it might be about discovering how a particular poem, or set novel, is using, adapting or subverting a style or convention, making it unique and special.

Creative writing to develop critical analysis does not have to be full-blown, time-consuming, all-singing-and-dancing, nor, if it's carefully thought through in terms of purpose, need it be a distraction from 'the real business' of learning to write critical essays. It can consist of brief experiments, little playful try-outs – or what we call, on our courses and in publications, 'micro-interventions', where some small aspect of style and language is changed, to transform the text and see what the impact has been. So, for instance, one might try omitting all the adjectives and adverbs from a particularly rich passage from *The Great Gatsby*, to reflect on what the impact is, and by extension, what their effect was in the original. (Fitzgerald's lush, over-abundant prose, juxtaposing romantic and modernist imagery, is created in large part through the use of adjectives and adverbs.) At GCSE, one could change the narrative voice at a key moment in *A Christmas Carol*, to move either into free indirect style, or away from it, to explore how Dickens directs our sympathies through subtle shifts in the third-person voice. Ten or fifteen minutes on this kind of activity can pay off in terms of students getting under the skin of the writer's craft. 'We haven't got time for nice things like that,' isn't an argument if 'nice things like that' actually teach ideas about the writer's craft really well.

Reflecting on what's been learned by doing creative writing around texts is vital. It's fun to try writing yourself, or make changes to a text, and, of course, it has its own independent value but in the end, as part of critical analysis, the key point is to understand what you've learned about the text under scrutiny.

One example

Here's an example of me testing this out for myself. I did it alongside teachers on a recent course, using a short extract from *Jane Eyre*.

The extract from *Jane Eyre*

'What dog is this?'

'He came with his master.'

'With whom?'

'With master – Mr Rochester – he is just arrived.'

'Indeed! and is Mrs Fairfax with him?'

'Yes, and Miss Adele; they are in the dining room, and John is gone for a surgeon: for master has had an accident; his horse fell and his ankle is sprained.'

'Did the horse fall in Hay Lane?'

'Yes, coming down-hill; it slipped on some ice.'

'Ah! Bring me a candle, will you, Leah?'

Leah brought it; she entered, followed by Mrs Fairfax, who repeated the news; adding that Mr Carter the surgeon was come, and was now with Mr Rochester: then she hurried out to give orders about tea, and I went upstairs to take off my things.

My microintervention – changing dialogue to narrative voice:

I asked Leah about the dog and whose it was. She was slow to respond, infuriatingly so, as I had already recognised the dog and was in a state of high anxiety, wondering how on earth its owner had ended up in the house. Finally, she told me that it was Mr Rochester and that he had had an accident. Of course, I knew that it was the man I had helped but still I couldn't refrain from confirming that it was definitely him, and then discovered to my shock that it was none other than my master, the owner of the house.

Exploratory thoughts on my creative writing experiment

I've discovered that the use of dialogue only leads to the absence of any exposition of Jane's feelings. This creates an extra frisson of anxious excitement. I was fully aware of Jane's shocked discovery of who Rochester was, though Leah wasn't, and of how she carefully disguises her agitation. The lack of description of her emotions paradoxically makes her likely inner turmoil all the more heightened. We are also with her in the moment of discovery, rather than hearing about it retrospectively, as in my example.

My critical writing as a result of reflecting on the creative writing experiment

Through the use of dialogue, Brontë heightens the moment of Jane's discovery that the man she helped in Hay Lane is in fact Mr Rochester. The lack of narrative explanation first has the effect of the events unfolding for us as they do for Jane, in the moment, and without any retrospective reflection. This makes it more immediate and dramatic. At the same time, it means that Jane's feelings are withheld from the reader. All we have is the words she uses to Leah, with no explanatory speech tags, indicating her reactions. She is forced to keep the exchange entirely emotionless, yet as readers, we read into this her shocked realisation and recognise that this is a highly charged and significant moment. Her factual account of going up to her room, at the end, suggests her need to recover from her agitation, without revealing this to Leah or anyone else in the household.

The whole process took about twenty to twenty-five minutes. (Obviously for students this might be a little longer.) Like me, the teachers who try this kind of approach on our courses tell us that it gives them real insight into the text and would be very beneficial in terms of students' ability to write about passage-based questions in exams, and in teaching them about how literary texts work.

The evidence? Brilliant critical writing at GCSE and A Level

As I'm suggesting, we have long been convinced of the value of these kinds of approaches to critical writing. But something happened recently to absolutely confirm this for us: the Forward/*emagazine* Student Critics' Competition, which in this its first year had three entry groups (14-16, 16-19 and teachers) and two categories (Critical and Creative-Critical). Lucy Webster and I, as editors of *emagazine*, did the initial read-through of entries, before passing the shortlist on to Sarah Howe, a poet/critic whose own view of reading and writing as complementary acts is very much in line with our own thinking. The quality of entries, in both the 14-16 and 16-19 age groups was exceptionally good in both categories. But what was particularly startling was the extraordinarily high standard of the creative writing and the critical commentaries that went with it. The students who chose this option not only commented with critical acuity about their own writing but also wrote brilliantly about the poem that stimulated their own work. Both at 14-16 and 16-19, it was very clear that there was a depth of insight, freshness of response, clarity of thought and personal, critical voice that were, at times, quite remarkable. These GCSE and A Level students were doing in their critical observations, exactly what the GCSE and A Level Literature Examiners' Reports say they would like from students – fresh observations, talking about what's significant, writing concisely and with relevance, thinking independently, showing depth of knowledge of the text.

Not only at GCSE and A Level, but long before that, at KS3 (and well after, at university level), critical analysis can be enriched by students writing themselves. As the Forward/*emagazine* winners show, it gives them a lot to say about texts, and the kinds of things they have to say are grounded in a strong sense of how writing works and genuine ideas about what writers are up to. It's not a lovely little optional extra, but one of the strongest weapons in our armoury, a really powerful way of teaching critical analysis.[1]

From the Forward/*emagazine* Student Creative Critics Competition

Ravinthiran writes about watching both the present and the past through observing a loved-one: an ambiguous 'you'. The piece is titled 'Dubrovnik', but is as much about the echoes of Sri Lanka later in the poem, described in beautifully evocative images and subtle rhymes ('bitten', 'smitten') that tie the poem together. I loved the idea of the observer that begins 'Dubrovnik', and so have tried to respond to this by creating my own, who watches her mother swimming and, much like that of Ravinthiran's, thinks of a past and future.

In Ravinthiran's poem, there is a strong sense of two separate places, with the act of swimming as a bridge between them. I decided to write about multiple places that intertwine as a result, some more domestic and maternal – our bath at home, and ultimately the womb, all told through the inherited family memories Ravinthiran also writes of. I really liked the significantly implied female presence in Ravinthiran's poem – he refers to two mothers – which I wanted to draw on myself, applying this to my own personal history of my mother and grandmother. I chose the same setting of Ravinthiran's poem – the sea – which seemed apt, as a kind of mother to so many other living things.

'Dubrovnik' above all touched me for its beautiful and deceptively simple presentation of time passing. The poem jumps from the present to a 'later' to the earlier memory of Sri Lanka, and even the possibility of being 'pulled in and under and lost forever.' Both mothers at the end of 'Dubrovnik' act differently as the antitheses of each other – but neither seems less loving. Like my own mother and grandmother in this poem, two very different kinds of mothers, this

---

1. Since writing this blog, we now only offer one category in the Forward/*emagazine* Competition – the Creative-Critical – in recognition of the quality of writing emerging and as a low-risk way of demonstrating to teachers the value of integrating this approach to critical writing into their core work.

poem aims to recreate Ravinthiran's sense of tenderness in portraying loved-ones and motherhood.

Lucy Thynne reflects on her poem and the poem that inspired it, 'Dubrovnik' by Vidyan Ravinthiran

References for Chapters 6 and 7

Bullock, A. 1975. *A Language for Life*. London: HMSO.

AQA. June 2017, 2018, 2019. *GCSE English Language and English Literature Examiners' Reports*.

Bilston, B. 2017. *You Took the Last Bus Home*. (Unbound format).

Fisher, R., Jones, S., Larkin, S. and Myhill, D. 2012. *Using Talk to Support Writing*. London: Sage Publications.

Hirsch, E. 1977. 'An interview with Derek Walcott'. In ed. Baer. W. 1996. *Conversations with Derek Walcott*. University Press of Mississippi Jackson.

King, S. 2012. *On Writing: A Memoir of the Craft*. London: Hodder Paperbacks.

Langer, J. 2010 [2nd Edition]. *Envisioning Literature: Literary Understanding and Literature Instruction*. New York. Teachers' College Press.

National Writing Project (USA) https://www.nwp.org/

Prose, F. 2012 [2006]. *Reading Like a Writer: A Guide for Those Who Love Books and For Those Who Want to Write Them*. London: Union Books.

QMUL. Thinking Writing website http://www.thinkingwriting.qmul.ac.uk/thinking

Smith, J. and S. Wrigley. 2015. *Introducing Teachers' Writing Groups*. Abingdon: Routledge.

Wray, D. and Lewis, M. 1988. *Writing Across the Curriculum – Frames to Support Learning and Writing Frames: Scaffolding Children's Non-fiction Writing in a Range of Genres*. Reading: University of Reading.

Wray, D. 1996. *Writing Frames: Scaffolding Children's Non-fiction Writing in a Range of Genres*. Reading: University of Reading.

Wray, D. 2001. 'Developing factual writing: an approach through scaffolding'. Paper delivered to the European Reading Conference (Dublin, Ireland, July 1-4, 2001). Available at https://files.eric.ed.gov/fulltext/ED454534.pdf

Wolsey, T.D., Lapp, D. and Fisher, D. 2012. 'Students' and teachers' perceptions: an inquiry into academic writing'. In *Journal of Adolescent and Adult Literacy* Vol 55 Issue 8.

Further reading on creative critical work

At university-level, there is a long tradition of creative-critical work and a recognition of its value:

Knights, B. and C. Thurgar-Dawson. 2006. *Active Reading: Transformative Writing in Literary Studies*. London: Bloomsbury (Continuum Literary Studies).

Maxwell, C. 2010. 'Teaching nineteenth-century aesthetic prose: a writing-intensive course'. In *Arts and Humanities in Higher Education* 9 (2).

Pope, R. 1994. *Textual Intervention: Critical and Creative Strategies for Literary Studies*. Abingdon: Routledge.

Writers on reading literary texts from a writer's perspective

Herbert, W.N. (ed.) *Strong Words: Modern Poets on Modern Poetry* ed. W.N. Herbert Bloodaxe.

Howe, S. 'Prac Crit'. http://www.praccrit.com/. A website which brings together critical discussion of poems with interviews with the poets, exploring ideas and processes in their writing.

McCallum, M. 2012. *Creativity and Learning in Secondary English: Teaching for a Creative Classroom*. Abingdon: Routledge.

Padel, R. 2004. *52 Ways of Looking at a Poem*. London: Vintage.

Prose, F. 2012 [2006]. *Reading Like a Writer: A Guide for Those Who Love Books and For Those Who Want to Write Them*. London: Union Books.

8. Teaching Poetry

This is a new piece that draws on blogs about poetry and the many publications I have written for EMC, from *The Poetry Pack* on. Other sections of this book also deal with poetry – in discussions of our project *It's Good to Talk* and 'Writing as a Reader, Reading as a Writer'. While these are referred to briefly, the emphasis here is more on poetry itself – the importance and value of both reading and writing poetry in the English curriculum, what it should consist of and how it should be taught.

EMC has published several resources for poetry, of which the latest is *KS3 Poetry Plus* (2018). A quick backwards look offers a reminder of the approaches that have characterised our classroom work on poetry for the past 40 years. From the very earliest work in the 1970s, using DARTS[1] (with cloze procedures, jumbled poems, sequencing activities, titles left off, fragments, before, during and after reading activities), our approach has encouraged students to get their hands dirty – to plunge into anthologies, make choices about which poems to explore, mess with poems, experiment with them, re-write them, interrogate them and, above all, treat them as something very different from prose. To read a poem, we believe, is to appreciate its illusiveness and allusiveness, to withhold cold critical analysis and the yearning for certainty for long enough to allow complexity, ambiguity, sound, musicality, verbal and visual patterning to do their sub-, or semi-conscious work on our thoughts and feelings.

It's hard to explain to pupils what a poem is and what makes it special. In some ways, experience has to do some of that work for you. 'I like this', 'I love that', 'I'm not sure what on earth that's about', 'I wonder why the poet did this or that' can take you quite a long way with many poems though. It starts a conversation that, like a snowball rolled through thick snow, gets bigger as it goes. A blog, inspired by work with Richard Long's Year 7s at St Michael's High Wycombe, as well as all the other work on poetry in EMC's group work project (both explored in Chapter 5), show how starting with some enjoyable experiences, and then building up understandings of the genre through metacognitive conversations begins to teach students the terms of engagement. And it's the terms of engagement, rather than the literary terms, that we really need to pay attention to when children are beginning to study poetry. This means helping students to understand the ways in which readers read poems, why they read them, what there is to get out of them and how they differ from other kinds of texts. Literary terms are important, of course, but they can come relatively easily along the way, as part of explaining and exploring what's observed and finding the precise language with which to express this. If it's just pinning terms to features, however, then it is a thin gruel of knowledge, compared with the more complex, subtle, rich and intermingled

---

1. Directed Activities Related to Texts (DARTs) came out of the *Effective Use of Reading Project* (Lunzer and Gardner, 1979). Bob Moy and others working at EMC in the 1970s developed many DARTs activities that came to figure prominently in our publications.

flavours that come from examining ideas and feelings and discovering how they are conveyed through linguistic and literary choices.

Before we started working on poetry with his class, Richard Long asked his students what they thought about poetry. He asked for their honest responses and an account of their experiences in primary school or before. The answers were interestingly (and unsurprisingly) eclectic and seemed to depend very much on how they'd been taught in primary school – everything from 'I've never read a poem' to 'I write poems in my head almost every day', from 'I find poetry confusing and boring' to 'it's my favourite part of English'. Some expressed a bewilderment – a kind of 'I don't get it' response – that we would all recognise, I'm sure, as being the view of poetry of many students.

The 'I don't get it' response can, itself, be the start of a fruitful conversation about what poetry is. Poetry is language 'in orbit' (as Seamus Heaney said). It's 'language made strange'. The study of poetry needs to take this into account, embracing the defamiliarisation involved in reading the 'odd' language of poetry as a way into close linguistic exploration and analysis. This allows students to become explicitly aware of implicit understandings and expectations of different forms of speech and writing. Studying lots of poetry in this way provides an ideal opportunity for exploratory questioning about language, that can teach students about language itself.

Geoff Fox and Peter Benton, two titans of poetry education, wrote about the specialness of poetry and how teaching needed to reflect that in 1985 in *Teaching Literature 9-14* (Oxford University Press)

> Our approach to a poem must be less continuously linear than to a story. The very presentation signals this. Instead of the eye being channelled along regular lines of print, themselves justified left and right and framed in predictable margins, it is suddenly invited into a more or less varied activity where the shape of the text on the page assumes a special significance. The linearity of prose presentation reflects the importance of the passage of time in fiction. Basically, the reader of a story wants to know what will happen next and how it will end. By contrast, the infinite variety of ways in which poems are presented indicates different emphases where the sense of space is often part of the reader's response. The reader of a poem wants to move about within it, discovering what it means to him and enjoying the way it makes that meaning. [...]
>
> There is a riddling quality to poems, something in the way words are used and laid out on the page, as if the words are saying [...] 'we're special; we're the chosen few.' The problems of much current methodology is that far too often we imply that poems are riddles with single solutions, which we, the teachers, happen to know, rather than objects crafted in the medium of riddling word-play, yielding a range of meanings.

Poets themselves are constantly reminding us how different poetry is from other kinds of writing – how much more there is to it than a description of themes or content, a paraphrase or attempt to 'explain' the meaning. T.S. Eliot famously wrote in *The Use of Poetry and the Use of Criticism*:

> The chief use of the 'meaning' of a poem [...] may be [...] to satisfy the habit of the reader, to keep his mind diverted and quiet, while the poem does its work upon him; much as the imaginary burglar is always provided with a bit of nice meat for the house-dog.

More recently, Mark Yakich, poet, professor of Creative Writing and author of *Poetry: A Survivor's Guide* (2016) wrote:

> A poem cannot be paraphrased. In fact, a poem's greatest potential lies in the opposite of paraphrase: ambiguity. [...]
>
> A poem has no hidden meaning, only 'meanings' you've not yet realised are right in front of you. [...]
>
> A poem can feel like a locked safe in which the combination is hidden inside. It's okay if you don't understand a poem. Sometimes it takes dozens of readings to come to the slightest understanding. And sometimes understanding never comes.

Studying poetry with this awareness in mind is a very different experience to starting out looking for the right answer and expecting it to be 'given' to you precisely and clearly by your teacher. If you're looking only for 'the' meaning in a poem, it wouldn't be very surprising if you ended up not seeing the point of poems and failing to recognise the pleasures they can bring. You'd be chewing on the piece of meat, while the real action is happening elsewhere, unnoticed by you.

Mistaking the study of poetry for paraphrase is very unhelpful but equally so is making the study of poetry an exercise in feature labelling. Yet the richer experience that comes from a more open-ended, investigative approach takes longer and is not very amenable to the kind of short termism that schools often expect of teachers and students these days. It involves asking questions, developing a sense of what is possible across the whole genre, absorbing insights by many encounters with a variety of poems. It's deeply and unavoidably intertextual. You know what a ballad or a sonnet is and its parameters by reading several. If a poet stretches or subverts conventions, you only know that by familiarity with several examples. It's much easier to prove that a student has learnt what a simile is and how to 'spot' one than it is to teach them to 'appreciate' what's special about the way a poet uses similes in a poem, or why the poet has chosen a simile rather than a metaphor, or the characteristic use by that poet of similes. But the former task is narrower, less ambitious, and, in the end, far less interesting or likely to get students to write well about poetry, whether at KS3 or GCSE or beyond. It risks students getting permanently lost in a maze of detail, rather than having an overview, or map, which allows them to use detail at the service of bigger ideas. Long termism means holding your nerve and asking students to observe, think, respond, make judgements, play with possibilities, come up with authentic and significant ideas, which are then explored and exemplified through the details of poetic crafting.

Peter Barry, in his excellent article for *The Use of English*, based on a lecture given at an English Association conference at the Senate House, London, on 5th October 2013, argues strongly against the fixation on individual words in the study of poetry.

Often in essays or seminars, students tell us about a couple of words or phrases taken from a poem. For instance they detect and discuss assonance and alliteration, topics which all my life I have found tedious. The best response is 'Tell me something about the whole poem, not just about parts of it.' But of the naming of parts in poetry criticism there seems to be no end. It's a form of 'critical blazoning', akin in spirit to those Renaissance poetic 'blazons' which catalogued the parts of a woman's person without ever saying anything much about the person. So students blazon away, with talk of lexical sets, metrical patterns, consonantal rhymes, and so on, all of these having been snipped out from the living form of the poem.

He is writing about his experience with university-level students but it seems to me to be highly relevant to our own experiences with students at school. We have to start to recognise – as the Awarding Body Examiners' Reports themselves do – that 'snipping out' what's in a poem and 'critical blazoning' are neither a good way to teach poetry, nor a good way to prepare students to write well about poetry in exams. Interestingly, this was proved when Richard Long's Year 7s came to write about an unseen poem, having been encouraged to think in bigger, more authentic and exploratory ways. They had something important to say about the poem – a broad understanding or insight into what the poem was about, what it was trying to say or make us feel, and how it went about doing that, as well as expressing strongly their own response to it. Whenever I show examples of these unseen responses to teachers, there are always cries of 'I wish my Year 10s or 11s could write like that!', which is telling.

So far, I have written about poetry reading and critical response. But what of poetry *writing*? Elsewhere in this book I have made a strong case for writing being an essential part of critical response (see Chapter 7 'The Critical and the Creative'). I won't repeat that here; however, poetry writing for its own sake is also a hugely important element in English classrooms that has often, sadly, been neglected in recent years. One reason for this may be that teachers themselves sometimes feel unconfident about teaching it and also about assessing it. Sue Dymoke's book *Drafting and Assessing Poetry* is a thoroughly researched text, drawing on classroom experiences and the work of writers to show how drafting can work in classroom contexts and exploding the myth that poetry cannot be assessed.

Many schools have found it very helpful to bring poets into their classrooms to work with students, or to have longer residencies to support the writing of poetry. These often have wider impacts, not just on students' writing of poetry but also on their whole educational experience. Peter Kahn, a Chicago-based poet who lived and worked in London schools for many years, came to EMC in 2019 with three of his ex-students, all national US Youth Poet Laureates. They spoke movingly about how poetry writing had opened their eyes to poetry more generally and turned around their attitudes to school. All three had gone on into higher education and were now working in academic settings and schools. Kahn worked with UK poet Raymond Antrobus (winner of the 2019 Folio Prize for his first collection, *The Perseverance*). Antrobus worked for several years as a spoken word educator at Cardinal Pole School in Hackney and recently talked to hundreds of A Level students at an *emagazine* conference on poetry. The work of these poet educators not only provides inspiration for young people to see themselves as potential writers of poetry but also provides an 'apprenticeship' into the form from those with knowledge and expertise in the form, its practices and processes.

One of the most powerful examples of this is the work of Kate Clanchy, poet, teacher and advocate for poetry writing in schools. Her book *Some Kids I Taught and What They Taught Me* offers as strong a case for poetry writing in schools as any I have read. Teaching in a multicultural comprehensive school in Oxford, she has allowed numerous students – often migrants and refugees – not only to give expression to their painful and complex experiences but also to find a poetic voice of immense power and quality, winning critical acclaim and national competitions. Their lives have been changed and their educational experiences enriched by poetry. One chapter in her book, called 'About Teaching English', draws out some of the lessons about how to teach poetry from an account of how a particular student wrote an exceptionally clever poem in response to another poem she shared with the group. She says:

> I could not have hoped for a more powerful or accomplished literary reply, in short if I'd lectured my MA students for an hour and set the task as coursework.
>
> But no lecturing had happened at all. No one mentioned iambs, or stereotypes, or subversion, or even gender. All we did, in our group of teenagers sitting round in the library – all I ever do, in fact – was read the poem, and chat, not about how the poem worked, but what it provoked in us.
>
> Though, as teachers we should and do, of course, end up talking about poems and how they work for literary critical essays, we should never forget the power of the individual response, of exploration, of personal connection and involvement, of implicit awareness and understanding, all of which can be developed through writing poetry and all of which have a part to play in the critical as well as the creative process.

A manifesto for poetry teaching

So, in summary, what should a teachers' agenda for poetry in the classroom look like? What would my 'manifesto' for poetry teaching be? Here are the kinds of poetry experiences I think every student should have, not only to develop them as critical readers but also for their wider educational development – as thinkers, users of language and young adults who choose to use literary experiences to make sense of their lives:

- Write poetry themselves, to get under the skin of the genre and understand what it means to write in a poetic form or forms. This might include writing their own poetry, writing back to poems, textual transformations and other experiments with poetry to understand the choices poets have open to them.

- Write poetry for its own sake, as a powerful means of expression and a way of making sense of one's life.

- Read poetry in a different way from prose, acknowledging what is unique about it as a literary form and enjoying the different kind of reading and critical thinking that this implies.

- Have an authentic response to it that is based on what really strikes them – the things that leap out at them as being interesting, unusual or special, trusting their own responses rather than assuming that someone else automatically has a more authoritative view that they need to adopt.

- Explore aspects of language and form in relation to the big picture of what the poet is trying to communicate, rather than as micro-analysis for its own sake

- Think about such issues as tone and have the confidence to make a judgment about whether a poem is serious and reflective, wittily playful, or sharply satirical, intensely emotional or highly philosophical.

- Subject their interpretations to scrutiny, so that they can justify to themselves (and to others), the grounds for their views and ensure that their readings are plausible and convincing.

- Read adult critical writing about poetry, to develop a sense of the kind of thinking they do and the unique ways in which they engage critically with this particular literary genre.

- Read widely, beyond the confines of examination specifications, to develop confidence, familiarity and pleasure in poetry.

References for Chapter 8

Barry, P. 2013. 'What we talk about when we talk about poetry'. In *Use of English* (65.1).

Benton, P. and Fox, G. 1985. *Teaching Literature 14-19*. Oxford: Oxford University Press.

Clanchy, K. 2019. *Some Kids I Taught and What They Taught Me*. London: Picador.

Dymoke, S. 2003. *Drafting and Assessing Poetry: A Guide for Teachers*. London: Sage Publications Ltd.

Eliot, T.S. 1987 [1933]. *The Use of Poetry and the Use of Criticism*. Cambridge: Cambridge University Press.

Yakich, M. 2016. *Poetry: A Survivor's Guide*. London: Bloomsbury.

9. Teaching the Novel

This new piece explores some of the educational shibboleths surrounding the teaching of the novel. It argues that the class novel remains a vital part of the English curriculum but suggests that we need to think harder about why we're teaching it, and, in the light of that, question practices that have become routine and ritualised.

The novel only emerged as a form in the eighteenth century. For a considerable period of time it was regarded with scorn as lightweight reading, mainly for young women, that had nothing to do with the high prestige forms of 'letters' – the essay, history – or the higher literary form of poetry. Yet by the twentieth century it had become – and remains – a staple of English classrooms, to be taught and studied rather than dismissed as inferior. A whole class experience of reading and talking about a novel is more-or-less taken for granted. Whether it's one a term, one a half term or more, from Year 7 to Year 13, we expend a large amount of class time in English lessons reading and talking about novels. But why is this? And what do we want students to learn from the experience?

Here is a list of ten reasons why we might think about teaching novels to all students in secondary classrooms. I'm sure others could be offered but this is a good start and I think it probably includes things that are sometimes forgotten:

1. To inculcate a predisposition towards reading for pleasure in students' future lives.

2. To teach literary, textual knowledge that will be required for further study in the subject (for instance, about genre, structure, language, voice, point of view).

3. To teach understandings of period and context that allow students to fit future reading in academic English into a broader picture of what the novel is and where it sits.

4. To teach an understanding of story (narrative) and what it means in our lives, building on the continuum between everyday anecdote, storytelling as a way of representing all aspects of our lives to ourselves, and the fully fledged big beast novel.

5. To develop students' thinking and feeling about life, humanity and society – extending experience beyond their own specific, narrow world and building empathy and understanding.

6. To encounter written text in one of its most highly-wrought forms, in order to feed other necessary aspects of language and literacy learning, for example vocabulary acquisition, the ability to grapple with complex syntax, to infer and fill in gaps in challenging texts.

7. To develop the interpretative and critical 'muscle' – allowing students to question, generate an interpretation, test it against others, hold complex and contradictory ideas in one's head, deal with ambiguity.

8. To provide a shared, sustained experience across a class, upon which other things can be pinned, with discussion of themes, character, debates about the issues themselves offering multiple starting-points for other aspects of language and literacy work.

9. To enjoy reading and sharing a text, in the way that friends, or a community of readers, such as a book group, might.

10. To prepare students to answer questions on novels in exams.

As with many aspects of the curriculum, the way in which we teach novels has, in recent years, been distorted by just one of these ten reasons, the last one. As early as Year 7, novels are often taught with future GCSE assessment in mind. Choices of text are made to prepare for those texts on the current GCSE specifications. The experience of reading a novel in KS4 has, all too often, been turned into a series of opportunities to learn how to answer questions on prose texts – whether fiction or not – in an English GCSE Language exam. For reasons of time, teachers have been quite sensibly blurring the Language and Literature distinction but this has had a troubling side effect: the novel has become the focus for preparing students to write a paragraph closely analysing language in a short extract, or exploring structure in a similarly brief piece of text. I would argue that what this exam emphasis has done is to risk side-lining many of the most important reasons why we might want to teach the novel in the first place. EMC's 'Teaching a Novel at KS3', born out of our group work project *It's Good to Talk* explored this issue in practice in one year group at a school in east London. We looked at the ways in which the class novel was being 'mined' for its potential to teach GCSE language skills, and narrowed to a focus on word and sentence-level techniques – metaphor, simile, grammatical choices and so on. We entirely re-framed the scheme of work to focus on many of the reasons listed above, and found that the whole experience was fundamentally different, not only for the students but also for the teachers themselves. They re-discovered a confident sense of what it is that the novel teaches and what we should teach about the novel. These two elements were tightly-bound together in our thinking.[1]

So, how should we be teaching a novel?

First, it seems to me that, just as with any other genre, we should recognise the nature of the genre and teach it accordingly. So, while a poem is often taken in (at least initially) in one gulp in a single reading, and bears the weight of close reading to look at its highly patterned and closely woven textures of language, imagery, form and structure, a novel is an extended read, experienced over many

---

1. There is a full write-up of EMC's *It's Good to Talk* – 'Teaching a Novel at KS3' project on EMC's website. This includes the whole scheme of work, examples of student writing, an analysis of the writing, a summary of the teacher and student questionnaires and other data, as a free downloadable PDF. There is also a 35-minute film of the teachers talking about the impact on their students and on themselves as teachers.

hours, days or even weeks. Its patterning is often more loosely woven, broader, bigger, different. So, as well as looking closely at short passages and establishing thoughts about the characteristic style of the writing, we will want to look too at the whole architecture of the text. Taking in the building in its entirety – its size, shape, defining features and the site upon which it has been built (alongside other buildings or in the style of others) – is vital. We need to know if we're dealing with a small cottage in the woods, a tenement block, an English country house, a Victorian terrace or a 'Grand Designs' architectural innovation. We cannot hope to describe the building or comment on its features if we've come into it blindfolded and only have the blindfold taken off when we are in a small room, in the attic or down in the basement. This requires bigger thinking of the kind that allows us to orientate ourselves; it requires an encounter, over time, with plenty of reading that cross-references and compares, to help students understand what novels can be like – from a big, rambling Victorian tome to a playful, modern multi-vocal text. So we need to know about genres (like romance, crime, Gothic, rites of passage, thriller), and about kinds of writing (realist, experimental, postmodern), and about key elements in all narrative texts (voice, point of view, plot, motifs).

All of this has a 'chicken and egg' aspect to it. We need to teach these things in every novel we encounter and students need to encounter plenty of novels to learn these things. With the first novel they study in Year 7, depending on their primary experiences, some of these ideas might be more implicitly understood than explicitly so. However, as time goes on, if the teacher builds on all the reading they have done in the past and develops links over the reading they do at KS3, they will develop this broader set of understandings. We saw this happening in the EMC novel project, where the students who had read *In the Sea There Are Crocodiles* went straight onto read *Great Expectations*, and, without prompting, began to make connections and comparisons of this kind: 'It's another rites of passage novel'; 'It has a really different narrative arc'; 'The voice is first person but very different', and so on.

Knowledge of how novels work comes from reading plenty of them. But knowing more about how novels work is only one of our intended teaching outcomes – essential for further literary study, for instance at A Level, but not the only reason for studying them. As the list on pages 154-155 shows, the experience of reading novels, at least at KS3, is an important way of developing students' understanding of themselves and of the world as well. In a filmed interview for EMC in 2000, Ian McEwan said of the novel:

> I think the novel as a form is a marvellous means of investigation into life, and I mean life in all its senses, daily life, ordinary life, emotional life, life as we try to give meaning to it and try to understand it. I think it does it better than any other form, largely because it can give the illusion of getting inside the minds of other people. And I think having a theory of other people's minds, having a sense of what it's like to be someone else, is one of the great gifts we have. It makes us capable of living with each other, because we have some sense of empathy, or what it might be like to be someone completely different from ourselves.

A study in 2013 by psychologists David Comer Kidd and Emanuele Castano, at the New School for Social Research in New York, used Theory of Mind techniques to measure the participants' ability to accurately identify emotional states in others. High scores correlated to those who had read literary fiction rather than popular fiction or non-fiction texts. Kidd said that,

> What great writers do is to turn you into the writer. In literary fiction, the incompleteness of the characters turns your mind to trying to understand the minds of others.

What are the implications of this for our teaching? It means that we shouldn't simply be thinking mechanistically and in an atomistic way about the literary features and techniques of novels but should be allowing personal response, feelings and ideas to flourish in tandem with, and in relation to, critical analysis. So students need the space to say what they have found moving, or interesting, or enjoyable in a text. They need to be able to express thoughts about the subjects under discussion, whether these be identity, migration, growing up, war, love, urban life or the natural world. They need to be offered texts that allow them to enter into the minds of others, that are age-appropriate and stimulating to them. This doesn't mean a crude notion of 'relevance' – for instance because the class is adolescent boys, they should only read about adolescent boys. But it does involve a sophisticated consideration of which texts will allow students to think about 'what it might be like to be someone completely different from ourselves'. So *Great Expectations* might do that brilliantly. But so too might a contemporary YA novel by Sarah Crossan or Elizabeth Laird. Perhaps *Frankenstein* might do it for A Level students but not for younger students at KS3. As a teacher, you will know what is achieving this strong and authentic response by observing what happens. If you try teaching *In the Sea There Are Crocodiles*, for instance, and you find the students bursting with ideas, expressing empathy, wanting to talk about their own experiences, as we did in the EMC project, you might decide to teach it again the following year. If the students are disengaged, unable to connect with what's happening, not just in small stretches but for long periods, then perhaps the book isn't the right one.

We are also teaching novels to develop students' reading skills, their ability to navigate difficult texts, as a way of developing their vocabulary and understanding of language more broadly, and of increasing their appetite for reading. Julia Sutherland et al (based at Sussex University), in their 2019 research on 'faster immersive reading', tested out the idea of reading two texts back to back, relatively quickly, stopping only for clarification, response, exploration of inferences, prediction and so on. This contrasted with the halting, stop-start process of the reading they saw in many KS3 classrooms, where each small chunk of reading was constantly being interrupted to do detailed linguistic analysis and written work, slowing the whole process down and making it feel very unlike the experience we have as adults when we enter the world of a book. The new trial approach aimed to give students – particularly less able ones – the experience of reading a whole novel quickly and keeping it in their heads, with a second novel following swiftly after, to allow for comparison and connections to be made. The outcomes were measured in terms of a reading comprehension test and the students were found to have made significant leaps in their reading ages as compared with what one might have expected. They also showed much greater enjoyment of the texts. This kind of research is early work; more needs to be done. It is frustrating to me, as I'm sure it is to the research team doing this work, that important subject-based and classroom-focused research such as this should struggle to attract funding, while generic, cross-curricular testing of sweeping pedagogical ideas (particularly if associated with psychology and cognitive science) is deemed more important and finds it easier to attract funding.

For me what's refreshing about the Sussex research is that it asks some serious questions about what we do in the classroom when we work on a novel. It tries out something different to see what happens. I think there's an urgent need for this (perhaps not just with the novel but for the purposes of this chapter, let's stick with that). If we go right back to first principles and ask ourselves why we're teaching novels (my list of 10 reasons and perhaps others too), then perhaps some of the things that have been taken for granted and have become part of classroom rituals, should be seriously questioned. So here are just a few examples.

1. If one reason for reading novels is to inculcate a disposition towards reading them in future life, is the way we're doing it designed to achieve that? Should we not, for instance, be linking a pleasurable, quick read of a class novel to other texts that students might go away and read privately? Webs of inter-related wider reading could be on offer. Students could then bring back ideas from those texts to inform their earlier reading of the novel and bring those texts into conversation with it.

2. If a novel at KS3 is never going to be examined as part of national exams, why do we need to treat it as if it is? Why do students need to know every bit of it at the same level of detail, spend as long on Chapter 1 as on Chapter 7, as 9, 15 or 20?[2] Once some key ideas have been established, and some important thinking and discussion has developed, perhaps going at a slower pace at first, why not speed up and do very little on the later chapters (unless of course there's a significant new idea to raise)? In planning the teaching, one text might require two lessons on Chapter 1, just one on the five subsequent ones as a whole, one on the next rather crucial turning-point and then a race through to the end. A different book might require a different approach. Equally, is what we do with the book always carrying false assumptions of a test at the end? Is it important to remember minute details of plot and character with a KS3 book, or is it more important to focus teaching (and formative assessment) on core ideas to carry forward (such as understandings about the use of voice and point of view, genre, intertextual

---

2. John Brown and Terry Gifford in their excellent book, *Teaching A Level English Literature: A Student-Centred Approach* (1989) draw on Frank Kermode's idea that it is, in any event, an illusion to think that a novel is 'available' to anyone in its entirety. They argue that our teaching of novels should recognise this fact, rather than making students feel inadequate because they never manage the impossible task of 'knowing' a novel in its entirety.

connections and so on)? Might our formative test, having read a novel of one kind, be to offer a short extract from another with some points of connection, and see how far students are able to *apply* their newly acquired literary understandings to this new text?

3. Might we teach novels in different ways *deliberately* to offer different kinds of experiences of reading? So, for instance, might some of the novels at KS3 be read mainly for pleasure, for discussion, for encouraging wider reading whilst others are taught in a different, more 'literary' way? Might some be deliberately canonical and others more diverse, some highbrow, others light reads, to make sure that we're giving students a varied experience, and meeting the needs of all of our students?

4. Might we encourage the development of 'taste' in our students by offering small ways in which they can make choices – for instance, 'here are the opening chapters of three novels that are in the stock cupboard. The class can vote for the one it likes best.' Students argue why and then the one that is voted the winner is the one the class reads.

5. If we think reading good books makes you a better writer yourself, how about peppering the study of novels with opportunities to write – not always big, formal, assessed pieces but little experiments, chances to do creative responses for homework. Why not create a reading notebook, in which students can choose to write their own work, inspired by the novel they are reading?

If approached in this way, the novel can do many things for students and fulfil much of what we want to teach in English. The fact of it taking up time isn't a problem, if we're making sure that its potential is fully recognised and realised in the practice of the classroom. I believe that we can make it do all of those things on my list at the beginning of the chapter – even, I would argue, the last one. Students who have had a fulfilling and varied experience of novels in all of the other respects, *will* end up writing very well about narrative texts in exams.

References for Chapter 9

Brown, J. and Gifford, T.1989. *Teaching A Level English Literature: A Student-Centred Approach*. Abingdon: Routledge.

Kidd, C. D. and Castano, E. 2013. 'Reading literary fiction improves theory of mind' in *Science* 342 (6156).

Geda, F. 2012. *In the Sea There Are Crocodiles*. London: Vintage.

McEwan, I. 2000. EMC interview.

Westbrook, J., Sutherland, J., Oakhill, J. and Sullivan, S. 2019. 'Just reading: increasing pace and volume of reading whole narratives on the comprehension of poorer adolescent readers in English classrooms'. Available at http://sro.sussex.ac.uk/id/eprint/70702/

10. Assessing English

Assessment is one of the thorniest aspects of English teaching. I was tempted to avoid dealing with it head-on in this book because of its complicated history, multiple changes by accretion, and the problem of finding a shared language about it (for instance what we really mean by formative and summative assessment). It is also extremely hard to come up with practical solutions, given the labyrinthine nature of national assessment structures, combined with local school requirements and individual teachers' practices, all of which seem to be in constant flux.

In addition to all of this, there is the risk that, in questioning some of the practices that are current now, I might look as if I'm both glorifying the past and critiquing the work of the teachers of today. That is not my intention. Current assessment structures have undoubtedly led to more uniformity than in the past and perhaps avoided the very worst laissez-faire practice, where teachers were free to do more as they pleased. But they have also become unwieldy, burdensome and disproportionate, taking up too much teacher time in relation to the benefits and sometimes even distracting teachers from the realities of how to really move students on in their learning. Teachers coming on EMC courses are sometimes despairing of the processes they are 'required' to go through within institution-wide systems that often seem to them to be of little value.

Some things have undoubtedly been lost as a result of a tick box culture that expects learning to be demonstrated via the 'mastery' of small objectives. A more holistic approach to assessment – not only in summative assessment but also in formative work with students – seems to struggle to gain credence with senior leaders and national bodies, even though 'big picture' achievements and more complex, intertwined elements of knowledge and skill are likely to be far more significant. Though there is a lot of emphasis on formative assessment nowadays, and many teachers are working exceptionally hard on different ways of doing it, this form of assessment often mirrors summative assessments too closely. In asking good questions like, 'How can we work to help students to achieve x?', that 'x' is all too often a small, atomised objective rather than a more holistic one. It is usually one that relates to an external examination further up the line. I have seen careful, meticulous, time-consuming marking of KS3 student work that seems to me to have its eye on the wrong thing in terms of helping students to develop their thinking and writing.

I believe that the English teaching community needs to argue hard for forms of assessment (both formative and summative) that suit the subject better. This might be assessment that is quite different from that of other subjects, where simple right and wrong answers and set formats are, perhaps, more appropriate. It might make our forms of assessment in English messier and more complicated but it would allow us to actually assess, formatively and summatively, the things that we value in student work, rather than valuing the wrong things in order to comply with a simple assessment structure designed to work across the curriculum.

English requires a wider and more flexible range of assessment than most other areas of the curriculum. We believe that rigid syllabuses are not the best means of achieving this and that there should be an increase in school-based assessment with external moderation. (11.39)

The Bullock Report (A Language for Life), 1975

The Bullock Report (known as *A Language for Life*) of 1975 is as wise about assessment as it is about many other areas of the curriculum. The statement that English requires a different kind of assessment system than some other subjects speaks not only to the particular context in the 1970s but is of equal relevance now. Teachers of English have always struggled with imposed cross-curricular assessment systems because they have been aware that the subject doesn't work in the 'tidy' ways that some others might. For a start, English students are doing many different kinds of things. They are learning 'how to' as well as 'what', learning how to write for different purposes, how to read challenging texts, how to respond and interpret. English learning also doesn't happen in neatly linear or hierarchical ways. You can learn many interrelated elements alongside each other, or in a variety of different sequences. You don't need to know *this* before *that*. The messiness of this is its strength, not a weakness. Once you decide to pull it apart to assess the parts, the whole becomes a lot less elaborate, sophisticated and interesting and a lot less true as an account of what it means to make progress in the subject. In her book on assessment in English, *Testing English*, Bethan Marshall suggests that English is as much an Arts subject as anything else, a subject that develops aesthetic judgement, as well as the ability to create aesthetic work – 'language arts'. She quotes Eliot Eisner, writing in 2002 in *The Arts and the Creation of Mind*, that artistry

consists in having an idea worth expressing, the imaginative ability needed to conceive of how, the technical skills needed to work effectively with some material [in English the medium being words], and the sensibilities needed to make the delicate adjustments that will give the forms the moving qualities that the best of them possess.

These aptitudes, abilities, sensibilities and judgements are not easily assessed by atomised lists of objectives in a tick box format. Yet that seems to have been where assessment of English has been going. Ironically, in final summative examinations, there has been a growing awareness in recent years of the danger of this, and the need for more holistic thinking and grading, yet in the KS3 assessment structures within which many English teachers are required to operate, the patterns of assessment have all been about assessing only what can be easily assessed, breaking things down into small objectives rather than capturing the more complex and messy realities.

Sometimes it's helpful to think backwards, to what the world used to be like, in order to put the here and now into perspective. It can be hard for a new teacher to see that practices that seem natural or commonplace now are anything but. Nowhere is this more true than in the world of assessment. Many of the words like levels, targets, flight paths, assessment criteria, even assessment objectives, didn't even exist, or, if they did, exerted very little influence up till the early 2000s. I hope that by looking back, I can throw some light on current concerns, give a few pointers as to what might be important ways of addressing these and flag up some directions for the future. I will not be suggesting a magic bullet 'answer' to the assessment problem, but rather offer some thoughts to help anyone thinking about formative and summative assessment and the role they play.

Before levels, flight paths and datadrops

What follows is an account of what assessment was like for me when I first started teaching in 1977. The unsystemetised nature of what I was doing may seem a little surprising and even disconcerting to some in today's terms but it did avoid one doing things for form's sake, just because one had to, and allowed for flexibility and for meeting individual needs. Some teachers reading this may recognise some of the practices and even do some of these things themselves, though in a very different context of datadrops, statement banks and centralised systems.

Formative assessment in 1977 was largely through marking and dialogue with students. There was very little internal assessment by way of formal tests, mocks or exams apart from in the immediate build-up to external exams.[1] I marked my students' books. My school had its own marking policy and there were frequent discussions about whether to grade or not, usually leading to the decision not to grade or give marks because students became fixated on the marks rather than on developing their work. My marking was what one might call 'holistic' – in other words I wasn't marking to a set mark scheme, nor were students writing to one. I thought about the work and considered what would make the most difference to each particular student and wrote a comment at the end of each piece of work – sometimes shorter, sometimes longer (depending on the work itself but also on my workload!). Given that writing tended to be more extended – my Year 8s wrote a whole novel one term – marking load could be managed differently according to what students were engaged in. Marking along the way was usually light-touch – not every spelling or punctuation mistake, unless that was the thing I thought was the priority for that student. Here's the kind of thing I might have written at the end of a piece of work:

> *Great story Maria! I loved the climax, when you fell off the edge. Really well told, with that terrific fairground metaphor. A small point – you're still struggling with there/their/they're. Add that cluster to your list of 5 common spelling mistakes to focus on every time you write. Pin it to your next piece of work before you start.*

Or

> *Your points about the witches were interesting but I didn't think the one about Macbeth himself was valid. Is there enough evidence for that? Doesn't he only first think of kingship when they put it into his head? Think about that again.*

Or

---

1. O Levels and CSEs, in those days. CSEs were introduced in 1965 as an alternative for lower attaining pupils. Achieving a Grade 1 at CSE was equivalent to a C at O Level and allowed progression into Level 3 courses. O Levels and CSEs were replaced by a single GCSE qualification in 1986.

What a change! So much better now you're writing simpler sentences. That reading aloud seems to have made a huge difference. Keep doing that!

I had the authority to set my own 'targets' for my students. They weren't rigidly fixed to a set of class targets, school or nationally determined ones and they weren't called targets, though that's effectively what they were – things to be aiming for. I held in my head those students and their work and thought hard about where they were at, where they were heading and where I wanted them to be over time. Maria (for Maria was one of my actual students) shifted over four years under my care as an English teacher from being in her own words 'terrible' at spelling to being a confident and accurate writer, who did very well in her O Levels.

The targets I set were not a multitude of atomised ones. They were not closely tied to future examination requirements. They tended to be big broad areas that required attention, within which smaller items were nested. It seemed important for students to concentrate on prioritising and getting big things right – their grip on basic sentence structure, for instance, came before developing an intimate knowledge and sophisticated ability to use semi-colons. Prioritising what would make the most difference to a student's development was at the heart of this – something one became skilled at by getting to know the students and their work.

Because students were often working individually, in pairs or small groups, in a kind of 'workshop' where they wrote a lot, there was time to get to know students' work well, to have one-to-one conversations and intervene with advice and comment at the point of production. So conversations might have gone something like this:

Me: What's happened to the tense here?

Student: What do you mean?

Me: The tense. Present? Past?

Student: Oh. Dunno.

Me: Read it back over, aloud.

Student: (*Reads aloud*) Oh yeah. It sounds odd.

Me: Why?

Student: It's switched from present to past.

Me: Did it help to read it aloud?

Student: Yes.

Me: When I write, I usually stop at the end of every paragraph and read it aloud in my head. I notice things going wrong, or not sounding like I'd like them to sound and change them. It's a good thing to do.

Student: But it makes my work messy then.

Me: That doesn't matter. Messy on a first draft is OK. In fact it's good!

A conversation like this can offer all kinds of benefits:

- Addressing head-on the specific problem in that single piece of work.

- Making that problem something to learn from in future work, by drawing out the bigger idea, or bigger lesson to take forward.

- Intervening at the point of production, when things are fresh in the student's mind and when the intervention can actually change something before the work is even completed.

- Focusing on an issue for that particular student, rather than a set of general objectives for the whole class.

- Offering immediate solutions, rather than just identifying problems.

- Sometimes watching over, and supporting, as that solution is tried.

- Providing a chance to correct misunderstandings, for instance that neat first drafts are more important than making changes along the way.

- Allowing the teacher to bring to bear their own experience and knowledge – the 'master artisan' passing on their craft to the student.[2]

You may notice that I don't use the word feedback for what I was doing. Feedback seems to me to be an okay word but not the best one. It doesn't really encapsulate what's important about the kind of teacher intervention described above. I'd prefer to use the word 'dialogue', or 'response' or a combination of the two, 'responsive dialogue'. Feedback suggests a one-way process on something that is complete. The teacher 'gives' it; the student listens to it and acts on it (or not). Dialogue is the kind of thing exemplified above, an engagement between learner and teacher that includes more than just a comment on a piece of work but also an unveiling of processes and of thinking; a checking of what's been understood; an engagement with the content and the ideas as well as the formal aspects of student work, using the student's writing as a springboard for discussion of the matter at hand, whether it's the representation of Macbeth, or the ambiguity in a line of a poem. In a world where PEE has devalued the 'P' (the point, the ideas) and over-valued the form (first point, then evidence, then exploration no matter how good or bad the point may be), it seems to me to be really important to have a dialogue that focuses on developing students' subject-related knowledge and ideas as much as the form in which they are conveyed.

In 1977, there was little requirement to prove to the outside world (or even to senior management in my own school) that I was working with students in these formative ways. There was much less scrutiny of assessment during the teaching – though, of course, examination results mattered. The downside of this was that teachers, left to their own devices, and less regulated, might be hugely variable in their own practices. The upside was that they could use professional judgement over what they considered to be *genuinely* formative.

---

2. Arthur Applebee, in *Curriculum as Conversation*, talks of the relationship between students and teachers as between 'novices and master craftsmen and women'.

Summative assessment and accountability – final exams and their backwash

When I started teaching, there was a clear distinction between such 'formative' assessment as that described above and 'summative' assessment – a distinction that was probably a bit clearer than it is now. With no league tables or industrial-sized collection of data in schools, summative assessment meant, by and large, end of year exams and final exams (O Levels and CSEs, then GCSEs, and A Levels). Before final exams, students did mocks. Just once, in the December or January of their final year. Intensive exam preparation happened in the period after Easter. Prior to that, students were reading, writing, talking, learning. They did some timed writing and associated time-limited activities along the way to help them understand what was to come and begin to develop those skills, but they didn't do constant tests and certainly were not being examined endlessly in order to feed data into any school-wide machine.

Assessment, even in exam terms, involved coursework. CSE, taken by large numbers of students for whom O Level was not a very good fit, could, in those days, be 100% coursework, though later that was reduced[3]. Many students taught by me achieved the equivalent of an O Level pass and continued into Level 3 education. Within a few years of starting to teach, I was also teaching the AEB 660 English Literature for A Level. John Hodgson and Bill Greenwell's article in *English in Education*, 'The Work of the Course: Validity and Reliability in Assessing English Literature' (2017), traces the development of the AEB 660 A Level from its origins as AEB 753 in 1977 with 30% coursework, to its heyday in the late 1980s when, as 660, it allowed 50% coursework, had thriving moderation consortia and became an extremely popular specification (or syllabus as it was then called). The inclusion of coursework had massive implications. These were largely – though of course not entirely – helpful.

- The final assessment was a *selection* of the work of the course. What this meant was that the course itself was much more than just that which was assessed. Students selected their best work; they had done many other pieces as trials, experiments, enjoyable interludes. *Everything*, in fact, had this sense of low risk and freedom, because no one piece of work had to go in for assessment. Sometimes it was the more experimental pieces that ended up in the folder, sometimes not. (One downside of this, of course, was that if everything was low risk and might not matter, students didn't necessarily recognise the importance of any given piece of work. Without the exam monster breathing down their necks, forcing them to work consistently hard, they needed intrinsic motivation, based on the subject and on their own development. This could of course be viewed as an upside as well.)

- Because of the nature of the assessment – in teacher-assessed, moderated folders of work – teachers in all English departments spent considerable amounts of time looking at their own students' writing in relation to that

---

3. CSE Mode 3 allowed for 100% coursework.

produced in other teachers' classes. They were taken off timetable for final examination moderation but department meetings also included time to look at student work. This played a huge role in teacher CPD. It cannot be overstated. As a young teacher I would get to see the work of all the other teachers in my department. Some got fantastic work out of their students. Here was a chance to see that work, and talk about how those teachers had elicited it from their classes. I developed a strong sense of what was good and what wasn't – a standard by which to judge my students' work. There were no hideous surprises when my students got back their grades (either from exams or from external coursework moderation). Nowadays, in teacher CPD at EMC, I sometimes see younger teachers floundering when making judgements about student writing. Their chances to debate and discuss this together are fewer and less systematic. Though some Local Authorities and Multi-Academy Trusts (MATs) do moderate across schools it is rarer for this to happen as a matter of course, so ideas about standards can spring up within a school that are out of sync with wider standards, leading to big surprises in exam marking.

- Ironically, many of the schools who do constant testing and mock exams don't seem to do that much sustained moderation of work either, so the results from these internal assessments, used to accumulate the data on individual students and whole cohorts, can be grossly inaccurate and misleading. One teacher might see something as brilliant, while another regards it as very poor, but that mismatch in teachers' thinking stays undiscovered and unresolved. Despite this, these flawed results feed into both the data and into their teaching. A massive data-collection operation, involving vast amounts of work, can lead to statistics based on very poor judgement of student work.

- Coursework blurred the boundaries between developmental work and assessed work in a very helpful way. Nowadays, it is far more common for everything to be either for assessment (internal assessment for data collection and determining flightpaths, or targets), or seen as building towards final assessment. The notion of writing as a developmental process has largely been lost. At EMC we're constantly working to reinstate a view of writing dissociated from final assessment preparation, both through recommending varying the kinds of writing that students do and introducing much more 'exploratory' writing. Writing is a way of developing thinking. It's also a way of discovering how to come up with a big idea of your own, construct sustained arguments, write at length, develop a writing style, find a voice, draft and re-draft and self-critique. With the loss of coursework, many of these ideas have been lost. Drafting and re-drafting in particular have taken a big hit, despite these being aspects of adult writing that are of pre-eminent value and importance.

I haven't said anything yet about Controlled Assessment, the writing of pre-planned GCSE coursework under teacher supervision. The shift from coursework to Controlled Assessment (2010-15) was purely about policing results and ensuring that students didn't plagiarise (and teachers didn't cheat). It was an elaborate structure that was destined to fail in a context where fierce accountability measures meant that students' results were of supreme importance to the well-being of teachers and schools. Instead of putting coursework into a contained, well-monitored context, it led to even more gaming, with some teachers feeling compelled to allow students to learn essays off by heart in advance, or to soften the Controlled Assessment conditions to allow students to succeed. Both the unreliability of coursework and the failure of Controlled Assessment were features of accountability gone mad and a system that had stopped trusting teachers.

Self-assessment, responsibility for learning, metacognition

At a certain point, some time in the mid 1970s, teachers started talking more actively about the need for students to become aware themselves of what they needed to do to improve their work. There was talk of 'ownership of learning' and 'responsibility for learning', a recognition that students themselves needed to be part of the process rather than the passive recipients of teachers' instructions and exhortations. This nowadays would be described in other terms. At its least helpful, it takes the form of 'targets' which are not always fully understood by students, are sometimes woefully unrelated to the key priorities for improvement in individual students' learning and are used to drive the data machine rather than genuinely impact on student attainment. At its most helpful, these days, it relates to the idea of 'metacognition' – the notion that thinking and reflecting on your own knowledge and learning can help you learn better.

In the 1970s, the form that 'ownership' and 'responsibility' took in assessment terms was self-assessment. Students were required to assess their own performance. This stemmed from important underlying principles, not dissimilar to the idea of metacognition, but from my perspective fell into the trap that many assessment programmes fall into – that of assuming a single rigid, unchanging structure will solve everything. Self-assessment proformas, like many other similar ways of assessing, became a routine and a dreary one at that. And once that happened, it lost its force for students and teachers alike. Any form that has to be filled out at the end of every lesson, or once a week in tutor time, is bound to be done in perfunctory ways. The participants in this process start to go through the motions to 'get it over with' as quickly as possible. As *A Language for Life* stated, 'Assessment is not in question: it is when it becomes an automatic and unvaried process that it loses its value for both teacher and pupil.'

One sees examples, in today's world, of formative assessment and self-assessment practices that are vibrant and vital – not overly-generic, not stodgily prosaic, not bogged down in routines. Some work on 'assessment criteria' for instance, where students engage in writing their own before starting a piece of work, and then evaluating their work in relation to that, seems to offer a more engaged and fruitful approach to self-assessment. The assessment is in relation to the student's own purposes rather than detached from it. James Durran, a Local Authority English

Advisor for North Yorkshire, offers teachers a way of supporting students to create a set of their own criteria for writing linked to purposes. This is an excellent example of productive, reflective thinking about success criteria. Its value to teachers is clear from the number of tweets and hits on the blog where he explains what he calls 'boxed' or 'expanding success criteria'.

Peer assessment working to a set of criteria also seems to offer rich possibilities, where students judge each other's work according to some key notions, both helping the students evaluate success at a given moment but also giving a window onto the kinds of judgements that are made more generally about success in the subject. If the success criteria for a piece of work include 'choose a narrative voice that works well in developing a child's eye perspective', that is teaching students to think and operate within the discipline of English Literature. Equally, 'make at least three major points on *different* aspects of the writer's style', might help students understand that an essay shouldn't just bang on about a single feature, repeating the same point endlessly, with numerous forms of exemplification.

Comparative Judgement (promoted by Daisy Christodoulou through her organisation 'No More Marking') seems to have some elements of past practices that could make it a helpful tool, particularly if it is done by more than one teacher and involves discussion, as a way of sharpening up teachers' own (and collective) judgements about student work. But it must not be just focused on the writing but on subject content too. Comparative judgement is only as good as the 'judgement' of those doing the comparing, in determining what is high-quality writing in the subject. I have seen comparative judgements on pieces of writing from KS2 up where what is being valued in order to make the judgement is highly dubious. For instance, if you decide that including particular grammatical forms, or varying sentence structures is what makes a piece of writing 'good', you will come to a very different judgement than if you give more weighting to other things, for instance the validity of the ideas expressed, the ability to write simply and clearly, or having a strong sense of audience and purpose.

The element that is emphasised least in comparative judgement – the holistic aspect as opposed to the comparative element, favouring broad judgements over atomised assessment criteria – is, for me, the most valuable part of it.

What happened to cause these changes?

How did we arrive here, at a point where centralised assessment has become so dominant, with proof of teacher activity rather than student development leading the process? How has summative assessment become so dominant in our thinking, often leading to an approach that closely mirrors the summative tests several years down the line? Why has assessment become so overbearing and burdensome, ruling teachers' and students' lives to the detriment of genuine learning?

Some key changes occurred in the 1990s and early 2000s that led to distortions in the system, a move towards objective-driven assessment and a shift away from holistic formative assessment and marking towards a more artificial tick-box approach to assessment that then impacted on learning itself. These included: levels; SATs (first taken by KS3 students in 1991); League Tables (1992); Ofsted labels (beginning in 1992 with a 7-point scale from 'Excellent' to 'Very Poor'); the National Literacy Strategy (introduced in primary schools in 1998); the KS3 Framework of Objectives for Teaching English: Years 7, 8 and 9 (which extended the literacy strategy to secondary phase in 2001); and several years later Assessing Pupil Progress (APP) provided detailed Assessment Focuses (AFs).

A heightened focus on 'performance' at every level, from governors and Senior Leadership to Subject Leaders and classroom teachers meant that assessment was, for the first time, seen as being a way of judging teachers and schools rather than individual pupils. One of the consequences of this was teacher fear of student failure entered the equation. At the same time, the assessment focuses of Assessing Pupil Progress led to an overly fragmented and mechanised approach to assessment. Teachers and students alike came to understand the subject and their own work in terms of these atomised methods of assessment.

This whole approach turned everyone's attention to small things, individual, small-scale bits of knowledge or skill, the kind of thing that could be assessed. The big picture was lost. I sometimes wonder whether it has ever been recovered and, in bleaker moments, whether it's recoverable. In assessing only what seems assessable, in ways that are disconnected from the bigger picture, we have fundamentally distorted learning in our subject. For me, this is one of the biggest lessons of all. We should learn from this how to move on into a new phase of education, where the big picture of knowledge, learning and achievement is of paramount importance and the small detail fits into it.

Assessment for now and for the future

So where does all this take us now and in the future? Without re-stating arguments raised above, here are seven bald (and bold) suggestions to take us forward. Some of these are, of course, happening already, where schools and individual teachers have put their energies into thinking hard about genuinely formative approaches to assessment and resisted the temptation for all assessment to mirror the forms of GCSE examination.

1. Accountability measures need to look beyond student performance in internal and external assessments. (There is some indication that Ofsted are acknowledging this, in their new inspection framework guidelines and in their public statements.)

2. Summative assessment should not drive the curriculum. Courses should not become exam preparation only. Summative assessment should be a 'slice' of what's been learned, not the whole thing and students should be taught in a way that allows them to be confident that this is the case.

3. Coursework, or the work of the course, without the pressures of accountability, should play a bigger role in summative assessment. This would reinstate the idea of teachers' professional judgement being both valid

and important, but would also be a major impetus to develop and enrich teachers' professional judgement. From the point of view of students and the development of their writing in the subject, more coursework assessment both at GCSE and A Level would have a beneficial effect on what is taught and how. It would re-instate different kinds of writing – extended writing and writing in different forms beyond the academic essay, as well as bringing back into focus the vital processes of drafting and re-drafting.

4. Feedback to individual students (via marking or oral dialogue) could, and should, draw on past experience and understandings, to make it richer and deeper than in its current forms. In spoken dialogue, in the lesson, in relation to both a specific piece of work and broader ideas, it should be part of an ongoing relationship between students and teachers – a collaborative venture in developing their knowledge, understanding and expertise in the subject, with the teacher as 'master artisan', charged with developing the knowledge and tools of their apprentices.

5. Assessment should be founded on responsiveness and attention to individual needs. That doesn't mean differentiating all work for every individual but it does mean noticing what each student is finding difficult, spotting breakthroughs and identifying what next steps will take that particular student forward and prioritising those.

6. Metacognition and other forms of self-awareness about learning, whether through vibrant forms of self-assessment, peer assessment, or through student/teacher dialogue, should be a major element in formative assessment.

7. Atomised, small scale objectives need to give way to much bigger ideas about student achievement, so that we recognise what is most important in all aspects of learning, from student writing to subject content.

References for Chapter 10

Applebee, A.N. 1996. *Curriculum as Conversation: Transforming Traditions of Teaching and Learning.* Chicago: University of Chicago Press.

Bullock, A. 1975. *A Language for Life.* London: HMSO.

Christodoulou, D. 'No more marking – comparative judgement'. https://www.nomoremarking.com/

Durran, J. Blog 'Re-thinking success criteria'. https://jamesdurran.blog

Eisner, E.W. 2004. *The Arts and the Creation of Mind.* New Haven Conn: Yale University Press.

Hodgson J. and B. Greenwell. 2017. 'The work of the course: validity and reliability in assessing English Literature'. In *English in Education* 51 (1) Special Issue: Assessment and Learning.

Marshall, B. 2011. *Testing English: Formative and Summative Approaches to English Assessment.* London: Bloomsbury (Continuum Books).

11. Teaching English Language

This is a new piece, written for this book. It gives a broad historical context for the teaching of language in secondary English over the past 40 years, drawing out key issues and principles that continue to be at the heart of both policy-making and practical classroom decisions about content, pedagogy and the application of teachers' own knowledge and attitudes.

Thank you to Dan Clayton for his helpful contributions to this piece.

During the 40 or so years in which I have been teaching and working in education, one of the most contested aspects of English teaching has been the question of language, and knowledge about language. The fiercest of debates and fights over the curriculum and its content have raged around two areas in particular – grammar and Standard English. At the heart of all the arguments are some fundamental underlying ideas and questions that divide people. These are outlined below.

1. How far does one value students' own language – the accents they bring with them into the classroom, the dialects and varieties of English they may speak beyond the classroom in their own family and friendship environments and the other languages they may regard as their mother tongues? A corollary of this is the extent to which one views children though a 'deficit' lens, as having limited linguistic skills or experiences, 'impoverished' language, 'restricted codes' (as Basil Bernstein termed it in the 1970s), or 'gaps' that need filling?

2. How far is one influenced by the accumulated knowledge and consensus views of academic linguistics, as opposed to more 'popular' notions of correctness and rules, of what's acceptable usage and what children need to know in order to talk and write 'proper'?

3. How far should the idea of linguistic 'standards' be allowed to hold sway, so that those responsible for children's education, from government ministers and headteachers to classroom teachers, only look at language through a lens of anxiety associated with standards supposedly falling in children's language, both in their speech and writing?

4. Do we think that knowledge about language is of value in its own right, aside from any questions of improving usage, and should be taught to all students? Is it worthy of study as a subject or sub-section of the English curriculum, because of its intrinsic interest and importance? Should it be studied by all students at secondary level, as you might study Physics or History or Sociology, not just at A Level or at university level, in English Language or Linguistics degrees but by everyone? And should that study be broadly sociolinguistic – the study of language in relation to wider social factors?

These issues emerge again and again, not only in classrooms but at the level of government policy and regulation, both prior to the introduction of the first National Curriculum (first taught in 1989) and since. However, from my perspective, the fourth has always been significantly underplayed and undervalued in public discussions and policy making, in part because the first three have been stoked by the flames of publicity, playing out not only in educational spheres and in government but also on the pages of the *Daily Telegraph* and the *Daily Mail*. They have sucked the air out of any genuinely interesting exploration of what knowledge about language might be.

In 1988, after a period of scepticism about the value of formal grammar teaching and a questioning of the role of Standard English, the Conservative government led by Margaret Thatcher, commissioned The Kingman Enquiry into the teaching of language. This sought to definitively answer the first three issues listed above, focusing strongly on both grammar and Standard English, though inevitably also touching on the question of broader understandings about language. The government hope was that it would recommend formal grammar teaching as a corrective to the more 'progressive' policies that they believed had gained ground. They wanted finally to put paid to descriptivist liberalism and replace it with prescriptivist rules and the teaching of 'correct' language. Deborah Cameron later wrote about this in *Verbal Hygiene* (1995) where she talked about the link between grammar and a 'nostalgic yearning for grammar schools'. She says that 'grammar schools embody a lost tradition of selectivity in state education, and therefore come, like grammar itself, to be potent symbols of these cherished conservative values.' Those values she describes as being 'order, tradition, authority, hierarchy and rules'. More overtly politically, she argues that

> Conservatives do not advocate teaching grammar for purely instrumental reasons to do with enhancing linguistic knowledge and skill. Their preference for methods that do not work must be seen in the light of the moral significance they accord to grammar. If the lesson is less about language than about order, good behaviour and respect for authority, the value of drilling becomes much clearer.

The Kingman Enquiry consulted 239 individuals and organisations and included visits to 30 schools and six initial teacher training organisations. The *Report* was interestingly balanced in its conclusions. It certainly did not support a return to formal grammar, but neither did it entirely fulfil the hopes of those seeking a more enlightened view of the teaching of language in all its variety. A quotation from the opening suggests this careful balancing act:

> Nor do we see it as part of our task to plead for a return to old-fashioned grammar teaching and learning by rote. We have been impressed by the evidence we have received that this gave an inadequate account of the English language by treating it virtually as a branch of Latin, and constructing a rigid prescriptive code rather than a dynamic description of language in use. It was also ineffective as a means of developing a command of English in all its manifestations. Equally, at the other extreme, we reject the belief that any notion of correct or incorrect use of language is an affront to personal liberty.

We also reject the belief that knowing how to use terminology in which to speak of language is undesirable. Language is, as a matter of observable fact, plainly governed by a series of conventions related to the varying audiences, contexts and purposes of its use. Successful communication depends upon a recognition and accurate use of the rules and conventions. Command of these rules and conventions is more likely to increase the freedom of the individual than diminish it.

It seems to want to have its cake and eat it, both rejecting a 'rigid prescriptive code' and accepting the idea of 'correct and incorrect' use of language, at the same time as acknowledging that this comes from 'conventions' more than from inherent properties of the language itself. Looking back, it looks like a bit of a muddle. Its statements about the value of students' language in different contexts and the consequent ways that students might use language differently but with equal legitimacy, are more promising.

Children normally belong to at least three social groups – the family, the peer group and the wider group, in social terms, of their 'public' world. The public world of children is largely bounded by the school, where Standard English will be the norm. In each of these groups, the conventions of language behaviour are likely to be different and children ought, in our view, to be aware of how all three have their own legitimacy. These conventions may be associated with different accents, different dialects and (in the case of some communities) different languages.

On accent and dialect, Kingman is clear:

It is understandable that people feel themselves to be proprietors of their own language, and that they should feel their ownership to be violated by the use of language different from their own. The relationship between personality or identification with a community and the common ownership of a language is so close that there is a tendency for people to feel that their language is the best. But facts are otherwise. All languages are rule-governed systems of communication, and none is linguistically superior.

The Kingman Report wasn't received with any great joy by the government that commissioned it – after all, as far as they were concerned, it came to the wrong conclusions. But one of its major recommendations, the establishment of a National Language Project, was accepted and led to the establishment of Language in the National Curriculum, or LINC as it has come to be known. LINC was a game-changer – a national project with a significant budget, led by a renowned linguist, Ronald Carter. Ron Carter (who I subsequently got to know through his support for EMC's work) had everything required for the role of leading the project – impressive linguistic and academic credentials, strong relationships with educators and school teachers, a collaborative way of working and a clear vision of how this project could transform teaching about language and teachers' own understandings about the way knowledge works. A superb central pack of resources was produced. There were also many smaller, satellite initiatives, one of which was based at EMC. I worked on it while taking a career break to spend time bringing up my children. I produced materials on the language of children's books, exploring *Peter Rabbit, Where the Wild Things Are* and other children's books as well as offering ideas and information about how children first learn to read. It was written for a KS3 audience and subsequently some of it was adapted and updated for use in EMC's *Language Works*, in an attempt to sustain and give fresh impetus to this kind of work. I look back at it wistfully as an example of the kind of work that was possible in the 1980s and 90s not just with A Level students but with much younger pupils as well.

The central LINC resource had a massive impact on English teachers and English teaching at the time. For many, especially those who had only done Literature in their own degree, it was the first time they had encountered serious academic ideas about the way language works and how it can be taught. The materials combined practical classroom activities, documentation in the form of transcripts and videos from classrooms and other settings, and, most importantly, commentaries and discussion that acted as a brilliant form of CPD for any teacher using the resources. It changed my own way of approaching language in the classroom and I never looked back. Even now, people ask for the materials, refer to them, reflect back on them, make active use of them in their thinking about the teaching of everything from reading, talk and writing to grammar, discourse and semantics. It is a truly seminal piece of work.

Sadly, because its stance did not match that desired by the government, the plug was pulled on the project before the official release of the materials and plans for a big programme of CPD were abandoned. The resource, however, was shared unofficially and publicised by word of mouth.

Where are we now? The strides forward that were taken in those years, particularly in the area of language study, have sadly been halted and the same fights about the most contentious issues still rage. In the press, in government, in staffrooms and on Twitter, the arguments are played out repeatedly, in very similar ways, as if little has been learnt. Language is clearly a highly charged and politically inflammatory issue.

Two things have happened in recent years that have seriously impacted on language study in schools, turning back the clock after the LINC years. The first is the introduction of grammar tests in KS2, which have required the teaching of formal grammar and an extensive list of grammatical terms, at a very early age. Ex-teacher and academic linguist, Ian Cushing is doing continuing research on the effects of this and raises major concerns. His article, 'Grammar Policy and Pedagogy from Primary to Secondary School' (December 2018) published in *Literacy*, the journal of UKLA, explores the disjuncts between primary and secondary schools' teaching of grammar. He notes that secondary teachers report poor conceptualisation of grammar by children coming up from KS2; they often seem to view grammatical knowledge just as a list of technical terms. His ongoing research, based on policy statements, test questions and interviews with primary teachers, suggests a high degree of what he calls 'pedagogical coercion' to teach grammar in ways that the teachers themselves do not believe to be productive. The tests and policies fuel a prescriptivist view of grammar that runs counter to the thinking of most linguists. Language commentator Lane Greene talks about the effects of this in his book

Talk on the Wild: Why Language Won't Do As It's Told (2018). He says:

> The pedagogical pendulum has begun to swing the other way, especially in Britain. Children learn a blizzard of terminology in primary schools […] All this has been done in the name of raising standards. But there is no clear evidence that this actually makes better writers […] In short, kids need to read, read and read some more, starting as early as possible, so they become comfortable with what the good stuff looks like. This prepares the ground for learning abstract concepts, which should be introduced later. Over-emphasis on the rules before children are strong readers is counter-productive.

The second major change is the removal from the National Curriculum and from GCSE of any formal requirement to study language for its own sake, over and above the utilitarian teaching of grammar for purposes such as the intention of improving writing. The absence of rich language study from GCSE is the most damaging because it has had a knock-on effect on KS3 as well.

In the 2010-2015 iteration of GCSE, based on the previous National Curriculum, all students undertook a spoken language study as a Controlled Assessment. This was a wonderful opportunity for students to study language in its own right, including the differences between speech and writing, the issues surrounding Standard English, accent and dialect, language and identity, the use of different kinds of language in different contexts, code-switching and much more. It also gave students a window into what language study could be like, acting as a bridge to A Level and encouraging many students to opt for more specialist study at this level. Michael Gove dismissed such study in a speech at the University of Cambridge in 2011 as 'listening to tape recordings of Eddie Izzard and the Hairy Bikers', a statement that showed his ignorance of the rich range of serious linguistic investigations undertaken by GCSE students (as well as his ignorance of the insights that might arise out of doing these very things).

One additional, less obvious barrier to rich language study is the loss of 'ephemeral' or 'transient' texts in English Language GCSE – a Goveian prescription based on the notion that multimodal texts and online writing were of less value than substantial literary texts. When response to the language of texts shrinks to the language of literature one loses the richness and range of response to language in use, for instance the opportunity to comment on the language of the sports commentary, the advert or to consider the mixed mode features of a blog or website. This has been one of the worst aspects of Gove's reforms because it has prevented students from learning about, and engaging critically with, the language they are surrounded by and themselves make use of every day. In a world saturated in online communication, visual imagery and the multimodal collision of speech and writing, students don't study it at all and it's completely devalued. Generic understandings have shrunk to literary genres; understandings of the written form are no longer informed by awareness of how writing differs from speech; making meaning in different contexts and for different audiences and purposes is limited if all the texts under discussion have the same broad purposes – written with literary contexts and audiences in mind. (As earlier chapters have discussed, this also distorts the study of literature.)

Despite all of this, language study at KS3 is still possible – and highly desirable. In every year, there should be an opportunity to look closely and analytically at an aspect of language in use, whether it be to do with the language of a particular context, or the exploration of one's own idiolect, or an activity looking at the history of the language and the imports (and exports) from different languages, or an investigation into local dialects and accents, or a discussion of the arguments surrounding Standard English. At KS3, the curriculum is currently open enough for this to be possible, yet many schools have simply forgotten that it is a possibility, or decided that the lack of assessment at GCSE makes it a low priority, and/or have started 3-year GCSE courses, attenuating further the window for KS3 language work to be done. This I believe to be wrong-headed. Explicit exploration of ideas about language can do nothing other than arouse genuine interest in students for language itself. That has to be both good for other aspects of the subject and of immense value for its own sake.

Despite the lack of government support in subsequent years, the spirit of the LINC programme – proper linguistic knowledge applied to making judgements about what to teach and how to teach it, combined with a passionate interest in teaching children about language – has survived today, however patchily. As previously mentioned, it fed into EMC's *Language Works*, a resource published in 2007 on knowledge about language at KS3. It was also instrumental in *Investigating Spoken Language* (2009), EMC's publication for GCSE Controlled Assessment on spoken language and it continues to have an influence on our current thinking, for instance in our most recent publication *EMC KS3 Language Laboratory* (2018). EMC has always put a high priority on provision of resources to fuel knowledge about language for its own sake.

Thinking about the current state of play, I would pull out just a few people, pieces of research and arenas in which interesting and important work has been done and is continuing to be done, addressing some of the three fundamental issues raised at the beginning of this chapter.

On the teaching of grammar

Debra Myhill and her colleagues at the University of Exeter have done exceptionally interesting and important work on the teaching of grammar. Their substantial piece of research, *Grammar for Writing*, on contextualised grammar at KS3, explored whether or not grammar teaching might impact on student writing. This was of major significance, given that up to that point no study had ever been able to prove any connection between grammar teaching and improved writing. Even here, Myhill and colleagues were highly cautious in the conclusions they drew. It was only when grammar was embedded in the context of a text being read, or of a piece of the student's own writing, that any positive impact could be observed. Even then, it was most marked in the work of *higher* attaining students rather than *lower* attaining students, although the more recent research is more optimistic about the impact of embedded grammar teaching on the wider cohort too. The research also pointed up the fact that it seemed more important for students to notice and explore grammar in texts, than aim to be fully conversant with the grammatical terminology used to describe it. In fact, the Exeter report suggested that grammatical terms could get in the way, if they became the predominant focus of attention both for students and teachers. Students could talk well (or badly) about grammatical features both using the terms and not using them. One important aspect of the research was a recognition that teachers themselves often struggled with the grammar and the terminology and that a large-scale CPD programme would be needed to make any impact on this. The research stressed the vital importance of talk in teaching grammar for writing, drawing on the work of Barnes and Mercer (see Chapter 5 on 'Group Work and Talk in English Classrooms', page 94). Imitation, playfulness, experimentation and seeing grammar as a 'choice' to be explored in texts and taken on board in your own writing are fundamental to this view of how grammatical knowledge can be brought to bear on the writing process. Grammar as choice rather than rules is at the heart of the findings. This draws on Halliday, particularly, a huge influence (alongside Ron Carter) on contemporary thinking about language and education.

Myhill's research took place both prior to, and in the period after, the introduction of the KS2 grammar test and glossary, both of which have had a profound impact on the teaching of grammar at primary level. Despite some examples of particularly good practice, the KS2 approach has broadly run counter to Myhill's team's findings about embedding grammar in real contexts and avoiding an over-emphasis on the terms.

The most recent work of the Exeter team includes Debra Myhill and Helen Lines' fascinating longitudinal study for the Exeter Centre For Research in Writing, *Writing Conversations,* which set out to explore the relationship between students' grammatical knowledge and their development as writers, as well as the impact of grammar teaching on their writing.[1]

Here, Lines says:

> Our study shows if teachers explain grammar in a more practical and natural way regularly, other than something separate or abstract from other lessons, children will better understand.

> Over-focusing on labelling and identifying grammatical terms is not helpful and the Government and teachers need to think again about how children can gain a more sophisticated and enriched understanding of what grammar is. They need more space in the curriculum for children to express both their understandings and their confusions.

Myhill states,

> Children's writing does become more sophisticated as they become older, but very often they can use a particular grammatical structure in their writing before they can describe what they have done. We don't yet know if this is developmental, or linked to how students are taught. But what is clear is that teachers who themselves are comfortable with grammar are better able to handle children's confusions and help them become more thoughtful writers.

---

1. This work is written up in outline on the Exeter University website: http://socialsciences.exeter.ac.uk/ education/research/centres/centreforresearchinwriting

Helen Lines did a small-scale study in 2018/19, an analysis of examination scripts for OCR, in which similar conclusions are drawn about the ways in which grammatical terms can get in the way of valid and reflective writing about grammar in texts and need to be taught sensitively, contextually and without an expectation of their constant use as labels.[2]

A Level Language and Linguistics in the academic world

A Level Language has been hugely important as a site for the development of teachers' own linguistic knowledge and thinking. This has facilitated broader CPD in English departments. Those A Level Language teachers, often themselves having degrees that include Language, or having done MAs as part of their own professional development, have brought their expertise to bear on everything from debates about whether students should be expected to speak in full sentences, or in Standard English in the playground, to discussions on how to teach grammar at KS3.

There has also been very fruitful interplay between academics working in the field of language and linguistics and teachers and their students. Many universities (including Reading, York, Huddersfield and Queen Mary University London) hold events for teachers or students; EMC runs courses for teachers that draw in academic linguists; *emagazine* includes contributions from linguists and invites them to our conferences for students. They provide a body of sound academic opinion and knowledge to allow schools to counter damaging, popular notions of correctness and standards. So, for instance, Rob Drummond at Manchester Metropolitan University intervenes regularly in education debates on Twitter about accent and dialect, pointing teachers in the direction of research and linguistic thinking that counters the notion that some accents are 'better' than others, that some 'dialects' are more or less rule-governed, 'better' or 'worse' than others. David Crystal has spoken out against the KS2 grammar tests, speaks at many student events and is followed avidly by many teachers. Marcello Giovanelli and Ian Cushing, both once A Level English Language teachers themselves, and now academic linguists, have engaged passionately in debates around the teaching of grammar, language in context, the nature of the reading process and more. Giovanelli's work on stylistics, looking at the relationship between language and literature, has been very important and has engaged many teachers in thinking hard about the nature of the reading process. Many others have also contributed hugely to the development of language and linguistics in schools, in a spirit of collaboration and in order to further the subject at all levels.

The twittersphere and the internet

For all its downsides and damaging aspects, Twitter can play a really important role in disseminating information and ideas, especially in communities of interest.

---

2. Of the Exeter team's exceptionally important work, the article I would most recommend is 'Playful Explictness with Grammar: a Pedagogy for Writing', written by Debra Myhill, Susan Jones, Annabel Watson and Helen Lines (2013). It is a highly readable goldmine of important ideas and practices, based on the 2012 study undertaken by the Exeter team.

This is particularly true in the world of linguistics and education. There are many sources of information about language now available via Twitter and blogs that would have eluded many teachers in the past. Linguists are active, prolific and eager to debate and share what they know. Dan Clayton's @EngLangBlog, @GrowthThroughGrammar, Lynne Murphy's tweets on American English and English @lynnelinguist, Deborah Cameron's exceptional blogs publicised through her twitterfeed @wordspinster and the QMUL Linguistics Research Digest, make it possible for teachers to keep bang up to date with recent linguistic research, fuelling their own thinking about the educational debates that crop up in their schools. Journalists like Oliver Kamm and Lane Greene are equally active in critiquing populist peeves and ill-informed linguistic gripes. They stand side by side with teachers in providing a rigorous basis for making judgements on language.

So, I would argue that, despite the negative effects of recent government policy, grammar can be taught in 'playfully explicit ways', language study is still perfectly possible in the spaces in the curriculum at KS3 and students' own language can be both valued and validated in classroom contexts. A failure to do any of these things would be a dereliction of our duty to students.

References for Chapter 12

Bleiman, B., Oliver, K. and Webster, L. 2008. *Language Works*. London: English & Media Centre.

Cameron, D. 1995. *Verbal Hygiene – The Politics of Language*. Abingdon: Routledge.

Clayton, D. and McCallum, A. 2018. *Language Laboratory*. London: English & Media Centre.

Cushing, I. 2018. 'Grammar policy and pedagogy from primary to secondary school' in *Literacy. UKLA*.

Department for Education and Science. 1988. *Report of the Committee of Inquiry into the Teaching of English Language (The Kingman Report)*. London. HMSO.

Greene, L. 2018. *Talk on the Wild Side: Why Language Won't Do As It's Told*. London: Profile Books.

Gove, M. 2011. Speech at University of Cambridge on a liberal education https://www.gov.uk/government/speeches/michael-gove-to-cambridge-university

Language in the National Curriculum Resources (LINC). 1989-91. Available Nottingham University Online Store (https://store.nottingham.ac.uk/product-catalogue/schools-and-departments/english/linc-project).

Myhill, D., S. Jones and T. Bailey. 2012. 'Grammar for writing? An investigation of the effects of contextualised grammar teaching on students' writing'. In *Reading and Writing* 26 (8).

Myhill, D., Jones, S. and Wilson, A. 2016. 'Writing conversations: fostering metalinguistic discussion about writing' in *Research Papers in Education* 31 (1).

Myhill, D., S. Jones, A. Watson and H. Lines. 2013. 'Playful explicitness with grammar: a pedagogy for writing'. In *Literacy* 47 (2). UKLA.

12. Research, Theory, Practice and CPD

University lecturers in education departments have *always* seen research as a major part of their job, MA and PhD students have conducted it and trainee teachers have been introduced to relevant studies. In external CPD, organisations like EMC have referred to research and drawn useful ideas and supportive evidence from it. Teachers doing their own classroom research, supported by sympathetic academics, is not new either. One can see it in the 1970s, in the work of seconded teachers and practitioners at EMC (then the ILEA English Centre) and the ground-breaking work of John Richmond and others in *Becoming Our Own Experts*. Yet, more recently, the belief that teaching is not sufficiently informed by current research has become widespread in certain educational circles. Initiatives to bring it into a more fruitful relationship with practices in schools and classrooms have burgeoned. A few elements of these discussions have caused me concern: the question of what counts as legitimate research; the nature of the research being applied, particularly from the fields of psychology and science and whether it can be applied unproblematically to educational contexts; the complexity of classrooms as organisms and teaching as an activity, and the care with which one might need to import ideas from one context into another; the question of what research to prioritise; the notion that teachers' own observations and judgements should be subservient to some external finding, rather than a major part of the equation; the absence of attention to subject-based research, as opposed to broader, generic research. The two pieces that follow, one from 2013 and one from 2015, touch on all of these substantial issues.

12.1 Is 'What Works?' the only question educational research should be trying to answer

We have entered a new phase in education, the 'Research-led Education Phase'. In principle that's an excellent thing. Drifting along doing things in classrooms without considering their impact is not a good way of making sure that pupils get the most out of their education. The new focus can be seen on many new education blogs, and at events like 'researchED 2013 – Working out what works', where many different angles on educational research were presented and debated. Teachers learning how to read research, discuss and critique it, rather than simply accept it at face value, is undoubtedly a good thing.

But along with these critical views of research there is also a climate in which research has shrunk to something very narrow, based on quantitative testing and trials that are only designed to answer the question 'What works?'. This kind of testing, imported directly from research in other spheres such as medicine, provides a set of seemingly scientific answers to what are not necessarily the right questions. 'What works?' is only one of a range of questions one might want to research in classrooms, to examine what makes a difference to pupils' learning. 'What works to raise Ds to Cs?'[1] is a question that is frequently asked, but a whole range of other questions cluster round even this narrow, seemingly clear-cut, simple one. 'What works in the short-term?', 'Is this the same as the longer-term?', 'Does what works now last?' 'Does what works to raise Ds to Cs make pupils better learners in other aspects of their schooling, or in their future lives as literate and competent citizens?' Equally, altogether different questions, such as 'What do pupils need?' or 'Why do some pupils have blocks to certain kinds of learning?' might yield very different answers.

If we narrow our questions so that we only ask the 'What works?' ones, so favoured by government-assisted funding bodies like EEF and others, then we fail to ask the questions that might provide equally important steers for educational practice. We squeeze out any questions that can't be answered using numerical data. Many of these questions are the more subtle, important ones about the impact of schooling on pupils' attitudes to learning, their thinking, their enjoyment and their ability and enthusiasm for tackling problems, engaging with ideas and going on to learn more. 'How do you engage pupils in their own learning?' or 'How do you encourage pupils to read for pleasure?' are not easily measured by numerical tests, nor can they be assessed in a short timeframe. Finding out about the impact of different elements of education on reading for pleasure inevitably involves attitudinal research and long-term study, rather than quick data-driven tests, yet time and again reading for pleasure is shown to be a better measure of long-term educational success than any other. If we fail to ask questions about reading for pleasure because it's hard to measure, then we risk focusing our time, our funding and our collective efforts only on those things that are easy to measure.

By contrast with this kind of Gradgrindian obsession with certain kinds of data, there are some very important and serious ways in which teachers can and should be making use of research – a different kind of research. Along with the obsession with quantitative data has come a new kind of teacher education, in which university learning is eschewed in favour of training in a school context. I would hate to knock what schools can do for new teachers – some are brilliant at preparing them for a life of teaching. But there's another kind of research that all trainee teachers, of English or any other subject, ought to have had access to, and that's the kind of research done by key thinkers and writers, both from the past and present, who have been significant in developing philosophical, psychological, sociological, pedagogic and other ways of thinking. Here I'm thinking about writers like Jean Piaget, Lev Vygotsky, Douglas Barnes, James Britton, Harold Rosen, Jerome Bruner, Paulo Freire among others. Vygotsky wasn't worried about D to C grades – he was a seminal thinker about how it is that children learn language and the ways in which that is a social, rather than an individual process. Reading Vygotsky won't tell you how to get a D to a C in easy steps but it will

---

1. This was an overriding preoccupation of the early 2000s, which, since the introduction of value-added accountability measures, Progress 8 and a new grading system, has been less starkly presented but nevertheless still drives much thinking in schools. What works to raise results is still behind much of the funding decisions for educational research.

give you a deep and lasting underpinning for the principles of how children learn that will see you through all your teaching. It will allow you to ride the waves of educational reform and stay afloat, however small your boat, because you have a well-made, robust craft that can steer its own course through choppy seas.

Another form of research that is equally important and is perhaps gaining more credence in our current world, is teachers' researching their own practices. John Richmond and others, in the 1970s and 80s, led the way, with *Becoming Our Own Experts* (1982), encouraging teachers to see the relationship between theory and practice in education, by making their own classrooms arenas for serious research into pedagogy in English teaching. Having film clips, or transcripts of classroom interactions gave teachers a chance to analyse together exactly what was going on. Thinking about talk and group work, in particular, was hugely enhanced by close observation of the processes involved and the role of the teacher.[2]

The new development of blogs, Twitter, Teachmeets and other such innovations, has led to a wonderful burgeoning of teachers sharing their experiences, their thinking, their expertise and examples of their classroom work. However, it seems to me to be important that these kinds of sharing do not become an alternative to other more sustained forms of research, but instead, sit alongside them, providing a huge amount of energetic and vibrant thinking but also allying themselves to other valuable forms of research and CPD.

Sometimes one reads of people zealously proclaiming the virtues of one kind of approach over another. University-led training is dead! CPD by training organisations isn't the best way of doing it! And so on. The truth is that all of these forms of teacher development (self-initiated, in the school, led by communities of teachers in local areas, online, provided by universities, training organisations, books, blogs or whatever), have the potential to develop teachers' practice and change their thinking, if they are asking the right questions, and if they are drawing on a range of different kinds of research – not just the kind that can be created in a year of randomised controlled trials, or someone telling someone else what they did in their classroom to get a D grade student to reach a C.

---

2. This kind of close observational research, as opposed to that focusing only on outcomes of interventions for cohorts, is more rare but there are some excellent recent examples of it. Adam Lefstein and Julia Snell's *Better than Best Practice – Developing Teaching and Learning through Dialogue* (2013) is based on transcripts and video extracts, predominantly from primary classrooms but interesting for secondary teachers too.

12.2 What is good CPD in English?

In 2015 I was asked to contribute to a cross-curricular panel discussion on CPD as part of a DfE/Teacher Development Trust initiative on creating a set of new standards for CPD. Around the same time, I attended an RSA meeting on this same issue as an audience member. At these meetings, I found myself arguing very differently from those around me. I was disturbed by the lack of interest in, or attention to, subject-specific CPD. It was as if it had been entirely forgotten. All the arguments and the focus of the standards were on cross-curricular, whole-school CPD. My contribution was to point out this major omission and suggest that, in my view, at secondary level, subject-specific CPD was the most important kind of professional development of all. More recently, there seems to have been a greater acknowledgement of this. In the blog that follows, I set out some key ideas about my own view of what good CPD looks like, drawing on all the work I have done with colleagues at EMC over the years.

In March 2015, David Weston, chief executive of the Teacher Development Trust, wrote a very informative article for *SecED*, the online education magazine, about how the most effective schools run their CPD programmes. In the article he addresses seven common problems with CPD, most of which relate to internal school issues. However, he also draws attention to the need for high-quality external expertise, explaining that 'Our best schools have taken tough decisions to maintain or even increase CPD budgets while financial pressures grow. They have understood the research that shows external expert facilitation to be a key ingredient of professional development that genuinely improves student outcomes.' In working for EMC, which has provided external CPD for many decades, I would, of course, support this view. However, as Weston points out, external CPD needs to be of high quality.

What are the essential features of such 'high quality' CPD? EMC is in a particularly good position to be able to identify some of the underlying qualities of excellent CPD, partly because of our longevity but also because our track record is so exceptional. We are consistently rated very highly by participants, many of whom come from schools who return to us with great regularity and give us feedback over time, not just at the end of a single day. Many of our judgements about the underlying qualities of superb CPD would chime with David Weston's views. What follows on pages 184-186 is a brief account of the most important aspects.

1. Practice – theory – practice

EMC, from its early days, has always had a credo of 'practice – theory – practice', in other words the idea that you start with classroom practice, you consider theoretical or research material, with intellectual analysis that might generate deeper thinking about that practice, and then you return to practice, to try out how new insights might influence or impact on classroom work. This is something that David Weston draws attention to in his recent article. As part of this, we believe that CPD should draw on shared experiences of teaching and learning that can be reflected on and discussed, with general principles being pulled out to make the insights applicable to other scenarios or contexts.

2. Learning through experience – understanding how it works

CPD should allow teachers to actively experience aspects of classroom pedagogy while the course tutors model and explain how the teacher could get the best out of the approaches. Reflecting on how and why strategies can be used, unpicking the underlying pedagogy and rationale seems to us to be essential. It allows teachers to reflect on what the student is learning and leads to richer discussions about how the teaching could be adapted for different contexts, ability levels and so on. Teachers often tell us that a useful bonus of a course run in this way is to be reminded of what it is like to be a learner, for example working in a group, or being asked to share a piece of writing with peers. A few teachers tell us that they would prefer to be 'talked at' but most say that this model makes them more likely to put into practice learning from the course.

3. Beyond the whizzy activity or the narrow performance focus

David Weston particularly cautions against the type of CPD which focuses on performance and technique at the expense of a real consideration of how to move students on in their learning. This is something that we feel very strongly about. CPD should not simply be about offering a string of quick-fix techniques, or 'whizzy things' to do in the classroom. Offering classroom approaches in CPD courses is great but only when it is allied to serious thinking about how and why these approaches might develop learning, how they can be adapted or developed in other contexts and how they fit within a broader set of principles about how children learn.

4. Going away with high-quality resources

Teachers are under huge pressure and love being given tried-and-tested resources that they can take back and use in the classroom straightaway. The great thing about having tried them out on the course day is that they have been discussed, analysed, reflected on and modelled, so for teachers considering changing or tweaking their pedagogy to take on board lessons learnt, there are ready-made, well thought through and instantly available opportunities to do so. They can make small shifts in the confident knowledge that these new approaches have been done successfully with the group in the CPD session. We have found that this extra boost of both confidence and understanding of the underlying pedagogy is a strong encouragement for trying something new. It then provides a stepping off point for extending these new approaches into new texts, new topics or areas of work.

5. The CPD tutor as expert teacher

The modelling by the CPD tutor of excellent teaching can give teachers insight into how highly trained and experienced teachers teach. As Dylan Wiliam suggested in a 2015 *TES* article, judgement, expertise and experience are to be taken just as seriously as research-based knowledge; being able to draw on the experience of trainers with a track-record of highly successful teaching is extremely valuable. This is particularly so for new teachers, seeking to develop not only their thinking and their planning but also their classroom skills and ways of engaging with students. Teachers often comment on this aspect of CPD in their evaluations of EMC courses.

6. The development of subject knowledge

The development of teachers' own subject knowledge in relation to teaching is a key element of high quality CPD, for instance extending teachers' understanding of current practice in universities in relation to the teaching of Shakespeare, updating them on new developments in the teaching of critical theory or giving them access to current work and thinking on authors, texts or aspects of language. At EMC, we sometimes bring in an academic to offer an overview of a topic, or genre, or single text, to give teachers a significant input on that aspect of what they will go on to teach. This is then often followed up by discussion that allows teachers to consider the implications for their students or their classrooms. We always try to provide material that stretches and challenges teachers in relation to the subject itself so that they feel they've had an injection of fresh ideas and information.

7. Learning from others – beyond the school bubble

One important element in high quality CPD is the chance to go beyond one's own institution, to hear about the experiences of others, perhaps in similar contexts or alternatively in very different ones. Schools and colleges tend to be quite unique organisms and when CPD is always internal, however good it is, ways of teaching and planning for teaching can become a bit insular. Teachers in schools or colleges where there is little external CPD sometimes complain of being in a little 'bubble', where they are unaware of different ways of approaching similar issues or problems. On EMC courses, we find that teachers hugely appreciate the chance to exchange ideas and learn from each other, so that they can take back fresh ideas to their departments.

8. Thinking about what to take back to school and how

It is important, after one-day training courses, that teachers think about ways of incorporating their new insights or approaches into their own practice and consider how to share their new ideas with other members of staff. Sometimes teachers request that we come and deliver elements of the CPD they have experienced to the whole department. Others feed back to department meetings, or incorporate new resources in their planning and their schemes of work.

9. A chance to step back and reflect

Finally, one of the most important elements of CPD is that it provides teachers with an opportunity to stand back and consider what they are doing, to reinvigorate them, or re-inspire them. This is an understated benefit of external CPD. Squeezing it into an hour's meeting at the end of a long teaching day, or even holding it in the same old office or the same old classroom, doesn't have quite the same effect as giving someone a whole day, away from the school, to refresh themselves and their thinking. 'Inspired', 'refreshed' and 'more confident' are phrases which often crop up on our course evaluations and which give us great satisfaction as course providers.

10. Coffee and cake

I am only half-joking here! Schools and colleges are such busy places with little time to start, let alone finish, an interesting conversation about pedagogy or sharing ideas. A day away from it all with a nice lunch, the chance to chat, fresh coffee and stimulating sessions can send people back with renewed enthusiasm.

References for Chapter 12

Lefstein, A. and Snell, J. 2013. *Better Than Best Practice – Developing Teaching and Learning Through Dialogue*. Abingdon: Routledge.

Richmond, J. et al. 1982. *Becoming Our Own Experts*. The Talk Workshop Group: London.

Weston, D. 2015. 'Seven common CPD problems for schools'. In *SecEd* online article. Available at http://www.sec-ed.co.uk/best-practice/seven-common-cpd-problems-for-schools

Postscript: Harold Rosen Lecture

June 2019 NATE Conference, Chester

In June 2019 I was asked to present the annual Harold Rosen Lecture at the NATE Conference. I took the opportunity to present a different vision of English to that which has been emerging in recent years, in a world where teachers feel boxed in, constrained and stifled by external pressures and educational ideas that are inimical to some of the most important elements of the subject. It pulls together many of the ideas which have been discussed throughout this book, themselves the product of my 43 years of work in the subject.

Harold Rosen was Professor of Education when I trained as an English teacher in 1976 to 1977. His insights and understandings have remained with me ever since. That doesn't mean to say I haven't adapted and developed and enthusiastically taken on board lots of new things. But I also haven't abandoned some core principles and values that came from him, from thinkers like him, and ones before him. I was trained in a period when there were 'experts' like Harold. Expertise was valued.

For me expertise is a mix of two things – experience and knowledge. Older teachers or teacher/educators worked closely with younger ones like me. I remember in the late 70s and early 80s LATE workshops with people like John Dixon, or NATE 'strands' on poetry with the amazing Geoff Fox where I was given the opportunity to learn from these extraordinary English educators. They shared the knowledge they had accumulated over time, in the subject and in education more generally, from both a vast range of reading and substantial, significant, classroom experience, often as Heads of English. The two things together. Practitioners and theorists. Theorist/practitioners. And they were often conducting their own research too. Practitioner/theorist/researchers.

You'll notice I distinguish between research and theory. Theory seems to me to bring an additional dimension. It's not the here today, gone tomorrow research of 'what works' (or rather what might work in some contexts but not necessarily your own classroom). It's something more fundamental about political, societal, human values and ways of being. It's theories of language and thought, of knowledge, of human behaviour, of aesthetics and culture.

Something has changed. This kind of three-pronged expertise seems not to be valued so much any more, despite the fact that the knowledge of the past that I've described, combined with the energy, vitality and new vision of younger teachers is a potent mix. It has huge potential. But divorce one from the other and you risk English teaching becoming deracinated – losing its roots. Lovely looking shoots but nothing to anchor them firmly into the soil.

We can see endless new initiatives and ideas coming around and feel as if on a merry go round. Those of us who've been on it too long have begun to feel queasy. We saw something in other iterations. We doubted it then. We're sceptical now. We recommend care and caution. But no-one is looking back. No-one remembers what came before.

So I want to start my talk proper with a reference back. In my view it's an extremely important reference for English teachers, and it's to Harold Rosen himself and the insights this exceptional theorist, researcher, practitioner had to offer – and still does.

> English is nothing less than a different model of education; knowledge to be made, not given; knowledge comprising more than can be discursively stated; learning as a diverse range of processes, including affective ones; educational processes to be embarked on with outcomes unpredictable; students' perceptions, experiences, imaginings and unsystematically acquired knowledge admitted as legitimate curricular content.

This is powerful stuff. Important stuff. It was then and it is now. It has big aims for students and for the subject, big ambition, big ideas. Opening up, not narrowing or closing down, drawing students into the process not shutting them out, admitting rather than rejecting, allowing them to think big and think for themselves, and think beyond the limits of what the education system is currently imposing on them.

The rest of this talk is going to be all about that. The need to resist the subject shrinking only to what is assessable, to resist it becoming smaller and narrower and more limited but instead to allow it to be big, expansive, broad and inclusive in all kinds of different ways. If it sounds like I'm proseltysing, preaching, I am. This is a moment for beliefs and visions as well as facts. Ideas and values are what our subject is all about and I am unapologetic in stating that this is what I believe to be important. It comes from the experience, wisdom and knowledge of those, like Harold Rosen, who came before me.

So let's start with a text (see page 190) and some talk. Two vital things in anything to do with English teaching.

I want you to look at it and ask yourself four simple questions:

1. What are my first thoughts?

2. Am I puzzled or intrigued by anything about it?

3. What do I like about it?

4. Does it remind me of anything?

Now turn to the person sitting next to you and share your ideas.

Quend-Plage-les-Pins

This place would be beautiful
if it didn't exist. Well – the pines
can stay, and the dunes, with their strange
tenacious grasses; and the fine
falling sand, and the waves,
long and slanted, coming in
and coming in.
But it wouldn't need
this road, with its ribbons
and pennants, its kites and crêpes
and beach-toys. It wouldn't need
this fairground, this car-park,
this promenade. It wouldn't need
a name. It wouldn't need us.

Helen Tookey

This is not the way texts are currently being explored in many of our classrooms. What's your response and why?' has been supplanted by a focus on other things – often small things, at word, phrase or sentence level – small language techniques and devices. Vocabulary is one of the new 'obsessions'. The mantra, 'the more words you know the smarter you are' and the idea that students can't access texts without knowing every single word in advance (drawing on E.D Hirsch) has led to lots of pre-teaching of vocabulary. And lots of pre-teaching of context too, as if you can't ever approach a text without knowing everything about it first. As if it's risky and dangerous ever to just read and see what you make of it for yourself. As if texts don't ever explain themselves. As if they don't provide new knowledge. As if they're simply excuses for teaching vocabulary.

With the text I've shown you, you might start with something like this:

- Quend-Plage-les-Pins is a seaside resort in Picardie, in France.

- Here's a photograph of it.

- A pine is an evergreen tree.

- Dunes are mounds of sand on beaches.

- Tenacious means clinging firmly, determined, persistent.

- Pennants are flags.

- Crêpes are pancakes.

- A promenade is a walkway along a beach.

- You might pre-teach literary and linguistic terms like syndetic and asyndetic listing, caesura, alliteration, assonance, demonstrative pronouns and ask students whether they can find examples in the poem. In all instances, you can!

I'm exaggerating a bit of course, but not much. If you google 'vocabulary' and 'Strange Case of Dr Jekyll and Mr Hyde' for instance, you will find lists for each chapter that are pages and pages long, with comment to students telling them 'These are the words you need to know before even reading this chapter' or 'These are the words you need to know before your exam'. Given that the unfamiliar words in the first paragraph alone of Strange Case of Dr Jekyll and Mr Hyde include 'eminently', 'beacon', 'austere', 'symbols' 'mortify', 'a taste for vintages', 'approved tolerance', 'extremity', 'inclined' and 'reproved' this is very, very daunting.

Who would want to read the poem (or Strange Case of Dr Jekyll and Mr Hyde Chapter 1) if learning unfamiliar words is your main starting-point? Burrowing down into tiny details before even getting a chance to discover for yourself what kind of text this is going to be and what your first impressions are.

I might actually give you the information about where the place is, and perhaps even show you a photo or two. If a word stands in the way of your broad understanding perhaps I might also offer that to you.

But would you really need all the word information I gave you, up front, in order to talk interestingly about this poem? Were the pleasures and difficulties in the poem predominantly a question of words anyway? If you knew all the unfamiliar words would that, in and of itself, have opened up the poem for you? Could you talk about it without knowing all these words and this context, if some were missing? Could you work out enough for yourselves? And in doing that, would that not then stand you in really good stead for reading the next poem and the next one and the one after that? This is know-how in English literature alongside knowledge of a particular poem in relation to others – skills at the service of knowledge and vice versa. It's what Robert Eaglestone helpfully describes as 'doing English', or more humorously 'being an Englisher' in the way that others are geographers, historians or modern linguists, who discover the processes which subject disciplinary experts use to 'do' their subject.

How about, instead, if I had asked you to focus just on the first two lines and spend some time discussing those, perhaps in relation to other things? Can the students think of other things which would be beautiful if they didn't exist? How is that possible? Or if I asked you to think about that repeated phrase, 'It wouldn't need' and what 'it' is and what exactly 'it' wouldn't need and why? Wouldn't that take you further? Or in thinking about the question, 'what's puzzling or intriguing?' what if I asked you whether this is similar or different from other poems you've read. Are there aspects that aren't very poem-like? Or that are more poem-like?

If we narrow the focus to words only, to small detail, and always and only to the narrower questions of comprehension in a single poem, rather than big picture ideas, we risk becoming blind to the aspects of texts that are both most important and also cause students most difficulty. We focus students and their attention on little things and don't encourage judgement about what's significant and what isn't. We also narrow the conversation, confine it to elements that students cannot contribute much to, in which we are the sole experts and they must rely on us for answers, only to questions that can be answered. We deny the importance of their response and the fact that sometimes their response might collectively take the class further than just our own response, and take our own response further too.

English Literature is all about readers, writers and, crucially, the relationship between them. That's a complex business, nerves and muscle and bone and blood supply and chemicals and hormones all operating together to make the body work. If we look only at a small bone in the foot in isolation, not even at a whole skeleton, or at blood in a test tube, or at a single nerve twitching, we never see the whole body in motion.

To turn now to the question I asked about the poem, 'What does this remind you of?' it seems to me to be a particularly important one. The text might remind you of personal experiences and send the conversation outwards (and inwards) into life and mind and emotion – that's after all, what poems are meant to do – to connect with you personally, to make you think and feel. It might bring up strongly held feelings about the environment and nature.

How about, if I'd asked you to use the first two lines as a starting-point for a poem of your own? Or if I'd suggested that you write about a place that you think has been spoilt for you by people. (In my case, it might be the Alhambra, with all its tourists taking photographs – or my neighbours' new back extension, blocking out the light in my kitchen.)

But equally it might and should send you into other literary experiences and encourage you to make connections with other reading and writers. These kinds of conversations, with yourself and with others, are vital not only to reading literature but to studying it. They are a fundamental part of the way all thinking and all knowledge works – the categorisation of what we encounter – why a text is this, or this or this but *not* that, or that, or that.

So, encouraging those literary connections and comparisons is really important – going out from a text in big, expansive ways and then back in again. I recognise the poem as a poem only because of others that I've read. It's more like a lyric poem than a narrative one. It's short, intense and it has a point to make. I recognise it in these ways only because I've read other poems, ones that are both like it and not like it, lyrics and narratives. I automatically start to categorise it in my mind to discover what makes it special, where it sits in the world of poems and poemness. It makes me think of other sea poems, Matthew Arnold's 'Dover Beach' for instance – also questioning humanity in the wider landscape, both natural and spiritual. It makes me think of Anne Stevenson's 'With My Sons at Boar Hills', a very different poem – much more personal, using a memory of her sons as children to think about time passing. It's a bit more like Larkin's 'To the Sea' perhaps? But his vision is more photographic, and more about people and their lives, less about nature and what people do to it. It makes me think of William Carlos Williams – the simplicity but also that taking you out of a scene or a description into something more profound and yet still elliptical and uncertain. Or new ecological writing in other genres – Robert Macfarlane, for instance. And so on and so on. If I started to talk to someone else about this – any one of you for instance – I'd hear about other poems, I'd remember others myself, I'd refine my thinking not only of the specific poem but also of poetry in general.

Now obviously students don't have all these poetic reference points. But they have to start somewhere. And that's with us. In English classrooms. If you've read only a handful of poems in detail, that gives you limited experience. So students should be reading lots of poetry, in lots of different ways – sometimes close up, of course, looking at the brush strokes, but sometimes also just strolling through the gallery, noticing the different kinds of things on offer, and visiting many different kinds of galleries. We should be drawing them into the process of being able to refer back and forwards in this kind of way. Unprompted they might say, for instance, 'it's not at all like that other poem we read 'The Sea is a Hungry Dog' by James Reeves' and their teacher might ask why. And that opens up the conversation about themes and ideas, one being about this, the other about that, but also about the very different poetic stances, voices, stylistic choices. By the time they reach GCSE and unseen poetry, and then perhaps, hopefully, A Level, they will have broad experiences and big ideas to draw on, when looking at any single text – a rich context into which to put it.

As those of you have read my blogs will know, I'm very taken with the work of an American acolyte of Harold Rosen's called Arthur Applebee. Rosen supervised his PhD when he was living and studying in London. Applebee and his colleagues, undertaking research in 2002 into the most effective English classrooms in the US, drew attention particularly to this idea of connections – the linking of one of idea to another, the drawing of parallels and relationships, the bigger picture of literature and the subject.

Applebee's write-up of this research in *The English Journal* (2002) says,

> Interconnectedness is an important feature of effective curriculum and instruction at virtually every level, from the coherence and interconnectedness of classroom discussion on a particular day, to connections across school experiences and between school and home, to the interweaving of reading, writing, and discussion throughout a unit, to the exploration of key concepts and questions over the course of a semester or year. […] In contrast, the good but not exceptional classrooms that CELA has studied have been orderly and systematic, but they have tended to treat ideas and experiences in isolation from one another, as building blocks in the larger curriculum, rather than nurturing rich layers of possible links by inviting constant comparison, contrast, and the re-visiting of related ideas and experiences.

Applebee sees the English curriculum as one big, continuing 'conversation'. He sees knowledge as being about entering into subject disciplinary conversations and traditions of thought. I find this a very appealing and intuitively 'true' way of thinking about the English curriculum in schools. I can look back at my own teaching over thirty years and at the great teaching I saw both then and since, and this particular way of characterising it seems to me to have been a feature of the very best of what I've experienced, seen and still see in classrooms.

I'm going to take the time to read to you a few extracts from Applebee's book *Curriculum as Conversation*, because I think it has such important messages for us, particularly at this moment, when the curriculum and knowledge are being debated so passionately and when English departments are searching for a rationale and a set of principles for new thinking.

Applebee says to new students of English,

> English is like a long conversation through time. Like any conversation, it moves over various linked themes; it has quarrels and agreements; people talk at the same time, struggle to be heard or shout louder and louder to dominate the debate; people suggest fresh ideas ('what about this?') or respond to earlier ones ('can we just go back to…?'); there are newer and older participants; like all proper conversations, part of it concerns the point of the conversation itself ('can we please focus on why are we discussing this?'); and now you, doing English, have joined this conversation and will change what's said next.

He says,

> Schooling should be organised to help students enter into culturally significant domains for conversation, themselves representative of broader cultural traditions of knowing and doing. By placing the emphasis on entry into such conversations, I seek to ensure that students will emerge with knowledge-in-action rather than knowledge-out-of-context. By stressing culturally significant domains, I seek to ensure that education is organised around living traditions that look to the present and future as well as the past. And by stressing domains for conversation, I seek to ensure that there is an emphasis on the structure and interrelatedness of ideas and experiences within a domain.

What I love about this is the way it encapsulates everything I've said about the interrelationships between particular bits of knowledge and textual experiences but connects this with Rosen's and others ideas about the student's 'perceptions, experiences, imaginings and unsystematically acquired knowledge admitted as legitimate curricular content.' There is no need to exclude students' own experience from the conversation. In fact, the conversation can't really happen without it.

So, for the second part of my talk I want to focus on what actually happens when you construct your teaching in this way – where conversations about individual texts are at the heart of teaching but where those significant conversations go beyond the narrow confines of the single text and reach both back into memory (and sideways) into students own experiences of life and literature. And go forwards too, anticipating, prefiguring and developing the kinds of conversations that we hope students will go on to have about future texts and experiences of literature, both in academic study and in their reading lives as adults.

In our project, *It's Good to Talk*, as its name suggests, conversation is seen as a means of learning as a well as being fundamental to knowledge in the subject. In September last year we worked with a Year 9 cohort in a school in East London who were studying a novel. Half the cohort did their old scheme of work, the other half followed a new scheme written by myself and one of the teachers at the school, Lucy Hinchliffe, who at the time was working one day a week at EMC.

The project on a novel, that started with 'let's add in some group work' pretty quickly became engulfed in the much bigger questions of 'why are we teaching a novel?', 'What do we want students to know about this novel?', 'What kinds of conversations do we want our students to have about it?', 'What's important for them to learn about narrative texts that can be taken further into KS4?' and 'How important is it to know the book inside out as opposed to enjoying reading it and studying it in terms of what it offers as knowledge to take forward?'.

The book was *In the Sea There Are Crocodiles* by Fabio Geda. It is a novel based on a true story of the migration of a 10-year-old Afghani boy, Enaiat, who embarks on a 5 year journey to find a place of safety in Europe. Geda, the novelist, is the journalist who interviewed the boy on his arrival in Italy and turned his story into fiction.

The previous scheme proceeded, as many do these days, largely by PowerPoint – a sequence planned in advance by one teacher and followed by everyone teaching the book. It had several lessons of prior knowledge – slides with images of Afghanistan and historical information, followed by student research into Hazari and Pashtuns (despite the fact that many children in the classes were themselves Hazari or Pashtun and probably knew more than the teachers could tell them. In any event, the book itself gives you pretty much everything you need to know and teaches you all about the context.) The focus of this was all taking them out of the book into the wider context. Fascinating as that might be, it wasn't a literary experience.

Something very powerful and horribly upsetting happens right at the beginning of the book, in the first two or three pages – when the boy's mother leaves him, hoping that he'll have a safer, better life away from his village and suddenly he realises that he's on his own, having to fend for himself. The first time I read it, the tears welled up. I don't think I could read it aloud in class without choking. But there was little time in the original scheme of work for students (many of whom have personal histories of migration, in their own families), to talk about the impact of this on them and how the writer had conveyed the horror and the heartbreak.

The bulk of the study overall was GCSE exam-led, with a very close focus on language in preparation for the GCSE Language questions – a lot of PEETAL paragraphs on short extracts, concentrating on small details of language at word or, at most, sentence level.

There was very little of what I'd call bigger picture thinking:

- What's my response? Which was the most powerful moment for me? What does it remind me of?
- What kind of book is this?
- How does it compare with other novels I've read?

And so on.

The scheme Lucy Hinchliffe, the lead teacher, and I developed (which came to be known by the teachers as 'the EMC way') offered a radically different approach, that would encourage these kinds of ideas and insights, responses and thoughts, conversations that were serious and high level and personal and literary in their nature.

We asked ourselves what happens when you focus on big things – big ideas first, before small techniques:

- What is your response to the text and why (e.g. its subject, its events, what you find most interesting, moving, powerful)?

- Big ideas and concepts in literature (e.g. the novel, genre, fact/fiction).

- Significant narrative features (e.g. voice and point of view, narrative arc, dialogue, coherence, significant aspects of prose style).

- What makes the text distinctive? What are the 'characteristic' features and qualities of the text? Big patterns.

- Understandings about the way texts work that can be taken forward into the study of the next and future novels.

We had half the Year 9 cohort doing it the new 'EMC way' and the other half using the existing scheme of work.

Right from day one, lesson one, the students in the EMC groups were encouraged to think about these issues – to think big, not just in terms of the kinds of ideas but also in terms of questioning, drawing in previous experiences and knowledge. To think hard about important issues. In that first lesson, they were given fragments of the text to explore – to whet their appetite without spoiling the book, and to set them thinking about what kind of text this would be. Their first thoughts about what was most significant were collected on the whiteboard, in order to establish an on-going, class agenda – a kind of flexible, provisional, changing, developing, ever more sophisticated set of ideas about what's important to them about the book. It could be done differently, by reading the first chapter and then pooling ideas about important aspects of subject matter, themes, style, voice, genre and so on. In our case, we did it using these little fragments, that were explored in groups and then discussed in class.

> *Khasta kofta* means 'as tired as a meatball', because the women where I used to live made meatballs by rolling them and rolling them and rolling them for a long time in the palms of their hands. And that was how I felt, as if a giant had taken me in his hands and made me into a meatball.

How can you just change your life like that, Enaiat? Just say goodbye one morning?

> *You do it Fabio, and that's it.*

I read somewhere that the decision to emigrate comes from a need to breathe.

> *Yes, it's like that. And the hope of a better life is stronger than any other feeling. My mother, for example, decided it was better to know I was in danger far from her, but on the way to a different future, than to know I was in danger near her, but stuck in the same old fear.*

Now let's see where I was in time and in my story. I'd reached a point of no return, as you say here – because we don't say it, at least I never heard anyone say it – I was at such a point of no return that I'd even stopped remembering things, and there were whole days and weeks when I didn't think at all about my little village in Ghazni province and my mother or my brother or my sister, the way I did at the start, when their image was like a tattoo on my eyes, day and night.

He looked me up and down as if I was an insect, then said, First tell me who you are. Are you Shia or Muslim? Theoretically, they're the same thing, so it was a really stupid question. I got angry. Patience has its limits even when you're a child no taller than a goat.

We weren't just cramped, we were very cramped. More than cramped. We were like grains of rice squeezed in someone's hand.

Here's one example of a first lesson agenda.

- *Leaving home*

- *Unhappy*

- *Away from home and imagines going back*

- *Some is in italics, some isn't*

- *Some of the italics are used for words which are clearly from his home*

- *The use of dialogue between the teller and Fabio*

- *Moving to another family*

- *Money problems that cause the family to separate*

- *A background story?*

- *A move for a better life*

- *No speech marks for dialogue – why?*

- *A poor life – the teller is not rich*

- *Indentation seems to show importance to some of what he's saying.*

Usually short sentences.

- *Based in Afghanistan*

- *Men are often treating our storyteller badly*

- *The retelling of a story that happened to them*

- *Conversations about the story*

- *Formal and informal mix = teenager?*

- *Cultural references*

- *Enaiat and Fabio*

You can see how at this initial stage it's a loose collection of thoughts of different kinds – some about subject matter, some about narrative style, some about possible themes. It's impressionistic – a pooling of first impressions. But it starts to include some complex ideas, such as the 'metafictional device' of talking about the story being told – not in those terms, but still thinking about this aspect of the text.

I want to show you a tiny fragment from a student's exercise book, just to give you a glimpse of how these agendas developed over time. (The text is reproduced below for ease of reading.)

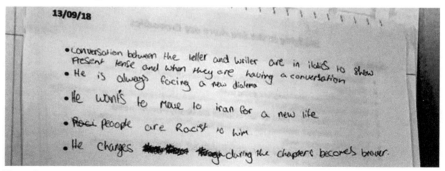

Figure 1

Conversation between the teller and writer are in italics to show present tense and when they're having a conversation.
He wants to move to Iran for a new life.
People are racist to him.
He changes during the chapters, becoming braver.

As lessons went by, new ideas were added, both collectively in class, and individually by students. So we start to hear, by lesson two, about how they've been discussing the fact that it seems to be non-fiction written in a fiction-like way, for instance, and what that means. (Incidentally, as an aside, it's worth thinking about the use of subject terminology here. The language of the subject is being included quite simply and naturally. No lesson time was given separately to explaining the meanings of words like protagonist, imagery, voice, rites of passage and so on but they were being used. In lessons, useful terms were used... when they were useful. They came up naturally in classroom conversations. No modelling was needed to incorporate them in writing because students had heard them said enough times to know how to do so. Students weren't rewarded for using, or not using, them. What was valued was good ideas well expressed in whatever way one can best express them.)

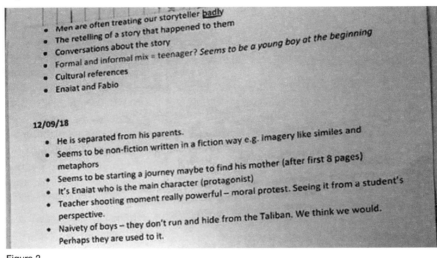

- Men are often treating our storyteller badly
- The retelling of a story that happened to them
- Conversations about the story
- Formal and informal mix = teenager? Seems to be a young boy at the beginning
- Cultural references
- Enaiat and Fabio

12/09/18
- He is separated from his parents.
- Seems to be non-fiction written in a fiction way e.g. imagery like similes and metaphors
- Seems to be starting a journey maybe to find his mother (after first 8 pages)
- It's Enaiat who is the main character (protagonist)
- Teacher shooting moment really powerful – moral protest. Seeing it from a student's perspective.
- Naivety of boys – they don't run and hide from the Taliban. We think we would. Perhaps they are used to it.

Figure 2

In Figure 1 (page 197) you see a student adding their own ideas to what's been discussed to the agenda – a rich mix of stylistic observations and ones about the events of the novel and what their underlying implications are. (We're at 13th September here – so just a couple of lessons in to the study of the book.) In Figure 2 you see the development the class's collective thinking.

This gives a sense of the range of thinking going on – uncompartmentalised, grappling with themes but also very strongly engaged with the subject, the characters, the events, the ways of telling.

In another lesson, Lucy gave her students the challenging statements on page 199 cut up in envelopes. They had to agree/disagree, pick ones they were most interested in, talk about them and then choose one to write about in an exploratory way. She read to them something she'd written herself about an entirely different statement, to show how she used writing to think and explore, to work out her own ideas about it.

Big issues – fact and fiction

1. Fiction and non-fiction are both entertaining. In lots of ways, they cross over.

2. Non-fiction can never be 100% fact. It's always going to have elements of forgotten memories or exaggeration.

3. It is not right to tell someone's sad story to entertain readers.

4. Non-fiction should always lead us to think about serious issues.

5. Non-fiction cannot be 100% not fiction if it is written to entertain.

6. Non-fiction is not written to entertain. It is only written to tell.

7. The truth can never be 100% the truth.

8. It is possible to tell both the truth and an entertaining story.

9. A person cannot tell another person's story 100% accurately. That would be impossible.

10. Children see things differently than adults. A child's perspective can be captured in writing though.

Here one student chooses to write about the statement 'It's possible to tell both the truth and an entertaining story.'

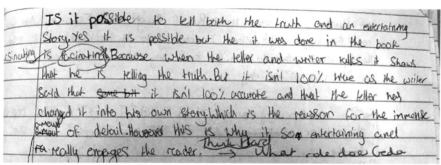

Figure 3

Now, if you were going to mark this on GCSE criteria, you'd probably complain about all sorts of things. You'd see it through a very different set of lenses to the ones I hope we can all see it through. The student is struggling a bit to express his ideas. But what he's trying to express is really difficult and interesting. It's at the heart of what makes this book especially complex and special – the telling of someone's real life story as fiction, but with the teller stepping out of the fiction from time to time, to include fragments of dialogue between himself and the real boy whose story he is telling.

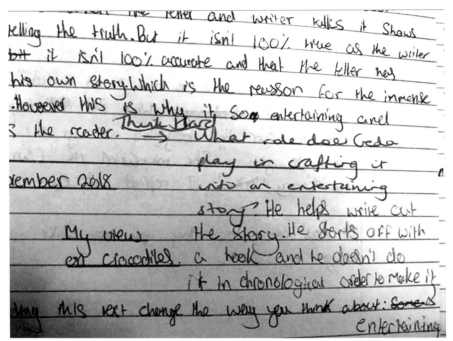

teller and writer talks it shows
telling the truth. But it isn't 100% true as the writer
but it isn't 100% accurate and that the teller has
his own story. Which is the reason for the immense
However this is why it so entertaining and
s the reader. Think Hard → What role does Geda
play in crafting it
vember 2018 into an entertaining
story? He helps write out
My view the story. He starts off with
en crocodiles. a hook and he doesn't do
it in chronological order to make it
ding this text change the way you think about. Some is
entertaining

Figure 4

One extra question from Lucy, as a kind of 'Think harder' question (shown in Figure 4), elicits a range of sophisticated thoughts about how the writer has crafted a 'novel' out of fact – the difference between Geda (the writer) and the boy (which involves the complex issue of voice and viewpoint, the sequencing of events, the hook at the start). Lucy's focus is on developing the student's ideas. There's no formalistic attention paid to a structure into which these ideas must fit. It's exploratory and developmental in nature, at this stage, not writing to a GCSE question task. And what emerges is good thinking in my view, for a Year 9. He's exploring the text in ways that will stand him in very good stead when he goes on to his next novel – in this case *Great Expectations* – allowing him to engage in Applebee's connected curriculum, in a long term set of 'conversations' between one text and the next. Lucy did, in fact, find that students drew spontaneous, insightful parallels and contrasts with *In the Sea There Are Crocodiles* as soon as they started work on the Dickens – exploring ideas about rites-of-passage novels, differing narrative arcs, child's eye perspectives and so on – often without prompting.

What kind of writing emerged from the EMC groups generally, as compared with the non-EMC ones, who were doing something very different in classwork (lots of PEETAL paragraphs and constant reference made to the demands of the GCSE Language paper)?

Here are a couple of short examples of writing taken from the student exercise books[1]. The questions, as you'll see were slightly different – in seemingly small but significant ways. The non-EMC questions always mirrored the GCSE Language

1. Student A and B were both relatively high-attaining pupils with similar predicted grades.

exam. The EMC questions varied but writing about extracts quite often took the form of 'In what ways is this extract characteristic of the rest of the novel?', with students being expected to draw into close reading their understanding of the text as a whole – small detail at the service of big picture thinking. I'm going to read the first one aloud.

Student A (non-EMC) classwork on an extract using PEETAL

Q: A student reading this extract said, 'In this extract Enaiat is clearly struggling to survive. It makes me feel sorry for him. To what extent do you agree?

I agree completely with the student who says that he feels sorry for Enaiat. When Enaiatollah is making his way to Van, he encounters 'wind that was like a razor.' This quote means that the wind was so incredulously cold that it felt like it was cutting at his cheek. This is a simile because of how it is comparing the wind to a razor. This makes me feel sorry for Enaiat because of how cold he must be feeling. A razor is sharp and would cut you, and this suggests that it was so cold during the journey that it felt like he was being pierced by a really sharp wind. Razor is a second key word. It's a noun that makes you feel sorry for Enaiat as the wind was so harsh and freezing cold that it cut your cheek, similar to a razor. Therefore, this leads me to agree with the statement because of the use of a simile.

[162 words]

What do we notice about this? For me, PEETAL has shrunk literary studies to words and phrases, disconnected from bigger, more significant meanings. Endless mining of single words or phrases means we have no sense at all about what makes this book special, why it's been written, what its impact is, what's been learned about how narrative texts work. And the exploration of the words themselves ends up being repetitive, banal, not very illuminating at all.

Here's an extract from a much, much longer piece by a student in Lucy Hinchliffe's 'EMC group'. It was written for homework. It was based on the student's own annotations of an extract.

Student B (EMC group) –on a different extract

Q: How is this extract characteristic of the rest of the novel?

This extract is characteristic of the whole novel in the way that something positive happens but it is always followed by something negative [...]

The way that parenthesis is used is similar to rest of the novel in some ways, as it keeps up the sense of a conversation. For example, Enaiat says 'I've already said – if I'm not mistaken' and he says 'and one of the most appropriate (so I believed).' This shows his uncertainty to his memories. Also it reminds us of the age that he is narrating and that it was long ago when it happened. It shows us the unreliability of his memories and it reminds us that the book is a work of fiction. Also it is a constant reminder that Enaiat is telling Geda about his experience.

[...] The way Enaiat has both adult and childlike qualities, and the way he yearns to remain a child, is also characteristic of the novel...

[Part of an essay – 6 sustained paragraphs, 3 ½ pages of an A4 exercise book, self-planned and written without any formula, 500+ words.]

In this you can see the use being made of the sophisticated thinking that started in the very first lesson, and in the lesson about the nature of fiction and non-fiction. Her reflections on the use of parentheses, is rooted in thinking about the nature of the narrative and the way it is told. Even in this tiny extract, one has a good sense of it being about this particular novel and what makes it special. Incidentally, being freed up to talk about what's genuinely interesting and significant means that the EMC students go into many more areas of language, in much more varied ways. The non-EMC students are so focused on proving their knowledge of language in PEETAL style, that they only ever talk about metaphors and similes, as if that's all language is.

What's interesting about the 'EMC way' students' writing is that, although there is a common spine to their writing – the things that have been emerging through the collective agenda – how they choose to write about these things and what they focus on is very, very different. Even writing about a short extract, they choose different quotations to focus on, they say different things, they say them differently. They select what they genuinely deem to be most interesting and important. No two pieces of writing read the same. By contrast, the students in the other group focus on just a handful of the same quotations that have been modelled in class. Across the whole book, when you look through their exercise books you see that they have only focused on a few quotations. They don't make judgements, decisions, choices for themselves, nor do they apply knowledge to fresh evidence themselves. They have some limited knowledge, but little know-how.

And one thing that is also really noticeable is the authenticity of the EMC students' response – the language in which they express it. So they use phrases like 'What stands out for me', 'What intrigued me the most' [as in this example], or 'I was struck by' or 'I think' or 'I hope that'. The students own 'perceptions, experiences, thoughts, imaginings' (as Harold Rosen describes them) find a valid, important place in their writing and their writing is all the richer and more authentically 'English' for that.

There's been a lot of interest in the novel project. But it's not just about novels. It's about everything. It's about how we work on texts across the whole landscape of English. So let me conclude by going back to the idea of how students work and think about poetry, which we examined earlier, when we looked at the poem about the beach in Picardy.

The brushstrokes of close reading are important, of course they are, but in the wider context of the painting, the movement, the whole gallery and many, many different galleries.

And here's what happens when you allow students to walk around a gallery, enjoying the art works, before looking at the brushstrokes of a single painting

– how you allow them to read openly, enthusiastically and develop points of reference and comparison of their own, engaging with important ideas.

Richard Long, a Head of Department in High Wycombe who has been a hugely enthusiastic, committed member of EMC's project, worked with me on poetry at KS3. Here's what happened in the first lesson:

1. The teachers chose a poem, read it to the class, talked about it – what they liked about it, what's puzzling, surprising, intriguing about it.

2. They gave the students a small cluster of five or six poems to choose between (individually), with the same prompts – what do I like, what puzzles me etc

3. Students worked in groups, presenting their poems to each other and picked one that the whole group liked. Prepared to read it and present it to the whole class.

4. Students individually wrote about one poem chosen from all those encountered in the lesson, in an open, exploratory way, on a class blog.

The student choices were fascinating, often not at all what their teachers expected. 11-year-old boys were choosing Maya Angelou and saying 'I really, really like that!'. Students were picking challenging and enigmatic poems, not the simplest – sometimes ones the teachers had been a bit reluctant to include. Naomi-Lee picked her favourite poem from the lesson to write about in the blog.

Here's the poem she chose.

This Poem

This poem is dangerous: it should not be left
Within the reach of children, or even of adults
Who might swallow it whole, with possibly
Undesirable side-effects. If you come across
An unattended, unidentified poem
In a public place, do not attempt to tackle it
Yourself. Send it (preferably, in a sealed container)
To the nearest centre of learning, where it will be rendered
Harmless, by experts. Even the simplest poem
May destroy your immunity to human emotions.
All poems must carry a Government warning. Words
Can seriously affect your heart.

Elma Mitchell

Her response was addressed to Richard and to the other students (reproduced here with her original spelling).

Hey everybody! It's Naomi-lee here! Today I will be discussing my favorite poem called 'this poem..'. This poem is so interesting and also very puzzling. I like this poem because it is funny and it is kind of like washing up detergent averts because one of the lines in the poem is 'it should not be left within the reach of children, even adults'. It is very comedic and made me laugh the first time I read it.

The thing that puzzles me about the poem is actually what another student, Kaiden, said which was 'is this really a poem?', this made me winder a little bit. Is it? This made me think in to my knowledge of poems and I came to the conclusion that I am in fact not sure and would like to hear another students ideas to help decide mine. I like the end line 'words can seriously harm your heart'. I like this because in a way it is true. Poems do have an effect on your emotions which is one of the things I love about poems. They can take you away from society and the real world.

Thank you for reading my responce!

For me, Naomi-Lee is fully entering our subject discipline and, aged 11, doing it with gusto. She's engaging in the big, important conversations of English. She's doing just what Applebee talks about in terms of engaging in disciplinary traditions, and, just what Harold Rosen describes as bringing in 'affective' and 'unpredictable' elements. For me (as in the work of the students on the Year 9 novel), this is indeed, 'knowledge made not given' and these students 'perceptions, experiences, imaginings and unsystematically acquired knowledge' have truly been 'admitted as legitimate curricular content'.

If we want our subject to thrive and grow, if we want students to choose to study it at A Level and at university, and if we want students to do well at GCSE, this is what it has to be – a subject with genuine intellectual interest, that brings students on board, that takes them and their own contributions seriously and allows them to take a full part in the conversation. It's what made the subject one we all chose to do ourselves and they have an entitlement to that. We shouldn't expect them to settle for anything less.

References for Postscript: Harold Rosen Lecture

Applebee, A. 1996. *Curriculum as Conversation: Transforming Traditions of Teaching and Learning*. Chicago: University of Chicago Press.

Applebee, A. 2002. 'Engaging Students in the Disciplines of English: What Are Effective Schools Doing?'. In *The English Journal* 91, (6). NCTE.

Mitchell, E. 1987. *People Etcetera: Poems New & Selected Poems*. Norwich: Peterloo Poets.

Rosen, H. 1981. 'Neither Bleak House nor Liberty Hall: English in the Curriculum'. In ed. Richmond, J. 2017. *Harold Rosen: Writings on Life, Language and Learning, 1958-2008*. London: UCL IOE Press.

Tookey, H. 2019. *City of Departures*. Manchester: Carcanet.

Appendix: An Example of an Agenda

murder

Utterson is Jekyll's friend

Genre- Horror
Maybe mystery

Hyde is wicked and rude

Can we go too far with science?

Is Jekyll in control of Hyde or not?
He seems to plan for Hyde's takeover
Yet he forges signatures so how is Jekyll good?

Jekyll is apologetic of Hyde
So is Hyde more in control?
Hyde is trying to take over Jekyll permanently by the end

Word play - hide and seek.

Hyde is different - he's not like a human.
Undeveloped form of human, unsocialised and uncivilised

Written in third person
Also written in first person
There seems to be some element of Jekyll-Hyde talking directly to us. Speech? Different points of view? Statements, letters

Jekyll - reputation/status - Dr
Degraded by Hyde?

Suspense needed
Big reveal at the end
The Victorian reader would be taken through not knowing that the two men were the same

Why would anyone want to be a bad guy?

Utterson - main narrator. Seeks the answer to the case. He is VERY on the case. He wants to find out what's going on. Utterson and Enfield are very formal the way they address each other

Jekyll is an unhappy man
Wants to be free like Hyde

Dark
Mysterious
Secretive

People of supposed class behaving oddly
Good characters in bad places and why??
3 men of very high class - lawyers and doctors hanging around at 3am.

Hyde is a result of Jekyll's pressure. Is Jekyll someone who is trying to hide the nastiness within him?
Suppression. e.g. Utterson and Enfield agreeing not to gossip!

Pressure of society - people who have a high status need to behave a certain way e.g. the doctor. But the doctor reacts strongly to Hyde when he should maintain his public face
This really shows how ugly/devilish Hyde must be
Needing an outlet
Did societal pressure create a 'bad side'?

Robert Louis Stevenson
From Edinburgh, not London
But Edinburgh has an Old Town and New Town, and at the time they were very different
New Town v respectable and middle-upper class
Old Town seedy and dark
Stevenson used to visit the Old Town after hours to drink and gamble
Inspired J&H?

'man is not truly one but truly two' - Jekyll has been doomed by the character that he has created.

This agenda is the result of a Year 10's first lesson on *Strange Case of Dr Jekyll and Mr Hyde*. It shows how the class began to pull out key ideas and ask questions that prime the reading.